North Dev

Cum

North Downs Way

Colin Saunders

Aurum

in association with

NATURAL
ENGLAND

Acknowledgements

Aurum Press and the author gratefully acknowledge the assistance of Tony Gowers, the current North Downs Way Trail Officer, in preparing the new edition of this book, and Mike Waite of the Surrey Wildlife Trust, who wrote the chapter about flora and fauna. The author is also grateful to others who have helped him prepare the book, especially Dr Alan Harrington, Jim Walker, the proprietors and staff of many establishments along the route who have readily answered the author's questions, and the creators of a multitude of websites.

The author of this new version, Colin Saunders, has written several books about walking during a career in the travel industry and event-organising. He is now retired, living in the northern outskirts of London, but continues to work on books and other activities connected with walking. The author of the original edition was Neil Curtis, whose introduction to it is still largely valid, so an updated version has been included in this edition.

This new edition published 2011 by Aurum Press Ltd
7 Greenland Street, London NW1 0ND · www.aurumpress.co.uk
in association with Natural England.
www.naturalengland.org.uk · www.nationaltrail.co.uk

Text copyright © 2011 by Aurum Press Ltd
and Natural England

The photographs on pages 12, 21, 26, 37, 83, 86, 121, 138, 154, 161, 175, 178 are by Mike Williams and are copyright © Natural England. All other photographs are copyright © the photographer/agency and are by: pages 31, 32, 33, 39, 40, 41, 48, 50, 52-3, 56, 59, 63, 79, 94, 106, 116, 119, 126, 133, 163, 171 Colin Saunders; pages 1, 2–3, 25, 28, 29, 35, 65, 77, 80, 137, 141 Alamy; pages 23, 73, 104, 149 Mike Waite; pages 100–1, 118 David Hiscock; pages 111, 151, 177 Anthony Gowers; pages 19, 139 Getty Images; page 20 Topfoto.

OS Ordnance Survey® This product includes mapping data licensed from Ordnance Survey® with the permission of the Controller of Her Majesty's Stationery Office. © Crown copyright 2011. All rights reserved. Licence number 43453U. Ordnance Survey, Pathfinder and Travelmaster are registered trademarks and the Ordnance Survey symbol and Explorer are trademarks of Ordnance Survey, the national mapping agency of Great Britain.

A catalogue record for this book is available from the British Library.

ISBN 978 1 84513 677 2

1 3 5 7 9 10 8 6 4 2
2011 2013 2015 2014 2012

Book design by Robert Updegraff
Printed and bound in Italy by Printer Trento Srl

Cover photograph: *Morning sunlight over the North Downs at Newlands Corner.*

Half-title photograph: *Canterbury Cathedral was journey's end for the Christian pilgrims of medieval times, and remains one of the most striking landmarks to visit along the North Downs Way.*

Title-page photograph: *The view over the North Downs from St Martha's Church in the Surrey Hills.*

Aurum Press want to ensure that these National Trail Guides are always as up to date as possible – but stiles collapse, pubs close and bus services change all the time. If, on walking this path, you discover any important changes of which future walkers need to be aware, do let us know. Either email us on **trailguides@aurumpress.co.uk** with your comments, or if you take the trouble to drop us a line to:

Trail Guides, Aurum Press, 7 Greenland Street, London NW1 0ND,
we'll send you a free guide of your choice as thanks.

Contents

How to use this guide

This guide to the North Downs Way is in four parts:

Part One: Introduction

Includes a historical background to the area, a general introduction to, and history of, the North Downs and the North Downs Way, and the flora and fauna you may see while walking. It also gives an overview of the Pilgrims Way and how it interacts with the North Downs Way.

Part Two: Practical advice

Advice for walkers on matters such as which of the two alternative routes to follow, how long it will take to walk the route, the best parts (for those who do not have time to walk it all), travelling to and from the route, refreshments, toilets, accommodation, equipment, maps, the different types of rights of way you will encounter, signage, safety issues and walking with dogs. There is also some information for cyclists and horseriders.

Part Three: Route description

This is split into 15 sections: sections 1–11 cover the 'Main Line', using the southern route from Boughton Lees to Dover via Wye and Etchinghill; sections 12–15 describe the 'Canterbury Loop', using the northern route from Boughton Lees to Dover via Chilham and Canterbury.

Under the heading for each section, its distance in miles and kilometres is shown, together with an estimate of its total ascent and descent and the lowest and highest altitudes reached, in feet and metres. A general overview of the section follows, describing the terrain and highlights. The next part draws attention to 'things to look out for' along the route, in the order that they appear, showing the feature reference point number (as shown on the maps) and its name in bold type.

The main part of each section consists of the actual route description, opposite the equivalent map for that part of the section. The names of 'things to look out for' are shown in bold **blue** type, together with the feature reference point shown on the maps. Also appearing within the text and on the maps are route reference point letters, and the 'Trail Guide symbols' and 'tourist and leisure information' as shown on the inside front cover of this book. Each section finishes with information about public transport, refreshments, toilets and accommodation.

Information that is not relevant to the actual route of the North Downs Way, such as links with railway stations, pubs and other refreshment opportunities nearby, are shown in italics. The station links are described in detail at the end of Part Three.

Part Four: Useful information

Contact details for public transport information, tourist information centres, connecting trails, and other organisations: throughout the book, **green** text indicates that contact details are shown under 'Useful information'.

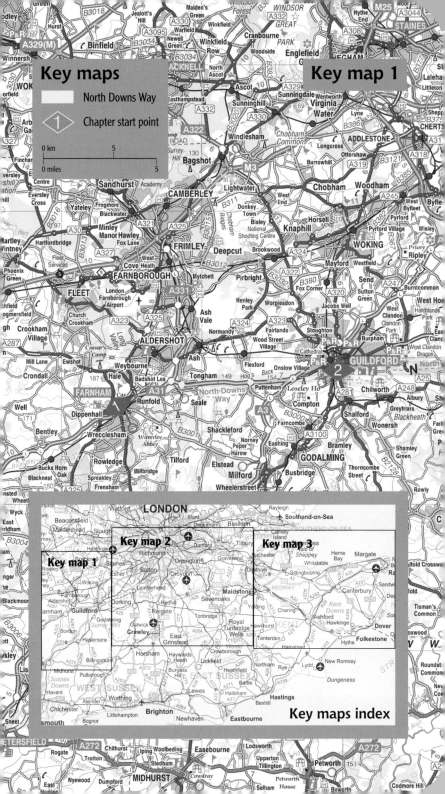

Key maps

North Downs Way

◇1◇ Chapter start point

0 km   5

0 miles   5

Key map 1

Key map 1

Key map 2

Key map 3

Key maps index

Key map 3

The Wye Downs and Wye Valley from Soakham Downs

Distance checklist

This list will assist you in calculating the distances between places on the North Downs Way where you may be planning to stay overnight, or in checking your progress along the route.

Location	Approximate distance from previous location	
	miles	km
Farnham	0.0	0.0
Puttenham	6.6	10.6
Guildford	4.4	7.1
Newlands Corner	3.4	5.5
Ranmore Church	7.3	11.7
Westhumble	2.2	3.5
Reigate Hill	7.9	12.7
Merstham	2.2	3.5
Oxted	8.0	12.9
Knockholt Pound	8.3	13.4
Otford	3.4	5.5
Wrotham	6.7	10.8
Cuxton	8.8	14.2
Blue Bell Hill	6.2	10.0

			Canterbury Loop		
Detling	5.9	9.5	Boughton Lees	0.0	0.0
Hollingbourne	5.3	8.5	Chilham	5.9	9.5
Harrietsham	2.3	3.7	Chartham Hatch	3.6	5.8
Lenham	1.6	2.6	Canterbury Cathedral	3.6	5.8
Charing	4.2	6.8	Patrixbourne	3.2	5.1
Boughton Lees	4.7	7.6	Shepherdswell	7.2	11.6
Wye	2.3	3.7	Dover	8.5	13.7
Stowting	6.7	10.8			
Etchinghill	4.6	7.4			
Folkestone (A260)	4.6	7.4			
Dover	7.5	12.1			

Preface

The North Downs Way National Trail stretches across south-east England from Surrey to Kent, finishing on the coast at Dover. The route is full of contrasts – you'll pass through dense woodlands, follow the chalk ridge of the Downs with its wide skies and open views, and wind through river valleys. The area is rich in wildlife – especially butterflies and wild flowers.

There are lengthy stretches of bridleway too, making it accessible to horseriders and cyclists. The many railway stations close to the route make it an ideal trail to reach without using the car and its proximity to London means it is an attractive and peaceful destination for day visitors and long-distance walkers alike. The relatively easy-going terrain and wealth of places to stop or stay make it an excellent route for the less experienced trail walker.

Like other National Trails, the path is waymarked with the distinctive acorn symbol which signals you are on the right route. This book has been completely revised and rewritten to reflect changes that have taken place along the trail. I hope that it will help you enjoy many happy hours on the North Downs Way.

Poul Christensen CBE
Chair
Natural England

PART ONE
Introduction

The village of Brook from the North Downs in spring colour.

Pleasures of the North Downs Way

With acknowledgement to Neil Curtis, author of the first edition of the North Downs Way National Trail Guide.

The 153-mile (245-km) North Downs Way offers tranquillity, rural beauty, historical and literary interest, and some splendid natural history to anyone willing to make the journey from Farnham to the Kent coast.

Unlike the most popular National Trails, where overuse has led to serious problems of erosion in places along the route, and where you can play 'follow my leader' along some sections, it is perfectly possible, even in the height of the summer holiday season, to spend hours or even midweek days negotiating the North Downs Way without meeting another traveller, except perhaps an occasional dog-walker or local cyclist or horse and rider. And this is particularly surprising when you recall that the route traverses England's thronging south-east region, which is networked with trunk roads, motorways and railway lines, and peppered with industry, suburbia and dormitory towns; this does, however, mean that the walker is seldom far from shelter or public transport.

This book describes the walk from west to east through two counties: Surrey (with 46 miles/74 km of the route) and Kent (107 miles/172 km). This means you can begin, conveniently, at Farnham railway station and your journey takes you to the sea – always a satisfying goal and a fitting climax to any walk on the wild side in an island country – and generally, because prevailing winds in Britain blow from the west, you should have any breeze at your back for much of the way to give you that little extra spur.

Anyone who has walked the South Downs Way will, at least for some years, find the North Downs Way a different creature, being generally more wooded and with less open, rolling grassland. The two ranges used to be more similar, when sheep grazing was widespread, and has remained so in the South Downs. However, during the 20th century farmers left much of the North Downs ungrazed, with the result that trees and scrub grew unchecked. This is beginning to change, however, with the National Trust, wildlife trusts and other nature conservancy bodies reintroducing livestock so that a more open landscape will in time return to the North Downs and allow the more delicate downland flora and fauna to return.

The North Downs Way is a National Trail of contrasts. For those who, especially on a hot day, prefer to walk beneath the shade of trees, Surrey offers large expanses of beech, oak, ash, juniper and yew woodland. But for others, there are few greater joys than striding across the springy, rabbit- and sheep-cropped turf on a chalk ridge crest with a light breeze blowing, fine open vistas spread below, and with the sea a distant blue-grey ribbon between sky and earth. From the Wye Downs across Cheriton Hill and Hangar Down to Creteway Down, the Kentish stretch offers just such inspirational journeying.

You will follow river valleys, such as that of the Wey, and cross other rivers, such as the Mole, on stepping stones when the water is not too high. You will need to haul yourself up to lofty beauty spots like St Martha's Hill, Box Hill and Newlands Corner, reaching an altitude of 853 feet (260 metres) at the highest point of the route – Botley Hill – but finally descending to sea level at Dover. You will walk beside motorways, pass beneath and over them, and you will be taken airily and noisily across the River Medway by the same construction that carries the M2 with haste towards Canterbury.

There are homely churches and awe-inspiring cathedrals to admire and explore. For the literary or artistically minded, there are connections with William Cobbett and George Meredith, with Dickens and

Tennyson, and with Graham Sutherland. There are reminders of almost every age of British life: the prehistoric long barrow of Kit's Coty, south of Chatham; the site of an Iron Age fort at Bigbury near Canterbury; across and along Roman roads; past Norman castles, medieval churches, 16th-century mansions, and Georgian country houses; and through relics of the Industrial Revolution.

The warming climate of recent decades has led to the reintroduction of vineyards in southern England, and you will pass three of them, including Denbies, the largest in Britain. Yet what could be more traditional than the round tower and conical chimney of an oast house, formerly used as a kiln for drying the hops that were, and still are, grown all around the 'Garden of England'? Apples and other fruit are also grown here, and approaching Canterbury you will wander through vast orchards.

There is industry too, though most of the chalk quarries and lime works are disused now. The Marley tile works at Lenham still seems busy enough, and as you follow the cliffs above Folkestone you will look down upon the vast complex of railway lines and loading ramps that surrounds the entrance to the Channel Tunnel. In several places you will encounter the high-speed railway line that carries Eurostar trains from St Pancras to Paris and Brussels, as well as the Javelin trains serving Kent.

However you choose to tackle the North Downs Way, it is there to be enjoyed and there is much to enjoy. From ridge top to valley floor, from shady woodland grove to open chalk downland, from Georgian town to ancient port, a traveller on the North Downs Way will usually have the songs of birds for company but, where hill or screen of trees muffles the roads and railways, the silence may be so deep and the solitude so complete that one's own inner musings may sound loud in the mind's ear.

History of the North Downs Way

The North Downs Way National Trail was formally launched on 30 September 1978 at a ceremony on Wye Downs in Kent, appropriately by the then Archbishop of Canterbury, the Most Reverend and Right Honourable Donald Coggan. So, if you happen to be walking the route on that date, propose a toast to the Countryside Commission (now Natural England), the organisation that was responsible for setting up the network of National Trails in England and Wales. And spare some of the contents of your glass for the two county councils – Surrey and Kent – without whose co-operation the creation and maintenance of the route would have been impossible.

The National Trails resulted from the National Parks and Access to the Countryside Act of 1949, which also created Areas of Outstanding Natural Beauty (AONBs). The North Downs were chosen for one of the trails as they include two AONBs – the Surrey Hills and the Kent Downs – and after 15 years of planning the North Downs Way became the eighth route in the network. There are now 15 National Trails in England and Wales, details of which can be obtained from the **National Trails** website, and a further four in Scotland (where they are known as Official Long Distance Routes), for which contact **Scottish Natural Heritage**.

There were time-worn precedents for this particular National Trail, as it follows roughly the same line as two ancient, parallel trackways: one along the ridge of the Downs, the other along a terrace near the foot – traces of both can be seen on Ordnance Survey maps. One hesitates to use the terms 'Ridgeway' and 'Terraceway' – the former is used for another National Trail; the latter has achieved great fame as the Pilgrims Way, and there will be more about that later.

In prehistoric times, when the lowlands were densely wooded, people travelling from east to west or vice versa would follow the sparsely vegetated ridge. In the Christian era much of the woodland was cleared for agriculture, many farming communities were established, linked by a network of tracks and each with its church and hostelry, so travellers (including pilgrims to Winchester or Canterbury) could more easily journey along the terrace, find lodgings and worship regularly.

It is no longer practical to follow the entire ridge of the North Downs, due to the inaccessibility or unsuitability of much of the land, so the planners of the North Downs Way decided to create a route that would make best use of both ancient trackways, with the result that it is fairly equally divided between the ridge and the terrace.

How the North Downs were formed

The North Downs run for about 100 miles (160 km) from the Hog's Back, near Farnham, to the chalk cliffs extending between Folkestone and Margate. The word 'downs' seems anomalous when applied to an upland region, but it actually comes from the Old English *dun*, meaning hill.

Both the North Downs and the roughly parallel South Downs were formed during the Upper Cretaceous period, around 85 million years ago, when this area was covered by sea, and layers of rock were formed from successive depositions of sandstone (during periods as sandy river deltas), clay (from the weathering of mineral rock) and, finally, chalk (from the skeletons of billions of marine creatures). The movement of tectonic plates forced the area to rise into a long dome, with an east–west axis, then erosion left the younger layers of chalk and sandstone exposed as elongated rings around what we now call the Weald, and with what we now call the North and South Downs forming high ridges on either

side. Soil and soft rocks on the south side of the North Downs have eroded to form a steep slope called a 'scarp', while the north side drops gently away – the North Downs Way often follows the top of the scarp.

The chalk originally extended further east, when Britain was joined to continental Europe, but in more recent times (about 10,000 years ago) rising sea levels at the end of the last Ice Age flooded the lower eastern parts. In more local terms, the chalk of the North Downs is underlain by a layer of greensand, which comes to the surface on the south side of the main ridge. The first 13 miles (21 km) of the North Downs Way, from Farnham to St Martha's Hill, lie on this sandstone outcrop, parallel to the ridge known as the Hog's Back, which is chalk.

Water from the greensand formed rivers that forced their way through the soft, porous chalk, creating gaps that facilitated north–south travel and where major settlements grew up. The North Downs Way encounters five such gaps formed by the rivers Wey (at Guildford), Mole (Dorking), Darent (Otford), Medway (Rochester) and Stour (Canterbury).

Another feature of chalk downland is the 'combe', or dry valley, and you will pass many of them, sometimes hardly visible due to tree cover, at other times curving away under a carpet of grass. They were formed during the last Ice Age by continual alternate freezing and thawing of the chalk: when it thawed, the frost-cracked chalk slid downhill, making the combe deeper. That process can be seen today along the south coast, where chalk cliffs continue to crumble into the sea due to frost action. The combes have since remained streamless because rain seeps into the porous chalk.

Chalk often contains nodules of a hard quartz called flint, usually dark and glossy on the inside with a lighter outer layer. As you progress along the Way, you will see them lying on the ground, broken open to reveal the dark interior, or used as building material for churches, cottages and barns.

The route clips the edge of the East Kent Coalfield, where a rich seam of coal was discovered under the chalk towards the end of the 19th century, resulting in the opening of 12 collieries. They were never really successful and, with the demand for British coal falling off during the 1980s, the last Kent colliery, Betteshanger, closed in 1989.

A historical overview of the North Downs

If you go back far enough, Britain was joined to the rest of Europe and early humans easily found their way here. Fossilised hominid bones dating back 700,000 years have been found here, as have those of woolly rhino, hippopotamus and mammoth. After the last Ice Age Britain became separated and started to develop its own culture, introduced by successive waves of settlers, latterly those of Celtic, Roman, Germanic and Norman origin.

The south-eastern Celtic tribes, the Regni and the Cantiaci, largely welcomed Roman culture, so in this part of Britain the Romans were able to develop farming and industry, and build their villas, in relative peace. They expanded existing Iron Age quarries and mines, relics of which are still visible beside the North Downs Way, which also encounters Roman roads at least three times.

In post-Roman times, from the late 5th century, Surrey became part of the kingdom of Middlesex, or the Middle Saxons. It was recorded in the 7th century as either Sudergeona or Suthrige, depending on your source of information – both mean 'South Region' (of Middlesex). Kent (its name derived from the Celtic tribe, Cantiaci) was settled by the Jutes, another Germanic tribe.

Although some historians maintain that Celtic genes are still strongly represented in the population of this area, it is the Saxons and Jutes whose place names have left the deepest impression, such as Farnham (Fearnhamme – ferny water meadow),

Dorking (Dorchingas – the name of the tribe that occupied the area), Merstham (Mearsoetham – marsh people's dwelling), Oxted (Acstede – oak place), Cuxton (Cucclestane – Cucula's stone), Harrietsham (Heriagierdeshamme – Heriagierde's water meadow), Charing (Ceringes – tribal name), Chilham (Cyleham – cold place) and Canterbury (Cantwareburh – stronghold of the people of Cantia).

In 1066 the Norman Conquest brought a new system, establishing Surrey and Kent as administrative territories, called counties, but ironically applying the Saxon term *earl* to the nobleman in charge. King William I ('the Conqueror') set about recording all the property of his new realm in the Domesday Book, completed in 1086.

During the Middle Ages, sheep farming became the most important economic activity throughout the region, but this later gave way to arable and the downland pastures were left to become overgrown with trees and scrub – this process is now being reversed with the reintroduction of livestock.

Hard, hot and dirty work: coal was difficult to extract from the coalfields of East Kent. This is one of the deep seams at Tilmanstone Colliery.

Existing small industries grew in importance, especially chalk quarrying. In the 16th century the abundance of water and trees led to the establishment of a paper-making industry in the Medway Valley, and you will see some of its vast paper mills in the distance from your North Downs Way vantage point, though they are currently being run down and closed. The growth of the 'throwaway society' during the 20th century has led to some former chalk quarries being used for landfill, though when full they have been grassed over to disguise what lies beneath.

The arrival of railways during the mid-19th century had a huge effect on culture and lifestyle. Much of south-east England became a dormitory for London, which is at most an hour or so away by train. Trains also made it possible for Londoners to visit the area in great numbers for the pursuit of leisure activities – and until the second half of the 20th century they could travel on many more railway lines. They went to the seaside, including Folkestone, or visited stately homes, such as Leeds Castle, or walked to beauty spots such as Newlands Corner or Box Hill.

The North Downs have been easily accessible to visitors from abroad for centuries, through the proximity of Newhaven, Folkestone and Dover, and more recently Gatwick Airport and Eurostar trains. But the 20th century saw an ever-increasing number of ramblers exploring the dense network of footpaths and bridleways that pervade these counties, providing a steady income for pubs, tea rooms, hotels and food shops, and seeking to improve their level of fitness. Long may this continue!

Human endeavour in the North Downs

Most early human endeavour in the North Downs took place slowly and steadily, though it was to have the most profound impact on the land: clearance of dense woodland to create fields for food production; establishment of family homesteads that grew into villages and market towns, and the development of trade and tracks between them; construction of places of worship; and removal of minerals for the benefit of agriculture and small-scale industry. All this

Short Brothers, whose factory was based at Rochester until 1947, built Britain's most famous flying-boats, including the celebrated Empire class that flew luxury routes to South Africa, India and Australia and were the civilian counterparts of the military Sunderland. Here a group of nannies and their charges watch the Empire flying boat Cambria taxiing up the Medway in September 1937.

With its curious mix of architectural styles, the Watts memorial temple, built partly by local craftsmen, is an extraordinary edifice.

went largely unrecorded until the late 11th century, when the Domesday Book meticulously took stock of everything of value, though intelligent guesses can be made at when, how and possibly at whose instigation such things had taken place over previous centuries. Now, planning regulations ensure that all developments are recorded in the minutest detail.

More recently, and on a higher intellectual plane, the idyllic surroundings of the North Downs have played host to a number of great creative minds. William Cobbett, author of one of the classic works of English travel writing, *Rural Rides*, was born in Farnham, Surrey, in 1763. E. M. Forster, author of two of the most highly regarded English novels of the twentieth century, *Howards End* and *A Passage to India*, lived from 1925 to 1945 at West Hackhurst, near Abinger, in the Surrey Hills. The composer Ralph Vaughan Williams lived for much of his life at Leith Hill Place, near Dorking (a statue commemorates him in the town centre). The Victorian painter George Frederic Watts lived outside Guildford and founded his Watts Gallery nearby. Though the origins of the Pilgrims Way may be a flight of fancy, it remains inextricably interwoven with the North Downs Way, and has inspired many works, from Chaucer's *The Canterbury Tales* to its modern wartime reworking in the classic Powell and Pressburger film *A Canterbury Tale*, and Hilaire Belloc's *The Old Road*.

But these artistic musings have been accompanied by the crash-bang-wallop of large-scale industrial activity and the pandemonium of war – the result of naturally occurring factors and proximity to London. The presence of chalk and other minerals has led to many scars along the green slopes. Huge paper mills dominate the Medway Valley, and Short Empire and Sunderland flying-boats thundered along the river's lower reaches. The discovery of rich seams of coal deep below east Kent brought clanking mineshafts and industrial strife, tempered by the sweet sound of a male voice choir. The ever-increasing demand for 'a home of one's own' has resulted in exponential growth of 'dormitory' communities enjoying clean air in and around the hills. And all this activity has spawned a tangle of roads and railways and a plague of edge-of-town supermarkets, sprawling motels and multiplex cinemas.

In times of war, the fact that London is the capital of the United Kingdom has made great impressions on the landscape and people of Kent and Surrey in their role as the last bastion against occupation of the capital: the coastal defences of the Napoleonic Wars, the string of Victorian forts along the North Downs scarp, the rash of Second World War pillboxes all over the place. But, surely, the most terrifying chapter of all this effort to defeat invasion must be the Battle of Britain in 1940: fighter aircraft were sent up from hastily constructed airfields that lay on or close to the North Downs (such as Kenley, Biggin Hill, West Malling, Detling, Lympne and Hawkinge), turning the sky above Kent and Surrey into a scene of ferocious dogfights, aircraft crashing into fields, buildings and woods, and the unloading of surplus bombs.

Think of these things as you progress along the North Downs Way. Then, on reaching the Battle of Britain Memorial near Folkestone, or the West Gate of Canterbury Cathedral, give thanks to our ancestors, because without their efforts and sacrifices none of us would have been able to enjoy the experience.

Flora and fauna of the North Downs

By Mike Waite of the Surrey Wildlife Trust

The North Downs Way traverses some of the richest countryside for wildlife in south-east England, with unique assemblages of special plants and animals, many of which have highly restricted ranges within the UK. Several sites are of truly international importance and are EU-designated Special Areas of Conservation.

The natural history of the North Downs is inextricably connected with chalk, the bone-white bedrock that gives the Trail its dramatic landscapes, seen most starkly in the famous white cliffs of far eastern Kent, as well as in a myriad ex-quarries, pits and dene-holes inland. Clearance of the original woodland for agriculture began in the Neolithic period and the open landscape it created was later maintained by generations of shepherds and their flocks. In contrast with the South Downs of Sussex and Hampshire, the North Downs seem to have retained significantly more of this 'ancient' woodland, especially in central and western Surrey. The steady demise of extensive sheep grazing from the end of the 19th century then resulted in a widespread return of regenerated scrub and woodland, but at the expense of the wildflower-rich chalk grassland of classic open downland. Still more of this grassland has been lost to post-war arable conversion and piecemeal urban development. This slow but relentless diminution has driven through successive Acts of Parliament to ensure the safeguarding of all that remains of this treasured habitat.

Today, the most important wildlife habitats along the North Downs Way include various types of woodland; the open chalk grassland with its associated fringing scrub; the narrow floodplains of some significant river valleys; and finally the coastal section between Folkestone and Dover. Some margins of long-established arable fields are also of prime botanical importance, particularly in one part of north Kent.

For the plant-lover, the North Downs are probably regarded most highly for their orchids. No fewer than 30 species may be found there – roughly 60 per cent of the British orchid flora. Several almost 'belong' here – for example the man and musk orchids for which the Downs are the national stronghold. Others are on the very edge of an otherwise continental range and thus found in Kent alone, like the late-spider and lady orchids. Orchid hotspots include Box Hill and its environs, straddling the Mole Gap in Surrey, as well as the Halling to Trottiscliffe escarpment and the Wye Downs National Nature Reserve in Kent. But in grassy margins anywhere along the route one can readily stumble upon pyramidal, common spotted, bee and fragrant orchids, often in spectacular local profusion. In the deep shade of the older beech woodland, bird's-nest and fly orchids, and white, broad-leaved and violet helleborines can be found. On the cliff tops above Folkestone, the early-spider orchid and delightfully named autumn lady's-tresses are both local specialities.

Where we cross the River Wey south of Guildford there are some rare surviving floodplain fen-meadows, in high summer full of ragged-robin, meadowsweet and pungent water mint, as well as several species of colourful marsh-orchids. A botanical reserve at Ranscombe Farm near Cuxton in Kent is owned by Plantlife, the wildflower conservation charity, to protect some of the rarest arable plants in the UK. Wild clary, blue pimpernel and night-flowering catchfly are just a few of these. Box Hill is so named for the country's finest native stands of the wild shrub, box. Also here and at a few other places nearby are the last remaining North Downs specimens of another native shrub, juniper, which is disappearing rapidly throughout lowland Britain.

A significant share of Britain's butterflies occurs on the North Downs, including several that are in sharp national decline. The 'blues' are particularly well represented. Chalkhill blue is still reasonably common, while the stunning Adonis blue is more restricted to the better-managed chalk grassland in nature reserves, as at Box Hill Country Park, on neighbouring Denbies hillside, and along the hill tops above Folkestone. The steeply declining small blue appears to have all but disappeared from the route, but this, the tiniest of our British butterflies, is easily overlooked. Also confined to its last remaining site is the Duke of Burgundy fritillary, a dapper little butterfly now present only at Wye Downs. On a positive note, the silver-spotted skipper is doing well in the Downs, having expanded along the scarp slope between Reigate and Guildford especially, as well as at certain sites in Kent.

Other, less spectacular invertebrates for which the North Downs have become something of a last bastion include the rare straw belle and black-veined moths, and the lemon slug in woodlands. The huge and somewhat pallid Roman snail, a veritable Moby Dick within the mollusc world, is now hard to miss in early summer along much of the North Downs Way. Our largest snail, it may have arrived with the Romans as a table delicacy. A late evening walk along rough grassy waysides in summer may also reveal the little green beacons of the glow worm, actually a predatory beetle preying on snails, and yet another waning species across the country.

The same walk could well reveal a badger about its business and the Downs in central Surrey are of major importance for bats, including uncommon species such as Bechstein's and whiskered bat, for whom the old chalk workings provide secure roosting quarters.

For the birdwatcher, the woodlands and coastal section are possibly the most rewarding, although the open downland landscape is where skylarks, yellowhammers, linnets, hovering kestrels and the few corn buntings remaining on the route may best be appreciated. Common woodland birds include the nuthatch and

The autumn lady's-tresses orchid is a local speciality on the cliffs above Folkestone.

various tits, with an apparently healthy population of the otherwise declining marsh tit, especially in central Surrey. Where the route bridges the River Mole north of Dorking, grey wagtails and kingfishers, as well as mandarin duck, can be found. Soaring buzzards are now regularly seen throughout the Downs, having staged a dramatic recovery from local extinction since the new millennium. Ravens may be beginning to follow suit; a good spot to see them is the viewpoint at Blue Bell Hill in Kent. When passing old chalk quarries, for example north-west of Reigate, keep an eye out for peregrine falcons. These magnificent birds, quicker in the air than any other on the planet, are probably easiest to observe between Folkestone and Dover, where several pairs breed on the white cliffs. Other cliff-nesters include fulmars, jackdaws, house martins and rock doves. Folkestone Warren is a good place to see rare Mediterranean gulls and marsh warblers, as well as resident rock pipits and the occasional wintering purple sandpiper.

The Pilgrims Way

The North Downs Way frequently encounters the Pilgrims Way – indeed, actually follows or parallels it for about a third of the distance. (To be pedantic, it should properly be written as either Pilgrim's or Pilgrims', depending on one's source of reference. However, you will most often see the term used as a road name without the apostrophe; therefore, for consistency, none has henceforth been used in this book.)

There is no historical evidence to show that the term 'Pilgrims Way' was used prior to the 19th century, and these days it is assumed that it was coined by someone, possibly an imaginative surveyor of the Ordnance Survey, as a romantic description of what was certainly a very ancient route that would have been used by pilgrims making their way to Winchester or Canterbury. The route has sometimes been called the Terraceway, as it largely follows a terrace near the foot of the Downs, and to distinguish it from the high-level Ridgeway.

Although the Pilgrims Way is one of the best-known historic routes in Britain, it is impractical to walk its entire length, as most has either become roads of varying degrees of traffic intensity, or has disappeared under the plough. However, enough of it remains as a quiet lane, byway or bridleway to provide some pleasant walking for North Downs Wayfarers.

The word 'pilgrim' means a person who travels to a sacred place for religious reasons, and derives from the Latin *pelegrinus*, meaning foreign. In AD 597, an Italian prior called Augustine landed in Kent, sent by Pope Gregory to convert the pagan Jutes to Christianity. Augustine died at Canterbury around 605, was buried in the abbey he had founded there (those walking the Canterbury Loop of the North Downs Way will pass its remains) and became revered as a saint. To travel long distances in order to see or touch the remains of a saint, or their container, has

long been regarded by many Christians as a way of demonstrating one's faith, so the faithful flocked to Canterbury to commune with the remains of Augustine.

Then Swithun, the pious Bishop of Winchester, died and was buried in that city in 862, and after he was canonised pilgrims made their way to what was then the capital of Wessex and later of England. So pilgrims were now heading in both directions, with Rochester Cathedral and many churches providing places to worship along the way. But the act that secured Canterbury's place as the prime destination was, of course, the 'murder in the cathedral' of Archbishop Thomas Becket in 1170.

While the presumed route of the Pilgrims Way no longer offers a practical way of reaching either destination on foot, the North Downs Way is the next best thing. If you wish to start your pilgrimage from Winchester, the 34-mile (55-km) trail called St Swithun's Way will take you from there to the start of the North Downs Way at Farnham. A route description can be obtained from **Hampshire County Council**.

The Pilgrims Way extends beyond Canterbury to Dover as part of the *Via Francigena* (Latin for Frankish Way), a historical route of about 1,050 miles (1,700 km) that has traditionally been followed by pilgrims travelling from Canterbury to Rome. From Dover, they crossed the English Channel to Calais, then continued through France, Switzerland and Italy to St Peter's Basilica in the Vatican City. The Council of Europe has declared the Via Francigena a 'European Cultural Itinerary', on a par with the better-known Way of St James to Santiago de Compostela in Spain. Pilgrims to Santiago carry a scallop shell, but those following the Via Francigena should carry a symbolic key to open the Gates of St Peter. As well as the National Trail acorn, North Downs Way signposts between Canterbury and Dover bear the 'pilgrim' logo of the Via Francigena.

PART TWO

Practical Advice

Newlands Corner in Surrey.

Which alternative?

The North Downs Way is 153 miles (245 km) long, if you count the two alternative routes at its eastern end, but walkers rarely undertake all of this, as time constrains their ability to cover both options. If you choose the southern route (the 'Main Line') past Folkestone, you will cover 125 miles (201 km). The northern route (the 'Canterbury Loop') branches off near Boughton Lees, near Wye, and if you go this way you will have walked 131 miles (211 km).

If you can spare the time to walk both alternatives, there are two practical ways of

Hop fields with their poles and strings near Chartham Hatch. During the summer the facing bank is awash with lavender, adding colour and fragrance to a day's walk.

doing it. On reaching Dover the first time, you can then take a train to Ashford, then bus or taxi to Boughton Lees to follow the other route. This way, you have the advantage of walking both routes in the same direction as described in this book. Or, on reaching Dover, you can just turn round and walk the other route in reverse, finishing at Boughton Lees and taking a bus or taxi to Ashford for your homeward journey; or you could walk the short distance to Wye and catch a train there. You would then have to ignore the route directions for the reverse part of your journey, but the maps in this book and the signage on the ground should be sufficient to guide you. And the 'things to look out for' mentioned in this book may still be of interest.

People ask, which is the better alternative? Undoubtedly, the southern route provides a more spectacular finish, with wider views, and most of its final 5 miles (8 km) lie beside the English Channel, with grand views of the Channel Tunnel Terminal, Folkestone, Dover Harbour and Dover Castle. It is also more strenuous, with many testing climbs. The views on the northern route are pleasant but rarely spectacular, and the terrain is gentler; however, for many people, the whole point of walking the North Downs Way is to make a pilgrimage to Canterbury Cathedral, so for them this is the only way to go.

How long will it take?

It is possible to complete the whole North Downs Way in a week, including both alternatives, averaging 22 miles (35 km) a day, and this will be perfectly feasible for strong walkers like members of the **Long Distance Walkers Association**. Occasionally, relay events are organised along the whole route with the aim of setting a fast completion time – 'crossings' of as little as 55 hours have been known.

But what is the point of hurrying when there is so much to see and admire? Most walkers can maintain a steady pace of 2.5–3 miles (4–5 km) an hour, in which case you should comfortably cover 12–15 miles (19–24 km) a day and still have time for refreshment stops. You will then need 8–11 days if you have time for only one of the alternative routes, or 11–15 days if you intend to walk both of them. If you are undertaking the whole route in one go, you may wish to add a day or two for rest or sightseeing. Some of the sections in this guide are quite short, which will allow you to have at least half a day's sightseeing in, say, Canterbury or Dover.

There is no need to follow slavishly the sections as described in this book: you can break your journey wherever is most convenient for you, and where public transport is available as described in the route description, or at any point by calling out a taxi (or a friend with a car) to collect you there.

Remember, though, that if you are travelling with a companion or in a party, you should not attempt more than can reasonably be achieved by the least fit among you. And bear in mind, too, that a steep ascent or crossing a large, freshly ploughed field can slow you considerably.

Potential walkers of the North Downs Way who are living or staying in the London area may find it more practical to make day or weekend trips, as there are such good train services from there to all the stations that the route passes. The Javelin high-speed trains from St Pancras and Stratford, introduced in 2010 by **South Eastern Railway**, enable even stations at the east end of the route to be reached in little more than an hour.

The best parts

If your time is too limited to undertake the full route, you can still sample the best of what the North Downs Way has to offer. Any list is necessarily subjective, but, in the view of the author and the National Trail officer, these are the parts you should not miss, all of which provide wonderful views over the Weald:

River Wey near Guildford to Newlands Corner (Sections 1–2, 3.4 miles / 5.5 km)
Lovely switchback walk past the atmospheric St Martha's Church.

Westhumble to Wray Lane Car Park (Section 3, 7.9 miles / 12.7 km)
Crossing the River Mole on stepping stones, classic climb up Box Hill, historic Reigate Fort.

Detling to Hollingbourne (Section 8, 5.3 miles / 8.5 km)
A demanding stretch offering superb views, ruins of Thurnham Castle.

Wye to Etchinghill (Section 10, 11.3 miles / 18.2 km)
Wye Crown, Devil's Kneading Trough, first glimpse of the English Channel.

Etchinghill to Dover (Section 11, 12.1 miles / 19.5 km)
Channel Tunnel Terminal, Battle of Britain Memorial, spectacular coastal scenery, Dover Harbour, Dover Castle.

Boughton Lees to Chilham (Section 12, 5.9 miles / 9.5 km)
Lonely Pilgrims' Church at Boughton Aluph, King's Wood, first distant view of Canterbury Cathedral.

Unlike previous editions, circular walks based on the North Downs Way are no longer offered in this guide. However, a wide choice of such routes is offered on the **North Downs Way** website.

Getting there

The North Downs Way enjoys some of the best public transport links of any National Trail. Twelve railway lines intersect the route, and 34 stations lie beside it or within a mile or two (1–3 km), with links to them from the route described on pages 179–186. Bus services supplement them at many places.

In this book, a summary of public transport services is given at the end of each route section. Further details of these services can be easily obtained by contacting **National Rail Enquiries** (for trains) or **Traveline** (for buses and trains).

E. M. Forster (1879–1970), who lived in the Surrey Hills, wrote outstanding novels such as A Passage to India *and* Howards End.

If there are two or more people in your party, it may be economical to hire a taxi, minicab or minibus from a station to your starting point, or back from the finishing point. Places where such services are located are shown in the public transport summaries. Further details can be obtained from **Yell**, **Talking Pages**, **Thomson Local**, or from online maps such as Bing or Google (just type 'taxis' followed by the name of your destination).

For some people it may be necessary or more convenient to travel by car; however, as the North Downs Way is a linear route, you will need either to find a way of getting back to it, or have one car at the start and another at the finish of your intended walk for the day.

Refreshments, toilets and accommodation

In this book, the locations of **refreshment facilities** are shown in route descriptions and on maps by the symbols 🍺 for pubs or inns and ☕ for cafés, tea rooms and kiosks. In general, refreshment facilities are shown if they are within about half a mile (1 km) of the route or its links with stations.

There are few **public toilets** on or near the route; those that exist are shown on the maps and in the text by the symbol **PC**.

Places that offer refreshments should have toilets, but usually for customers only.

Places within about 3 miles (5 km) that have **overnight accommodation** are indicated in the text by the symbol ⤳ but are not marked on the maps. In some cases, walking off route to accommodation may involve long stretches of roads, and you may prefer to call out a taxi. Some bed and breakfast establishments are willing to provide transport for walkers.

Budget accommodation such as hostels, camping barns and campsites is very limited along the North Downs Way. Within about 3 miles (5 km) of the route, we know of four youth hostels (Holmbury St Mary, Tanners Hatch, Gillingham/Medway, Canterbury), two camping barns (Puttenham, Coldblow Farm) and six campsites (Stansted, Wrotham Heath, Rochester, Dunn Street, Folkestone, Martin Mill). However, there are many motels within a few miles, managed by chains such as Premier Inn or Travelodge, which offer very low rates if you book early. Camping is not permitted on National Trust or Woodland Trust property, or on nature reserves. It may be possible on farmland but you must first get permission from the landowner.

In this book, a summary of refreshment, toilet and accommodation facilities is provided at the end of each section, showing the distance off route, where appropriate. The mention of an establishment should not be taken as a recommendation, and if the provision of any service is important to you, it would be advisable to check its availability by contacting the establishment. You are strongly advised to book overnight accommodation in advance. Due to limitations of space, it is not possible to give contact details in this book, but you can get further details of accommodation from the **North Downs Way** office, and of accommodation and refreshment facilities from online sources such as Google or Bing maps or **Yell**, from directories such as **Yellow Pages** or **Thomson Local**, or from a telephone directory enquiry service.

Equipment and maps

One of the joys of walking is that you do not necessarily have to buy any special gear, though this may make your journey more comfortable. If you have not walked long distances before, seek advice at an outdoor equipment shop. What you do need is a little bit of common sense: listen to the **weather forecast** and wear appropriate clothing. In cold weather, wear **several layers** that you can take off and put back on, as you will soon warm up while walking but then cool rapidly when you stop, especially in high places that are exposed to the wind. Young children and older people may need additional layers.

The most important thing about walking, though, is to have comfortable **footwear**, otherwise your walk will be spoiled, whatever the weather. So-called 'stout walking shoes' may be suitable, if you are prepared to let them get muddy. For many walkers 'light is right', and trainer-type footwear for walking can be very ('ultra') light. Others prefer a good, strong pair of walking boots in which to stride through whatever ground conditions you may encounter. It is a matter of trial and error, and personal preference. Footwear is available made from special 'breathable' materials designed to keep rain and water out, let perspiration out and air in. Rubber footwear (gumboots, wellingtons) may become uncomfortable on longer walks. If there has been much rain or snow, gaiters or anklets will help keep your feet dry.

Socks should be chosen with care, as rough ones can cause blisters. Wool is usually better than cotton as wool insulates more effectively and remains warm when wet, while cotton is liable to wrinkling, which causes blisters. Many walkers find that two, or even three, pairs are more comfortable than one, with one or two thin pairs under a thicker one. This, too, is a matter of experimentation. An advantage of wearing two or more pairs is that one can be removed if your feet tend to swell up when walking.

An umbrella may not be much use while walking, as rain is often accompanied by strong wind, turning your brolly into a windsail – you may come close to doing a creditable impression of Mary Poppins! It is usually better to wear a **waterproof and windproof jacket** with a hood, leaving both hands free. In really wet weather, **overtrousers** can give added protection. If you wear glasses, a **brimmed hat** or **peaked cap** will help keep the rain off. Try to avoid denims – when wet they take ages to dry and can become very uncomfortable.

Most regular walkers carry their extra gear (such as rainwear, camera, food and drink) in a **rucksack** to leave both hands free, and this is strongly recommended, as you will sometimes encounter steep gradients along the North Downs Way where two free arms will help keep your balance.

A **walking stick** or **retractable pole** (or two) provides support and helps keep your balance on gradients, steps and slippery surfaces.

Statue of Ralph Vaughan Williams (1872–1958) in Dorking. He lived nearby and wrote The Lark Ascending, *one of the most popular pieces of British classical music.*

As with all the National Trail guides published by Aurum, you do not need to buy **maps** as extracts of the Ordnance Survey Explorer series (scale 1:25000) are shown in the route description alongside the relevant text. However, if you plan to divert substantially from the route, to overnight accommodation for example, it would be advisable to obtain the appropriate full-size maps from the **Ordnance Survey**.

Explorer map sheets covering the Main Line are: 137, 138, 145, 146, 147, and 148. If you intend to follow the Canterbury Loop, you will also need sheets 149 and 150. Although they are not as good for walking, the Ordnance Survey's Landranger series (1:50000) provides a good overview of the area. The sheets covering the Main Line are: 179, 186, 187, 188 and 189, while 177 and 178 are also needed for the Canterbury Loop.

Two sheets published by **Harvey Maps** cover the whole route at 1:40000 scale.

There are currently no maps known to us that are being published at a smaller scale to give you an overview of south-east England. Ordnance Survey publish a Travelmaps series at 100000 scale, but the sheets 18 (covering the western half of the North Downs Way) and 19 (eastern half) were discontinued in 2010 – you may still be able to obtain copies at specialist map shops or online.

Public rights of way

Around 80 per cent of the North Downs Way is on 'public rights of way' (PROWs), which is a legal term covering footpaths, bridleways and byways. Their status is indicated on the Ordnance Survey Explorer maps used in this book by different types of green line (see 'Roads and paths' inside the front cover).

Footpaths are intended for pedestrians only. Cyclists and horses may not use them, but prams, pushchairs and wheelchairs can be taken along them. Signs on footpaths have yellow arrows or chevrons. Footpaths have their own special kind of furniture, which is designed to keep out (or make it difficult for) cyclists and horseriders: they include stiles, which are usually made of wood and consist of one or more steps across a fence or wall, and kissing-gates, which can be of metal or wood and consist of a hinged gate that swings inside a semicircular or V-shaped fence. You will also occasionally encounter squeeze-stiles, consisting of two sections that you must pull apart to pass through.

Bridleways can be used by pedestrians, cyclists and horseriders. Cyclists are expected to give way to walkers and horseriders. Walkers and horseriders should respect each others' right to use the route, and walkers should bear in mind that any noise or undue behaviour on their part may spook a horse. Signs on bridleways have pale blue arrows or chevrons.

There are two kinds of **byway**. A 'byway open to all traffic' (BOAT, normally just indicated as a byway) can be used by pedestrians, cyclists, horseriders, motorcyclists and motorists. However, in practice, most byways are very roughly surfaced and usable only by motorcycles and all-terrain vehicles. A 'restricted byway' is not legally accessible to motor vehicles, and may have some form of barrier at each end to prevent such use. Signs on byways have red arrows or chevrons.

Occasionally, the route follows a **permissive path**, where a landowner allows the public to use a path without formally dedicating it as a right of way; or an unclassified route that is not a public right of way, for example across a park or access land. The remainder of the route follows public roads, which may range from a quiet country lane to a motorway. Signs on these stretches have black arrows or chevrons.

Remember that, throughout its length, the North Downs Way crosses land that is

To open a squeeze-stile you just unclip the top and pull the two halves aside — making sure that you clip it back together again after passing through!

owned by someone, or some organisation, whether private landlord or farmer, a local authority, the National Trust, the Woodland Trust or a wildlife trust. Natural England and the county councils have spent many years negotiating new rights of way with landowners, and expend a good deal of time and money in maintaining waymarks and trying to ensure that the public rights of way remain open. Their work is not helped by travellers who do not respect the rights and wishes of the people and organisations who have given their consent for paths to cross their land, sometimes at direct personal cost in terms of repairing stiles or limiting their own use of land. So follow the **Country Code** (see inside back cover).

Closures and diversions. It is occasionally necessary to close a stretch of route temporarily, usually for maintenance or repairs. A warning notice should be put up

at each end of the closure, with a map showing how to get round it. Sometimes a stretch may be permanently diverted, usually to improve the route by taking it away from a road. Details of known closures or diversions are posted on the **North Downs Way** website.

Signage

The route of the North Downs Way is very well indicated by various types of signage. Most commonly, along public rights of way, you will see **discs** attached to gateposts, stiles or what are known as 'waymark posts', erected for the sole purpose of attaching such discs of the appropriate colour as described earlier. Discs should be attached to a post in such a way that the arrow points in the exact direction you should follow. In addition, the National Trail acorn logo appears either on the disc or on a separate plate.

Almost as frequently, you will see **fingerposts** – a tall post with fingers indicating the direction you should follow. In Kent, splendid and distinctive oak fingerposts were installed during 2009 at locations where public rights of way along the North Downs Way join a road. They indicate the status of the right of way by means of a chevron in the relevant colour. They also bear the National Trail acorn logo and pictograms of the types of traveller entitled to use the route: walker, cyclist, horserider, horse-drawn carriage, motorcycle and/or four-wheeled vehicle, as appropriate. Some fingers also show the distance in miles to significant destinations.

Elsewhere in Kent, and in Surrey, old-style metal or wooden fingerposts indicate the direction by means of plain fingers marked 'North Downs Way'. You may occasionally see low-level, concrete tablets on which 'North Downs Way' is engraved, together with a directional arrow.

Some of the oak fingerposts also carry a

plate marked 'E2', or 'E2/E9', where the North Downs Way is used by those **European Long Distance Paths** (E-paths). Route E2 runs for 1,910 miles (3,073 km) from Stranraer in Scotland to Nice in France via Harwich or Dover; route E9 for 2,800 miles (4,505 km) from the border between Spain and France to the border between Poland and Russia via Plymouth and Dover. Further information about these routes can be obtained from **The Ramblers** or the **European Ramblers Association**. The oak fingerposts between Canterbury and Dover bear a pilgrim logo, which indicates that this part of the route is also on the Via Francigena (see page 24).

Links between the North Downs Way and some stations near the route are in the process of being signed, using old-style fingerposts with white lettering on a brown background.

In the Kent part of the route, you will pass **North Downs Way 'milestones'** made of concrete. Do not expect to see them every mile: they are only milestones in the sense that they indicate the number of miles (and kilometres) to or from Farnham, Dover and Canterbury. The author spotted nine (as mentioned in the text), but there may be others.

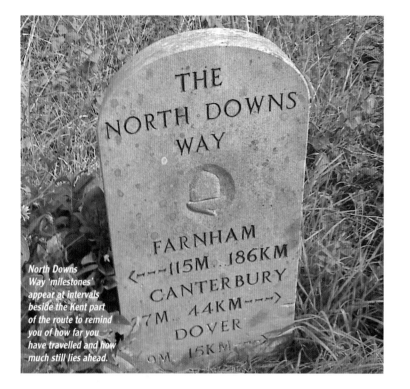

THE
NORTH DOWNS
WAY

FARNHAM
←---115M 186KM
CANTERBURY
7M 44KM---→
DOVER
0M 15KM

North Downs
Way 'milestones'
appear at intervals
beside the Kent part
of the route to remind
you of how far you
have travelled and how
much still lies ahead.

Potential hazards

Although every attempt has been made to devise a route for the North Downs Way that avoids **roads**, some use of them is unavoidable. Where a pavement or footway is available beside a road, this should of course be used, and they are usually provided beside busy main roads. However, most of the quieter roads or lanes you will encounter have no pavement or footway and this is indicated in the text of the route description by the symbol ⚡.

You will also need to cross many roads that have no protected facility for pedestrians. Most are quiet country lanes, but you should remember that, even on these, vehicles may arrive fast around a bend, unaware that you are there. Occasionally you must cross a busy main road unprotected, and in this book they are indicated by the symbol ⚠ on the maps

and in the text. You must take extra care in such situations: do not take risks, and do not attempt to stop traffic.

There are four places in particular along the North Downs Way where you may have difficulty crossing in the so-called 'rush hours' (around 7.30–9.30 am, and 4.30–6.30 pm): B3000 Puttenham Heath Road (Section 1), A233 Westerham Hill (Section 5), Rochester Road (Section 7) and A260 Canterbury Road (Section 11). The relevant highway authorities have been asked to try to improve these situations. Cross at the place that gives the best visibility for yourself and for oncoming drivers, and try to avoid them in rush hours, if possible.

Walkers are expected to use their common sense when walking along or beside roads, but there is no harm in reminding oneself of the precautions to be taken:

Do not linger on any road without a pavement, and try to keep to a part of it that provides best visibility for oncoming traffic. Take note of advice provided in the Highway Code for this situation: 'If there is no pavement, keep to the right-hand side of the road so that you can see oncoming traffic. You should take extra care and be prepared to walk in single file, especially on narrow roads or in poor light. Keep close to the side of the road. It may be safer to cross the road well before a sharp right-hand bend so that oncoming traffic has a better chance of seeing you. Cross back after the bend.'

Cross a road as quickly as possible to a place of safety.

If a path emerges directly on to a road with no pavement, always check that no vehicle is approaching before stepping out.

If you have to walk along a road with no pavement at night, or in poor light, wear something light on top and use your torch.

Barbed-wire fences are frequently used in the countryside and can cause damage to clothing or injury. Keep well clear, especially if the path is slippery. Some farms make use of **electrified fences**, usually a ribbon suspended between fenceposts. They are intended to control livestock and should not cause humans much harm, but it is advisable to keep well clear.

Stiles can be slippery or dilapidated, and injuries are often caused when walkers slip or fall off them. Take care, especially if there is barbed wire or a thorny bush nearby, and hold on to an adjoining post while climbing over, if provided. **Steep hills** or **steps** may be slippery in wet weather and you should take extra care when descending. In some places you may encounter **exposed roots**, **potholes** or other **trip hazards**, so take care, especially in poor light or if you have to walk at night – use a torch. And watch out for **animal droppings**!

On bridleways and byways you may expect to see a fair number of **cyclists**. They may occasionally be seen on footpaths, though they will be trespassing. Some stretches of the route are on 'shared-use' tracks that have been designed to be used by pedestrians and cyclists, often with a dividing line in the centre. Most cyclists are courteous and will wish you a good day, but bear in mind that there may be rogues in a hurry who have little regard for other users and will take corners and descend hills at speed, or approach from behind without warning. Keep to the outside of bends so that you can be seen.

In general, **livestock** encountered on farms should not cause any harm to humans, but always exercise caution. Cattle or horses that approach you are probably just curious and should come to an abrupt halt if you stop and look at them, shout, clap your hands or wave a stick. Horses may think you are going to feed them, but you should refrain from doing so as they may then pester other walkers in expectation of a lump of sugar. Avoid getting between a cow and its calf – it may become alarmed and attack, especially if you have a dog. Keep your dog on a lead whenever there is livestock in a field, but if a cow attacks let it off the lead as this should divert the cow's attention, and your dog probably has a better chance of outrunning it. Potentially dangerous bulls are not allowed to be kept in fields that contain a public right of way, but bulls of certain breeds that are not considered dangerous can be.

Aggressive dogs should be on a lead or behind a fence, but if you encounter one running free a firm order to back off usually shows who is 'top dog'. If you have a walking pole or stick, do not use it to hit the dog (this may make it more aggressive) but stub it firmly on the ground between yourself and the dog while issuing your order.

Wild boar have been seen on at least one stretch of the North Downs Way – Soakham Downs and King's Wood on Section 12. They are not normally dangerous, but, like all wild animals, they can be unpredictable, especially if accompanied by piglets. They

A band of pilgrims on the road to Canterbury, depicted here in a 16th-century miniature.

prefer the undergrowth and are unlikely to be seen on well-used paths. They are likely to detect your presence and wander off long before you are aware of them. If you see one, stand still and keep quiet, then it should amble away. If it seems at all threatening, slowly back away.

Occasionally the route goes beside or across a **golf course**, where you should beware of the possibility of getting hit by a stray golf ball. Public rights of way across them should be clearly marked. Always allow golfers to finish their stroke before proceeding.

Picking wild fruit (such as blackberries, sloes, rose-hips or elderberries) and **mushrooms** from a hedgerow has long been the custom, and although this is not a legal right there is general tolerance as long as you are on a public right of way. Only

pick things that you know to be edible, are not within contamination distance of a road or factory, and are out of reach of passing dogs. Remember that the Country Code (see inside back cover) states that you should protect plants – this applies especially to protected species of wild flowers.

Armed with this guide and keeping an eye on the signage, one hopes that **getting lost** should never happen while walking the North Downs Way. However, a missing sign, an occasional lack of concentration or a misunderstanding of the route description may lead you astray. If you find that you have come to a turning point with no signs, and the directions given do not match up, retrace your steps until you reach a recognisable sign or point in the route description, double-check your onward route and try again.

Safety first

All walkers should carry a **first aid kit** that, at the very least, contains materials to cope with cuts, blisters, insect bites and a tick-remover – check your body at the end of the day for ticks. Outdoor equipment shops usually stock a good range of kits. If possible, **walk with companions**. This not only gives greater confidence in lonely areas but means that someone can go for help in case of an accident. If you are walking in the afternoon (especially in winter) or in bad weather, carry a **torch** in case you find yourself having to walk in poor light or darkness. Take a **compass** to check your route direction if in doubt, and a **whistle** so that you can attract attention in an emergency – the recognised procedure is six blasts every minute, or at night this can be replaced or supplemented by six flashes of your torch every minute. Take your **mobile phone** if you have one, but do not rely on it: there may be no signal.

Walking with dogs

The Ramblers recommend that 'dogs should be kept under close control at all times, and kept on a lead on roads, near livestock or sensitive wildlife, where the terrain requires careful footwork and wherever the law or other official regulations require it. Dog owners must ensure their dog does not alarm other people, and they must clean up after their dog.'

Cycling and horseriding

Unlike the South Downs Way, the North Downs Way is not intended or suitable for cyclists or horseriders. They are most welcome on stretches of the route that are bridleways or byways (these types of right of way are distinguished on the maps in this guide by different types of green line – see 'Roads and paths' inside the front cover) and on roads. However, nearly half of the route is on footpaths, where they would at least be trespassing and possibly breaking the law in some circumstances. Footpaths are also encumbered by stiles, kissing-gates, long flights of steps and ploughed surfaces, which would make cycling or horseriding uncomfortable, difficult or impossible. The North Downs Way oak fingerposts in Kent clearly show which categories can use a right of way: if no cycle or horse and rider is shown, these categories are not permitted.

An alternative route is being examined to take cyclists from Rochester to Canterbury; news of this will be posted on the **North Downs Way** web pages.

Other walks

There are many other excellent walks in south-east England. Three other National Trails are nearby: the South Downs Way (100 miles / 160 km from Winchester to Eastbourne), the Ridgeway (85 miles / 137 km from Overton Hill near Avebury to Ivinghoe Beacon near Tring) and the Thames Path (180 miles / 289 km from the river's source in Gloucestershire to the Thames Barrier in London). Official National Trail Guides to all three are produced by **Aurum Press** in the same series as this book.

The North Downs Way encounters 15 other named walking routes that have been devised by various organisations; indeed, the route is shared with some of them in places and you will see their waymarks. They are: St Swithun's Way, Downs Link, Greensand Way, Mole Gap Trail, Thames Down Link, Downlands Circular Walks, Woldingham Countryside Walk, Vanguard Way, Darent Valley Path, Wealdway, Medway Valley Walk, Stour Valley Walk, Elham Valley Way, Saxon Shore Way and White Cliffs Country Trail. More details are given at the appropriate points in this book.

There are many other self-guided short nature trails and similar routes in the area, and guided walks are organised by such bodies as **Surrey County Council**, **Kent County Council**, **Kent Wildlife Trust**, **Surrey Wildlife Trust**, **National Trust** and **Woodland Trust**, which you should contact for further details.

PART THREE
The North Downs Way

At Brockham the white chalk gleaming through the vegetation shows how extensively the lime-rich rock of the North Downs was quarried in the past.

Farnham to Guildford

through Puttenham and past the Watts Gallery
11 miles (17.7 km)

Ascent 666 feet 203 metres)

Descent 765 feet 233 metres)

Lowest point Shalford Park: 118 feet (36 metres)

Highest point Puttenham Little Common: 404 feet (123 metres)

A comparatively gentle introduction to the North Downs Way. The chalk ridge to the north that is the Hog's Back – the true North Downs hereabouts – is unsuitable for walking, so this section goes through rolling farmland and heathland on sandy soil. Indeed, you will sometimes be walking on pure yellow sand, while layers of the crumbly, orange and yellow rock can be seen on either side in places where the path has been worn into it over the centuries. Leave some energy for a sting in the tail: much of the last 2 miles (3 km) is on soft sand and you will feel as if you are walking uphill on a sandy beach.

The section starts in the market town of Farnham and finishes on the outskirts of the cathedral and university city of Guildford – both full of interest and well worth a visit or a night's stay. The route passes through or skirts the villages of Runfold, The Sands, Seale and Puttenham, but the highlight must be the Watts Gallery and its tea shop right next to the Trail towards the end. The North Downs Way encounters the Pilgrims Way for the first time just over halfway along.

Things to look out for

1 Farnham is a pleasant and ancient town that is worth a look round if you have time to spare before setting off along the North Downs Way. It is now predominantly a commuter town for London, but it was once an important market town. You may be struck by the large number of alleyways that lead off the main streets – reminders of dozens of inns that once served the coaching trade in the 18th and 19th centuries; one of them, Lion and Lamb Yard, was converted in 1984 into a thriving shopping mall. The Georgian elegance of Castle Street has been enhanced by some 'orangery' type market stalls that look antique but were installed in 2008.

Farnham Castle dates from around the mid-12th century and later became a residence of the Bishops of Winchester. It is now a conference centre and is open to the public. Hops were once a major crop in the area and at one time the town had five breweries. By the late 20th century this had fallen to zero, but following the recent revival of real ale, four small, independent breweries have been established in and around the town.

2 Farnham Maltings, on the south side of the River Wey, is another relic of the town's brewing history. It started as a tannery in the 18th century, became a brewery in the 19th, then in 1969 the people of Farnham saved it from demolition so that it could be converted into an entertainment and exhibition centre. A market is held there on the first Saturday of each month. Nearby is the birthplace of William Cobbett (1763–1835), whose *Rural Rides* is an account of his journeys on horseback around southern England between 1821 and 1830. The building is now a pub of the same name, and Cobbett's tomb lies prominently outside the entrance of St Andrew's Church, which dates from the 11th century.

3 The **River Wey** has two sources: one (north branch) near Alton in Hampshire, the other (south branch) near Blackdown in West Sussex – you are beside the north branch here. The two branches join at Tilford, 5 miles (8 km) south-east of Farnham, then the river flows on through Godalming and Guildford to join the Thames at Weybridge. The lower reaches have been canalised: as the Godalming Navigation from Godalming to Guildford (see below), and as the Wey Navigation from Guildford to Weybridge.

4 The **North Downs Way seat** is one of two (the other is near Dover) commissioned from local artists by the then Countryside Agency to mark the start and finish of the route, or as near as was practical. Carved into its back rest is an impression of a bee orchid, while an inscription around the seat's rim tells you that there are 153 miles to Dover; however, if you have read the introduction to this guide you will realise that this is misleading: it is actually about 125 miles (201 km), taking the shorter 'Main Line', or 131 miles (211 km) by the 'Canterbury Loop'.

5 **Moor Park House** was the home of Sir William Temple (1628–99), an author and politician of some note in his day. The grounds can be visited by following a short (0.9 miles / 1.4 km) heritage trail, which passes the house, the ruins of Waverley Abbey, a Stone Age camp, and a cave that is associated with the legend of a white witch called Mother Ludlam.

6 **Runfold Wood Nature Reserve** is an area of predominantly broadleaved woodland, managed by the **Surrey Wildlife Trust**. Its resident fauna include roe deer, dormice, great spotted woodpeckers, blackcaps, nuthatches and stag beetles. The removal of rhododendron and cherry laurel has allowed a wider range of flora to flourish, including bluebells in spring.

This elaborately carved seat, with its 'bee orchid' back rest, was commissioned specially to mark the start of the North Downs Way.

7 The **Hampton Estate** comprises a vast area of 2,250 acres (910 hectares), based around Hampton Lodge and its lakes to the south-east. It is privately owned, with activities divided between agriculture and forestry, but much of the woodland areas (including Binton Wood to the south) are open for pedestrian access.

8 The **Hog's Back** is a narrow ridge that forms the westernmost part of the North Downs, cut off from the rest by the Wey valley. Once known as Guildown, it is 7.5 miles (12.1 km) long and reaches 499 feet (152 metres) above sea level at its highest point. It would have made a fine walking route, were it not for the A31 dual carriageway from Guildford to Dorset, which 'hogs' most of the ridge.

9 **Puttenham Common** is part of the Hampton Estate but is managed by the **Surrey Wildlife Trust**. Once a much larger area of heathland, the main part of the common is now predominantly silver birch woodland, but the heather, bracken and gorse that typifies heathland still grows in abundance, around clumps of oak and Scots pine, at Puttenham Little Common, which you go through later. Roe deer may be seen among the trees and adders are quite common in the open heathland.

10 **Puttenham** is a rather quiet village that achieved some notoriety when it featured in Aldous Huxley's *Brave New World*, published in 1932, which is set in a future society where humanity reproduces itself by technological means and is educated by sleep-teaching. St John the Baptist Church dates from late Saxon times, but most of it was added in stages, the last being the 15th-century tower. The 13th-century Lady Chapel was destroyed by fire in the 18th century and was not restored until Victorian times.

11 The **Watts Gallery** celebrates the work of the English artist George Frederic Watts (1817–1904). He was one of the foremost portrait painters of his day and many of his

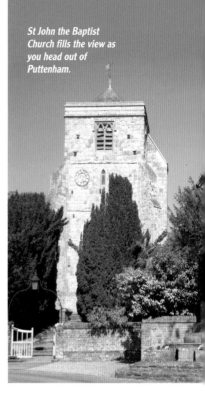

St John the Baptist Church fills the view as you head out of Puttenham.

works are on display at the National and Tate Galleries. He lived in a house nearby, and towards the end of his life decided that paintings that remained in his possession should be put on display to the public. Thus came into being the Watts Gallery, designed by his friend Christopher Turner, which opened in 1903, just a year before Watts died. Admission is free and the gallery boasts a rather fine tea shop. If you have time, a visit to the remarkable Watts Cemetery Chapel, 330 yards (300 metres) to the south along Down Lane, will be well rewarded. It was designed by Watts's wife Mary and completed in 1904 with the help of the villagers of Compton.

12 **Loseley House** has been the home of the More-Molyneux family since 1562, when it was built at the request of Elizabeth I, who stayed there several times, as did James I. It is open to the public daily except Mondays from May to September (also open bank holiday Mondays), and has a walled garden, a fine tea room and a shop.

There is an admission charge for the house and garden, but entry to the tea room and shop is free. The world-famous Loseley ice cream and yogurts originated from this estate, but have now far outgrown that source; production has moved to Wales and the Loseley Estate no longer has any connection with its eponymous ice cream.

13 St Catherine's Chapel was built in the early 14th century as a 'chapel-of-ease' for local people, who needed a more convenient place to worship than their parish church in Guildford. It fell out of use in the 16th century and is now a ruin, but panels beside the chapel show a reconstruction of how it may have looked in its prime.

14 The **Godalming Navigation** is, in effect, an extension of the River Wey Navigation. In 1653 the Wey was one of the first rivers in England to be made accessible to barges, as far as Guildford, and the opening of the Godalming Navigation in 1764 allowed chalk from nearby quarries and other heavy goods to be taken to London. From 1816 it was possible to continue to the south coast at Littlehampton, following the opening of the Wey & Arun Junction Canal, which linked to the Arun Navigation, but that fell into disuse and final abandonment in 1871. The Wey & Arun Canal Trust aims to restore this link, but that will take many years. In 1964 the River Wey and Godalming Navigations were donated to the **National Trust**.

15 Shalford Park was once part of the grounds of Shalford House, which was demolished in 1967. As you pass through, note on your left a group of little wooden structures made by the **Surrey Wildlife Trust** to provide homes for small wildlife. The park is the venue for occasional open-air concerts and other events.

The Godalming Navigation, part of the River Wey, is used mostly for quiet recreation nowadays, but in earlier times quarried chalk was carried on barges to London.

Route description

*To start your walk along the North Downs Way, from the main exit of **Farnham Station** ***A*** *go ahead down Station Hill to the traffic lights at the junction with the A31 Farnham bypass. Cross to your right to find a North Downs Way information board and signpost* ***B*** *marking the actual start of the route.*

🚌🛒🍺🛶 *If you wish to visit **Farnham** ***1*** *town centre, keep ahead at the lights, or for **Farnham Maltings** ***2*** *cross ahead then turn left beside the brick wall into Abbey Street.*

From the information board, walk beside the A31 for 150 yards (140 metres), then bear right along shady, tree-lined Darvills Lane. At a T-junction with another lane (Snailslynch) turn right, then bend left to pass a gate into a filling station **C**, which has a shop and café 🍵. You soon find yourself walking beside the north branch of the **River Wey** **3**, which, with its meadows, makes an attractive buffer between the walker and the A31.

Continue along the pleasant lane beside the river, where you may be lucky enough to spot a kingfisher. Pass Snayleslynch Farm, then at the next house (The Kiln) **D** turn right, away from the river, along a footpath to go under a Victorian brick railway bridge. You are now walking along a pleasant woodland-edge footpath with broad water meadows on your left. Shortly pass a path junction, then in a further 275 yards (250 metres) turn left at another path junction. In 60 yards (55 metres) turn right through a gate to find an elaborately carved **North Downs Way seat** **4** on your left.

You are now on a grassy track through fields with mature deciduous and coniferous trees all around, including a splendid European larch. In 325 yards (300 metres) pass through a gate on to a road (Moor Park Way) 🌲, where you turn left to a road junction **E**. Take great care here, as approaching traffic may be blind to walkers. Turn left along Moor Park Lane, which crosses the River Wey's north branch. You now walk between a lime hedge and a brick wall to reach a crossroads at the entrance to **Moor Park House** **5**.

Keep ahead up Compton Way, a very steep but mercifully short hill. When the road bends right **F**, turn left along a footpath beside a drive and gateway, soon turning

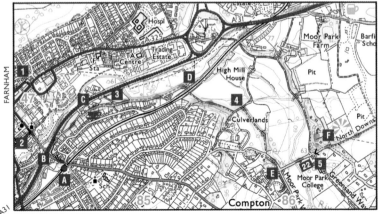

Contours are given in metres
The vertical interval is 5m

right to regain your original direction. You are now on Wey Hanger (*hanger* is an Old English word, widely used throughout this part of England, for a wood on the edge of a steep hill), but sadly the fine view to your left that used to exist here has been blocked by an embankment constructed around a recycling facility. Nevertheless, this is pleasant walking country and it is good to be well away from the town and traffic.

Go through a gate and keep ahead along the left-hand side of a large field, where yellow ragwort thrives. Pass through another gate into **Runfold Wood Nature Reserve** and follow the well-worn track ahead through mixed woodland and bracken, with old sand workings on your left. At a T-junction (with a Runfold Wood information board) continue ahead.

At the next junction descend steps , then turn right. You are now walking along a broad, slightly sunken track. At a fence corner, turn left to walk beside a high wooden fence, behind which is a private garden. After passing a house and garden on your left you come to Crooksbury Road on the outskirts of the village of Runfold. Turn left along the road ✖, then in 20 yards (18 metres) turn right through a barrier. Follow a short, fenced footpath leading to Sands Road ✖, where you turn right. Take care, as there is a blind right-

hand bend over the brow of a hill – you may find it best to keep to the left-hand side until after the brow.

Pass between Holly House, on your right, with its impressive grove of Scots pine trees, and on your left the golf driving range of Farnham Golf Club. You can now use a footway on the left-hand side of the road to reach the golf clubhouse opposite the Sandy Farm Business Centre.

🚰 *If you wish to visit the Barley Mow at The Sands, keep ahead along Sands Road for 330 yards (300 metres) to a crossroads, then keep ahead for a further 220 yards (200 metres).*

Turn left into Blighton Lane ✖ and follow it for 475 yards (435 metres). Soon after a brick postbox , where the road bears left, turn right over a small wooden footbridge to follow a footpath into trees then along the left side of the golf course (beware mishit balls). In 550 yards (500 metres) cross Binton Lane and continue along an enclosed footpath, which soon bears right, through a wooden gate, to lead beside open fields. In 275 yards (250 metres), at a grove of Scots pines take the right fork to follow a fenced footpath beside several more fields for 0.6 mile (1 km).

At the end of the first field, go through a metal gate into another field to continue in the same direction along its left edge,

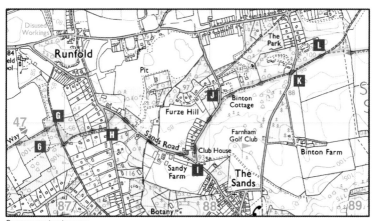

Contours are given in metres
The vertical interval is 5m

passing under a power line. You are now in the vast **Hampton Estate** **7**. Cross a sandy, sunken lane at an information board for Binton Wood **M**. Follow the third field to Elstead Road **N** at the south end of the village of Seale.

☕ *To visit Manor Farm Craft Centre tea room, go left for 440 yards (400 metres).*

Turn right along the road for 22 yards (20 metres), then turn left through a gate to find 'Tree House 4B' – an artistic, possibly ephemeral creation by person or persons unknown of knick-knacks festooning a sweet chestnut tree and its surroundings. Follow the shady footpath through Payn's Firs for 330 yards (300 metres), then turn sharp left beside a large garden **O** containing a brick wall feature. In 150 yards (135 metres) go through a gate and turn right

along a grassy footpath, with a young plantation on your right and heathland falling away to your left. There are now pleasant views across the valley towards Puttenham and the **Hog's Back** **8**.

Descend to pass through two gates into woodland, crossing the ditch and embankment of an old earthwork. Continue down, crossing a wide farm track to follow a sunken track to reach Totford Lane **P** at Totford Hatch, beside a red-brick bungalow with the date 1893 on its chimney. Turn left along the lane to pass through a five-bar gate, then turn right on to a fenced lane in woodland. You have now entered the main part of **Puttenham Common** **9** and will be following this sandy track for the next 0.8 mile (1.3 km). It is marked as a 'BOAT' (see page 30).

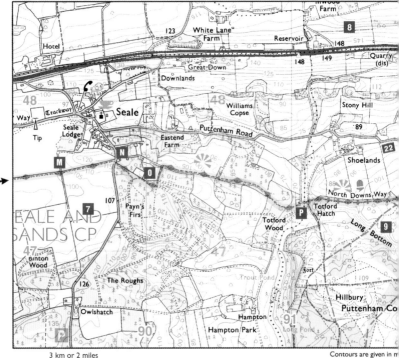

3 km or 2 miles
Elstead

Contours are given in m
The vertical interval is

Cross the stream (which feeds the lake at Hampton Park then flows on to join the Wey) and keep on up the lane beside Puttenham Little Common. At the top, with a red-brick house ahead, take the left fork and follow this as it winds and undulates through woodland, with views to the left of the Hog's Back. At metalled Lascombe Lane ◻ keep ahead to join Highfield Lane ◻ and continue down to **Puttenham 10**. Continue along its main road, The Street, which is where the North Downs Way first encounters the **Pilgrims Way**.

After passing the Good Intent ◻ ◻, you climb out of the village. On your right is the church of St John the Baptist; on your left is Puttenham Camping Barn ◻. At the top is the busy B3000 Puttenham Heath Road ◻ ⚠; cross and turn right, taking great care, as there is no dedicated pedestrian facility.

◻ *To visit the Harvester pub-restaurant, turn right before crossing the B3000.*

In 150 yards (140 metres), opposite the Harvester ◻, turn left and keep ahead along the left-hand of two drives serving Puttenham Golf Club; this is a public bridleway. In a further 240 yards (220 metres) you pass Clear Barn Farm ◻ to reach a fork, where you bear left (the right-hand fork leads to Puttenham's cricket ground). In another 240 yards (220 metres) pass **Greyfriars Vineyard**, which grows Chardonnay and Pinot Noir vines and has occasional open weekends. Keep ahead (signed '10th tee'), following a track that leads through the heart of the golf course. A belt of trees on either side should protect walkers from stray golf balls.

Continuing down the gravel track, at the isolated community of Monksgrove fork left and continue past Questors. Keep ahead

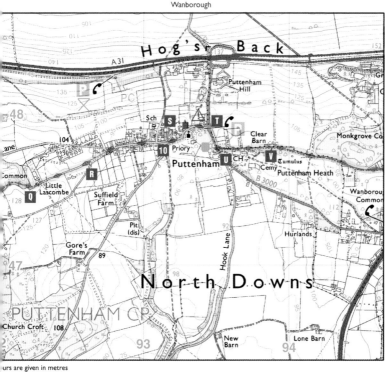

where several tracks and paths meet . After passing some large barns, the track narrows; keep ahead into woodland, with the sound of the A3 getting louder. Emerging from the woods at Monkshatch , bear right along a metalled lane to pass under two bridges: the first carries the A3, the other a slip road to the B3000. The two crosses on the latter mark the presence of the Pilgrims Way below.

At the T-junction , turn left along Down Lane to the **Watts Gallery** **11** ☕. Bear right on a bridleway to the right of the gallery. This part of the route is notorious for long stretches of deep sand. At first it climbs a sunken lane into woods, then levels out between fields with farm buildings on your right . The track narrows as you keep ahead uphill into overgrown old coppice. This is West Warren, part of a nature reserve in the Loseley Estate. Descend to a track junction **AA** in a dip between woods.

☕ *The broad track to your right is not a public right of way, but the Loseley Estate is happy for North Downs Wayfarers to use it to reach* **Loseley House** **12***, 0.5 mile (0.8 km) to the south.*

Continue to a junction with a footpath and keep ahead for 110 yards (100 metres) to a fork **AB**. The North Downs Way leaves the bridleway here to take the left fork, a public footpath, bending left then right. In 660 yards (600 metres) you reach a T-junction **AC** with a farm drive, where you turn left then shortly right, signed Stephenson Plastics. Pass Piccards Farm and continue for 825 yards (750 metres) between fields on your left and woodland on your right to reach a road (Sandy Lane) **AD**. Turn left down to the A3100 Old Portsmouth Road opposite Ye Olde Ship Inn **AE** 🍺. Cross with care ⚠ and turn right beside the inn, then in 50 yards (45 metres) turn left into Ferry Lane opposite the College of Law.

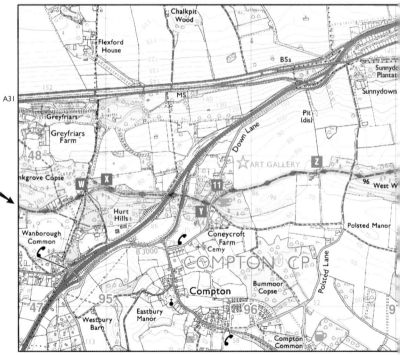

Contours are given in
The vertical interval

*A short, steep diversion up the footpath on the right is **St Catherine's Chapel** 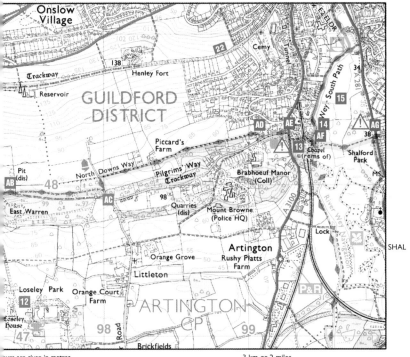. There is a shortcut from here straight down to the footbridge over the Wey, but it is extremely steep and not recommended. Instead, retrace your steps to Ferry Lane.*

Continue along Ferry Lane, which follows the line of an ancient track that took the Pilgrims Way down to the former ferry across the River Wey. Cross the railway line, then descend steeply past Ferry Lodge. At the bottom pass a little bower with a rocky seat and 'pixie's bridge' to reach the River Wey ⬛, here forming the **Godalming Navigation** ⬛.

⇌🚌 *The link with **Guildford Station** and bus station starts by turning left here (see page 179).*

Turn right to cross the footbridge, then turn left beside a carved post commemorating the Shalford House Estate. Follow the gravel path as it bends right, away from the river, to cross a wooden footbridge into **Shalford Park** ⬛. At a line of trees go through a gap and take the left-hand footpath across a playing field. Head for a pair of wooden five-bar gates to the right of the tallest pine tree and pass them to reach the A281 Shalford Road ⬛ and the end of Section 1 of the North Downs Way.

🚌 *Frequent buses go from the bus stop on this side of the road into Guildford town centre. Buses on the far side go to Cranleigh, Horsham, Dorking or Redhill.*

⇌ *The link with **Shalford Station** starts here by turning right, along a cycle track, just before reaching the road (see page 179).*

To continue to Section 2, cross Shalford Road with care ⚠, using the pedestrian refuge to the left if traffic is heavy, and keep ahead along Pilgrims Way.

Public transport

Farnham (on route) ⇌ 🚌
Guildford (1 mile / 1.6 km) ⇌ 🚌
Runfold (0.5 mile / 0.8 km) 🚌 Not Sundays
Seale (0.3 mile / 0.5 km) 🚌 Not Sundays
Puttenham (on route) 🚌 Not Sundays
Old Portsmouth Road (on route) 🚌 Not Sundays
Shalford Road (on route) 🚌
Shalford (1 mile / 1.6 km) ⇌
Taxis/minicabs: Farnham, Tongham, Farncombe, Godalming, Guildford

Refreshments and toilets

Farnham (0.3 mile / 0.5 km) 🍴☕ Wide selection
Farnham Maltings (0.3 mile / 0.5 km) ☕
Snailslynch (on route) ☕ Filling station
The Sands (0.3 mile / 0.5 km) 🍴 Barley Mow
Seale (0.3 mile / 0.5 km) ☕ Manor Farm Craft Centre
Puttenham (on route) 🍴 Good Intent, Harvester
Compton (on route) ☕ Watts Gallery
Loseley House (0.5 mile / 0.8 km) ☕
Old Portsmouth Road (on route) 🍴 Ye Olde Ship Inn
Guildford (1 mile / 1.6 km) 🍴☕ Wide selection
Shalford (1 mile / 1.6 km) 🍴 Queen Victoria
Food shops: Farnham, Snailslynch, Puttenham, Guildford, Shalford
Public toilets: Farnham, Guildford

Accommodation

Farnham (0.3 mile / 0.5 km) Wide selection – contact **Farnham Tourist Information Centre**
Runfold (2.3 miles / 3.7 km) Princess Royal
Seale (0.5 mile / 0.8 km) Ramada Jarvis Hotel
Elstead (2.9 miles / 4.6 km) Hunter's Lodge
Puttenham (on route) Puttenham Camping Barn
Guildford (1 mile / 1.6 km) Wide selection – contact **Guildford Tourist Information Centre**
Broadford Bridge (1 mile / 1.6 km) Parrot Inn
Shalford (1 mile / 1.6 km) The Laurels, Northfield

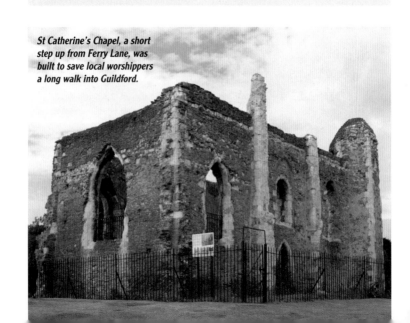

St Catherine's Chapel, a short step up from Ferry Lane, was built to save local worshippers a long walk into Guildford.

2 Guildford to Westhumble

via St Martha's Church, Newlands Corner and Ranmore Common
13 miles (21 km)

Ascent 961 feet (293 metres)

Descent 945 feet (288 metres)

Lowest point Shalford Road: 128 feet (39 metres)

Highest point White Down Lease: 722 feet (220 metres)

You reach the chalk of the true North Downs on this section. It is longer and a little more strenuous than the first, with more ascent, but the climbs are not steep, except in a few brief stretches. The route continues along the Pilgrims Way at first, but leaves it about a third of the way along to move abruptly from sandstone to chalk. You will pass through several nature reserves and Sites of Special Scientific Interest (SSSI), managed by the Surrey Wildlife Trust (SWT) or the National Trust (NT). Much of the route is in woodland, but you should often have magnificent views to the south over the Tillingbourne Valley towards the Greensand Ridge, the High Weald and even to the South Downs in places, given clear weather.

You will pass St Martha's Church, one of the highlights of the whole route, and Newlands Corner, one of its busiest honeypots. Then you march in the footsteps of the Canadian Army at one of their Second World War training camps. Finally, you survey the largest vineyard in Britain and preview the start of the next section: Box Hill.

Things to look out for

1 Chantry Wood (also called The Chantries) is so named as it was bequeathed to Holy Trinity Church in Guildford to pay for a licence for a chantry there, where the priest would pray for the soul of Henry Norbrigge, a 15th-century wool merchant and nine times Mayor of Guildford. The mixed woodland covers 188 acres (78 hectares) and was opened to the public after its acquisition by Guildford Borough Council in 1938.

2 Pewley Down sits on the chalk ridge that you will soon be joining to continue along the North Downs Way. Just before the First World War a proposal to build houses on part of the down was defeated. After the

war, a local brewery acquired the land and donated it to the people of Guildford as a memorial to those who lost their lives.

3 St Martha's Church, also known as St Martha-on-the-Hill, or 'the church on the North Downs Way', was built in 1850 from the ruins of a 12th-century church on the site of an earlier Saxon church. It is thought to be a place where pagan Saxons burned Christian martyrs and there is a (probably apocryphal) story that this, rather than the saint, may be the origin of the name. During the Second World War the church was disguised to look like a clump of trees to avoid its being bombed. At the east gate of the churchyard is a small memorial to

This view of Pewley Down behind South Warren Farm was saved from the blight of a housing estate.

Yvonne Arnaud (1890–1958), a French actress who settled in England and after whom the theatre in Guildford was named; her ashes were scattered nearby. St Martha's Hill is a SWT nature reserve, where adders may be seen. From this exalted location (573 feet / 175 metres above sea level) you have splendid panoramic views: south-east across the Tillingbourne Valley towards Blackheath and the Greensand Hills; north and north-west across Guildford and the Wey Valley.

4 The **Downs Link** is a 37-mile (59-km) bridleway that connects the North Downs Way with the South Downs Way at Botolphs, near Steyning, then continues to finish at Shoreham in West Sussex. Launched in 1984, it mostly follows a disused railway line.

5 The **Greensand Ridge** (sometimes called the Greensand Hills) follows a band of sandstone running parallel to, and around 4 miles (6.4 km) south of, the North Downs. Its highest point is Leith Hill, which you can see from Albury Downs and which at 965 feet (294 metres) above sea level is

also the highest point in southern England. In 1765 a tower folly was built on the summit to take the altitude up to 1,029 feet (314 metres) – by some definitions, this makes Leith Hill a mountain! The valley that lies between the North Downs and the Greensand Ridge is sometimes referred to as the Vale of Holmesdale.

6 **Newlands Corner** is one of the busiest honeypots that you will encounter (or endure) along the North Downs Way, and no wonder, for this is one of the finest viewpoints in Surrey. As well as a refreshment kiosk, picnic tables and toilets, there is a visitor centre, which offers internet facilities. In 1926 Agatha Christie's infamous 'staged disappearance' from here started a womanhunt throughout the nearby Downs.

7 **Netley Park**, part of Shere Woodlands Nature Reserve, was the Second World War training ground of Canadian armed forces, who arrived in 1943 to prepare for the Normandy landings of June 1944. The concrete water tanks that you see are relics of their occupation. For 1.3 miles (2.1 km), the North Downs Way follows what is known locally as the Canadian Road, as it provided access to the training ground; it once had a tarmac surface but that is gradually wearing away.

8 **Blatchford Down**, part of White Down Lease, has been named in honour of Alan Blatchford (1938–82), one of the co-founders of the **Long Distance Walkers Association**. Later in this section you will encounter Steer's Field, which commemorates Chris Steer (1919–92). The pair jointly founded the LDWA in 1972 – a matter of some serendipity, as Chris spotted a card that Alan had placed in a post office window asking for walking companions.

9 **'Pillbox'** is the nickname for a miniature fort, so called because the construction is reminiscent of the boxes that used to contain medicinal pills. They were used on First World War battlefields, but during the early part of the Second World War, when an invasion of Britain by German forces seemed imminent, some 28,000 were erected at strategic locations. Around 6,000 remain, and you will pass at least 12 as you progress along the North Downs Way, including seven in this section. The plaque by the entrance of the first one invites you to enter with care; the second is in a dilapidated state and should be given a wide berth. The pillboxes you will see are mostly hexagonal in plan, constructed of brick or concrete, with a slot in five sides from which to observe or shoot. In wartime they would have had some form of camouflage and were manned by the Home Guard. Further information can be obtained from the **Pillbox Study Group**.

10 The **North Downs Line** is the name given to both the cross-country railway line linking Reading with Gatwick Airport via Guildford, Dorking, Reigate and Redhill, and to the train service (operated by **First Great Western**) that runs along it. The line runs roughly parallel with the North Downs from Ash to Redhill, but in this area it makes its closest approach to the escarpment, cutting through the foot at one point.

11 **Dorking** is an ancient market town at the south end of a gap through the North Downs created by the River Mole. It is dominated by the spire of the parish church of St Martin – one of the tallest spires in England at 210 feet (64 metres), completed in 1877. There has been settlement in the area since Roman times, as Stane Street, running from London to Chichester, went through here. The town grew in importance after 1750, becoming a staging post when a turnpike road to Brighton was built through it, and many old buildings remain from the coaching era. Since the railway from London arrived in 1867, Dorking has increasingly become a commuter town. From 1929 to 1951 it was the home of the composer Ralph Vaughan Williams (1872–1958) and there is a statue of him in the High Street.

12 **Ranmore Common** is a vast tract of open access land on top of the North Downs, much of which is common land or owned by the National Trust. It is a Site of Special Scientific Interest due to the many rare species that can be found (white admiral butterfly; satin-wave moth; birds such as woodcock, tree-pipit, nightjar, redstart and hawfinch; flora such as yellow archangel, tutsan, sweet woodruff and enchanter's nightshade).

13 **Steer's Field** (see also point **8** above) is a steep, grassy slope that forms part of the Denbies Hillside National Trust property. For a while, the orange waymarks of the Denbies Hillside Nature Trail accompany the National Trail acorns.

14 **The Weald** is the name of the area that lies between the North and South Downs, though it is rarely seen from the western part of the North Downs, as the Greensand Hills are in the way. 'Weald' derives from a Saxon word meaning woodland or forest, and the whole area was heavily wooded in Saxon times. Looking south-east from here, the rich farmland beyond Dorking is the Low Weald. A great chunk of it 10 miles (16 km) away has been taken up by

Box Hill provides the backdrop for the visitor centre and winery of the Denbies Wine Estate and some of its 300,000 vines.

Gatwick Airport and you may see aircraft using it. The higher ground on the horizon is St Leonards Forest in the High Weald, which has been designated as an Area of Outstanding Natural Beauty.

15 The **Greensand Way** is a long-distance walking route, which runs for 107 miles (172 km) along the Greensand Ridge from Haslemere in Surrey to Hamstreet, near Ashford, in Kent. It is roughly parallel with (and has several links to) the North Downs Way. The original route in Surrey only, launched in 1982, was the idea of the late Geoffrey Hollis, then in 1989 the Kent Area of **The Ramblers** extended the route into Kent. Publications are available from **Kent County Council** and **Surrey County Council**.

16 **St Barnabas Church** looks much too large for its remote location, and like St Martha's has been called 'the church on the North Downs Way' due to its size and lofty position – it sits on the 185-metre contour line (607 feet) and the spire soars a further 46 metres (150 feet), making it visible for miles around. It was built in 1859 by the great Victorian architect Sir George Gilbert Scott, initially for the private use of the Cubitt family of builders, but its services are now open to all. The School House nearby, also built by Cubitt, no longer functions as a school.

17 **Denbies** was the 100-room mansion of the Cubitt family of builders. Thomas Cubitt (1788–1855) built much of Bloomsbury and Belgravia in London, also parts of Buckingham Palace and Osborne House. The mansion was demolished in 1953; part of the estate was handed over to the National Trust, but most of it was sold to Adrian White – see below.

18 **Denbies Wine Estate** is England's largest vineyard, covering 627 acres (254 hectares) and stretching for over a mile (1.6 km) west of the A24. Most of Thomas Cubitt's Denbies Estate was bought by Adrian White, chairman of Biwater, the water-treatment company,

who set about developing the vineyard – as it happens, close to the location of a Roman vineyard. The estate includes Bradley Farm, where the villa-style visitor centre and winery now stand. It is open to the public, has a shop and restaurant and the farmhouse offers bed and breakfast.

19 The **Thames Down Link** is a 15-mile (24-km) walking route that links two National Trails: the North Downs Way at Westhumble and the Thames Path at Kingston. Further details can be obtained from **Surrey County Council**.

Route description

🚌 **Alight at the Pilgrims Way stop. If arriving from Guildford, you are on the correct side of the road to turn left along Pilgrims Way. Arriving from the south (Shalford), you must cross the A281 with care (use the pedestrian refuge to the left if traffic is heavy) then keep ahead along Pilgrims Way.**

Section 2 of the North Downs Way starts at the junction of the A281 Shalford Road and Pilgrims Way **A**. Use the footpath along the left-hand side of lime-tree-lined Pilgrims Way for 440 yards (400 metres), passing Clifford Manor Road. As Pilgrims Way bends left to become Echo Pit Road **B**, cross over, turn left, then immediately bear half right along a metalled drive past Rodings. At a junction by a small car park, keep ahead past Chantry Cottage and bear left with the track, which climbs steadily in trees beside **Chantry Wood** **1**. Follow this track for 1.1 miles (1.8 km), passing an opening in the trees near South Warren Farm (a riding centre), with a fine view to the north of **Pewley Down** **2**.

The track emerges from the trees to pass between fields by Whinny Hill, then plunges back into woodland to reach Halfpenny Lane

C. Turn left along the lane for 35 yards (32 metres), then right, across the entrance to Southernway Cottage. Keep ahead up a steep bridleway to a junction with a car park on your left. On your right is Southernway house and a rather charming, timber-framed thatched cottage, looking sadly neglected.

Keep ahead up a sandy, post-lined track for 660 yards (600 metres) to **St Martha's Church** **3**. Leave the churchyard by the gate at its far (east) end, beside Yvonne Arnaud's memorial stone, and keep ahead along the broad, sandy ridge for 450 yards (415 metres). As the gradient steepens, keep to the left (higher) fork, then the right fork to descend a narrow, sandy path among heather. At a broad, sandy 'beach', keep to the left fork then join a broad, sandy ride, descending gently to a major junction **D**.

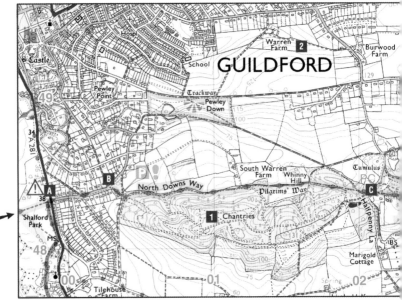

SHALFORD

Contours are given in r
The vertical interval i

� 🚌 *The link with **Chilworth Station** starts here by turning sharp right (see page 179), following the **Downs Link** 4. The Pilgrims Way continues ahead.*

Go half left to descend a bridleway for 330 yards (300 metres) to White Lane at the timber-framed Keepers Cottage E. You have now left the sandstone and are about to climb up to the typical chalk of the North Downs. Turn left past the cottage, beside a five-bar gate, then immediately right to follow for 460 yards (425 metres) a footpath that runs roughly parallel with the lane, bending left as it passes White Lane Farm. Eventually the path descends steps to the lane F. Take great care as you cross, watching especially for vehicles approaching blind both ways. Go ahead through a barrier and climb steeply, soon taking the right fork (ignore side turns) to emerge on to Albury Downs – you have reached the chalk escarpment and start to enjoy the true character of the North Downs.

Follow the higher path, beside trees, which describes a huge arc along the left side of the grass slope. The dominant feature of the view to your right is the **Greensand Ridge** 5.

Eventually the higher path rejoins the lower, which bends left on gravel and starts to climb steeply until it peters out among the sparse vegetation below **Newlands Corner** 6.

☕ **PC** *If you wish to go to the visitor centre continue up the hill. From there you can turn right, through the car park and along the access road, to rejoin the North Downs Way at the fingerpost beside the A25 Shere Road* G.

If you decide to eschew the delights of the visitor centre, when the path peters out go half right towards a gap in the trees and keep on to the fingerpost in the distance, which lies beside the A25 Shere Road G.

☕ *The Barn restaurant and coffee shop lies to the left here, and the Manor House Hotel 🛏 is a little further along the A25.*

At a fingerpost go half right on a bridleway beside the A25 for 75 yards (69 metres).

🚌 🛏 *If you wish to visit Albury, turn right to stay on the right-hand side of the A25 and follow the byway downhill.*

Carefully cross the very busy road ⚠ on to a bridleway that bears right (past a

A25 West Clandon 2 km or 1 mile

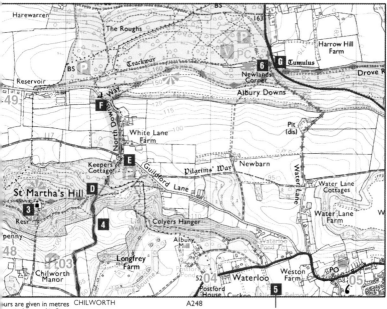

Contours are given in metres CHILWORTH   A248
vertical interval is 5m

St Martha's Church is one of the best-known locations along the North Downs Way, with outstanding views.

North Downs Way information panel) into woodland and continue along it for 1.6 miles (2.6 km).

About two thirds of the way along, at the second junction **H***, where you can turn right if you wish to make a diversion to Silent Pool, a famed beauty spot in this area, but note that it is 820 yards (750 metres) off route, steeply downhill and then, of course, steeply back up again.*

Towards the end of this stretch go through West Hanger, part of Shere Woodlands Nature Reserve (SWT), to a car park beside Staple Lane **I**. Cross the road and keep ahead for 220 yards (200 metres) to another road (Coombe Lane) beside a concrete dew pond. Turn right for 22 yards (20 metres) then bear left along a track. In 200 yards (185 metres) join a wide drive coming in

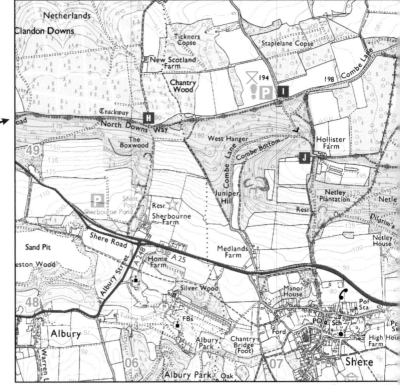

Contours are given in m
The vertical interval is

from the right, then in a similar distance, at Hollister **J**, turn left with the drive.

🍴 📂 ☕ *If you wish to visit Shere, 0.7 mile (1 km) to the south, keep ahead here.*

Go to the right of farm buildings, then pass a six-bar gate and keep ahead into trees. Follow this track for 330 yards (300 metres) to a junction, beside which is a disused concrete water tank, in **Netley Park 7**. Turn right then immediately left to continue in the same direction, following the 'Canadian Road' (bridleway), which swings left then right. In 0.8 mile (1.3 km) you reach a junction known as Gravelhill Gate **K**, by another concrete water tank.

Keep ahead to pass a viewpoint (Little Kings Wood), then fork right to leave the Canadian Road. In 55 yards (50 metres) turn right through a gate into Hackhurst

and White Downs (NT), with fine views to your right of the High Weald. The deep, tree-filled cleft on your right is Colekitchen Hole. At the next gate, fork left uphill beside a fence. After passing a gate you reach a gravel track, signed here as Public Byway 515 but known locally as Beggars Lane **L**.

🚃 🚌 🍴 *The link with **Gomshall Station** starts by turning right here (see page 179).*

Keep ahead, then bear half left. The path soon turns sharp right to reach a junction, where you pass through a gate into White Down Lease (NT), with a splendid view to the south. At the next crossing track and gate you enter **Blatchford Down 8**. Descend ahead, past bench seats and the first of seven red-brick **pillboxes 9**. Keep to the track as it climbs steeply past the

East Horsley
4 km or 2 ½ miles

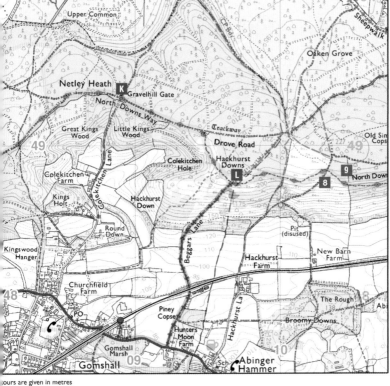

ours are given in metres
vertical interval is 5m

taller and somewhat ruinous second pillbox, which you should not enter. Leave White Down Lease at the next gate . The third pillbox lies well hidden on your right, then the track snakes steeply up through woodland.

At a junction with a minor footpath turn sharp right to descend in a gully to White Down Lane . Turn right downhill, then almost immediately turn left, past a bollard and along a chalky footpath into woodland, where you pass more pillboxes. The route now contours the hillside for the next 2.5 miles (4 km) at an altitude of around 640 feet (195 metres). Into view now come the southern outskirts of Dorking, while the **North Downs Line** runs parallel below.

Descend to a junction (another pillbox) 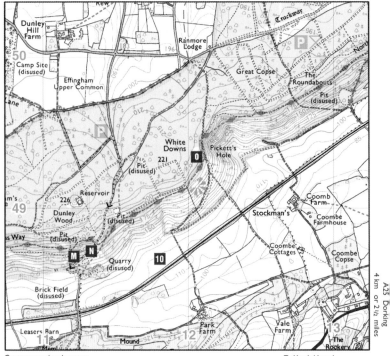, keep ahead through a gate, then climb into more woodland. In 130 yards (120 metres), by an information panel for White

Downs (NT), fork right on a footpath. Follow the path as it veers right, around the lip of another cleft, Picketts Hole. Ignore all paths leading off to the left, and be reassured by a Forest Enterprise sign declaring 'Walkers Welcome Here'. Follow this generally level woodland path for the next 1.3 miles (2.1 km), keeping ahead at three junctions. There are magnificent views at several places, at first down to Westcott, but beyond that, spread out like a view on Google Earth, lies the North Downs 'gap town' of **Dorking** (**11** on map page 60). You have now entered **Ranmore Common** **12**, where eventually you leave the woodland to enter **Steer's Field** **13**.

↘ *If you are staying at Tanners Hatch Youth Hostel (1 mile / 1.6 km), from here you will need to go half left up to the car park (which often has an ice-cream van), where you will find, on the far side of the information board, a poster giving*

Contours are given in metres
The vertical interval is 5m

To Youth Hostel
3 km or 2 miles

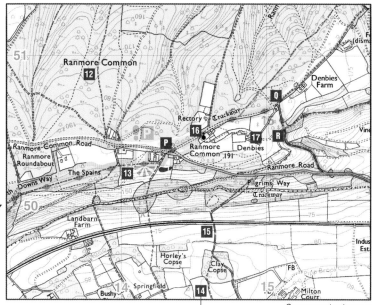

Contours are given in metres
The vertical interval is 5m

instructions for reaching the hostel. For Westcott, take the footpath down to the right just before reaching the end of the woodland.

Take the right-hand mown path, heading a little to the right of a church spire. The view to the right now extends beyond Dorking into **The Weald 14**. Head for a little gazebo behind a garden hedge, then turn left beside the hedge. *A signed link with the **Greensand Way 15** goes off to the right here.* Go through a kissing-gate, then bear half right to Ranmore Common Road **P**, which comes in from the left and continues ahead (the road to the right is Ranmore Road). Cross with care and keep ahead, using the grass verge and footpath along the left-hand side as the road has no pavement.

You soon pass **St Barnabas Church 16** and the neighbouring Old School, still keeping to the left-hand side of the road for another 550 yards (500 metres). When the road turns sharp left **Q** keep ahead, past the gate marked **Denbies 17**, into a meadow. In 33 yards (30 metres) turn right on a bridleway between fences, with an

Italianate, white-painted house away to the right. At a concrete track **R** turn left on a footpath into woodland.

⇌ *The link with **Dorking West Station** starts by continuing ahead (see page 179).*

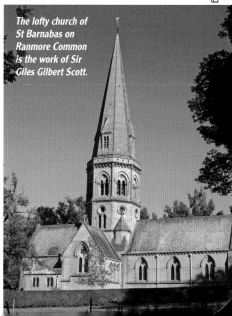

The lofty church of St Barnabas on Ranmore Common is the work of Sir Giles Gilbert Scott.

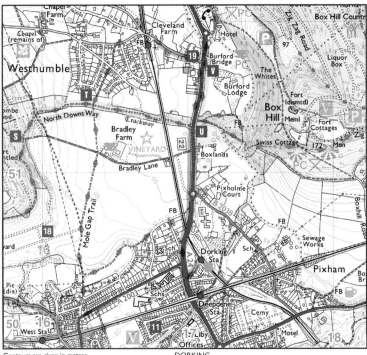

Contours are given in metres
The vertical interval is 5m

DORKING

In 165 yards (150 metres) go through a pedestrian gate to the right of a large pair of vehicle gates in a deer fence. On your right now is another fabulous view, with Dorking **11** providing a backdrop to a small part of the 300,000 vines that make up **Denbies Wine Estate 18**. Do look to your left too, where the field is graced by many fine specimens of tall deciduous and coniferous trees. As you carry on down the gravel lane, the wooded slopes of Box Hill creep into view. Pass through another gate in the deer fence and the view of Box Hill is now complete, with the Denbies visitor centre and winery amid a vast sea of vines.

Ahead now is the village of Westhumble, where Box Hill's railway station is located. The track, now concrete, bends left to a junction **S**, beside which a towering O2 mobile phone mast attempts a poor impersonation of a pine tree. Bending right, the mast's access drive now has a tarmac

surface. In 190 yards (175 metres), where the access drive turns sharp right, keep ahead on a gravel track, which shortly swings down to the right. In 440 yards (400 metres) keep ahead at a crossing footpath **T**.

If you wish to go to Denbies Visitor Centre or are staying at the farmhouse, turn right at the crossing footpath; this is the Mole Gap Trail (6 miles / 9.7 km from Leatherhead to Dorking) which also provides a pleasant route into Dorking town centre).

In another 440 yards (400 metres) go through a gate, past a bungalow and under a railway bridge to reach the A24 London Road **U**.

*The link with **Dorking Station** and **Dorking Deepdene Station** starts by turning right here (see page 180).*

Although the North Downs Way continues on the far side of the A24, regrettably there is no formal pedestrian link and crossing here is not recommended ⚠. Turn left beside the A24 for 440 yards (400 metres) to the junction with Westhumble Street 🟥, where Section 2 of the North Downs Way ends and the **Thames Down Link** 🔟 starts.

≋ 🚇 *The link with **Boxhill & Westhumble Station** starts by turning left here (see page 180). The bus stop for services to Leatherhead, Surbiton and Kingston is on this side of the A24 shortly*

before reaching Westhumble Street. Buses into Dorking stop on the far side of the A24, a short distance along Section 3.

To continue on to Section 3, or if you feel in need of a hot drink before catching your train or bus, go past the junction and through the subway. Turn right for the North Downs Way, or left for the Burford Bridge Hotel 🛏 and Ryka's Café ☕ **PC**, which is very popular with leather-clad bikers but provides a nice cup of tea and a variety of fry-ups.

Public transport

Shalford Road (on route) 🚌
Shalford (1 mile / 1.6 km) ≋
Chilworth (1.3 miles / 2.1 km) ≋ 🚌
Albury (1 mile / 1.6 km) 🚌 Not Sundays
Shere (0.6 mile / 1.0 km) 🚌 Not Sundays
Gomshall (1.1 miles / 1.8 km) ≋ 🚌
Westcott (1.2 miles / 1.9 km) 🚌 Not Sundays
Dorking West (1 mile / 1.6 km) ≋
Dorking / Dorking Deepdene (0.8 mile / 1.3 km) ≋
Westhumble Street (on route) 🚌
Boxhill & Westhumble Station (0.3 mile / 0.5 km) ≋
Newlands Corner is served by a Monday–Friday school bus; details from Traveline
Taxis/minicabs: Guildford, Shere, Effingham, Bookham, Westcott, Dorking

Refreshments and toilets

Newlands Corner (on route) ☕ Visitor Centre, The Barn
Shere (0.6 mile / 1 km) 🍺 White Horse, William Bray ☕ Lucky Duck
Denbies (0.3 mile / 0.5 km) ☕ Visitor Centre
Dorking Station (0.8 mile / 1.3 km) 🍺 Lincoln Arms
Westhumble Street (on route) 🍺 Stepping Stones
Burford Bridge (0.1 mile / 0.2 km) ☕ Ryka's
Food shops: Shalford, Shere, Dorking
Public toilets: Newlands Corner, Burford Bridge

Accommodation

Chilworth (1.3 mile / 2.1 km) Boors Green Farmhouse
Newlands Corner (0.4 mile / 0.6 km) Manor House Hotel
Albury (1 mile / 1.6 km) Drummond Arms Inn
West Clandon (2.2 miles / 3.5 km) The Oaks
Shere (0.6 mile / 1 km) Rookery Nook
Gomshall (1 mile / 1.6 km) Compasses Inn, Hop House
Holmbury St Mary (2.8 miles / 4.5 km) Bulmer Farm, Holmbury Farm, Youth Hostel
Abinger Common (2.8 miles / 4.5 km) Leylands Farm
Wotton (1.7 miles / 2.7 km) Wotton House Hotel
Ranmore Common (1 mile / 1.6 km) Tanners Hatch Youth Hostel
Westcott (1.2 miles / 1.9 km) Corner House
Dorking West Station (1 mile / 1.6 km) The Pilgrim
Dorking (1.1 mile / 1.8 km) Wide selection – contact Mole Valley Visitor Information Centre
Dorking Station (0.8 mile / 1.3 km) Lincoln Arms
Denbies (0.3 mile / 0.5 km) Denbies Farmhouse
Burford Bridge (0.1 mile / 0.2 km) Mercure Burford Bridge Hotel

3 Westhumble to Merstham

over Box Hill and Reigate Hill
10 miles (16 km)

Ascent 1,450 feet (442 metres)

Descent 1,260 feet (384 metres)

Lowest point Stepping Stones: 144 feet (44 metres)

Highest point Reigate Hill: 770 feet (235 metres)

You cross the celebrated stepping stones over the River Mole then face one of the longest and steepest ascents along the North Downs Way – up the scarp of Box Hill – though with the assistance of (by the author's counting) 273 steps. One would have thought it should then be possible to stay at a high level all the way to the next break in the range – the Coulsdon Gap – but this would involve too much walking along roads. So our route soon plunges down to rejoin the Pilgrims Way for several miles, before re-ascending to the ridge at Colley Hill.

Much of this section is wooded, but you can still enjoy excellent views, especially from the viewing platform on Box Hill, and from Colley Hill and Reigate Hill. Evidence of past quarrying may detain the industrial archaeologist at Brockham Lime Works and, whether or not you are interested in history, the recently restored remains of Reigate Fort provide a fascinating insight into 19th-century soldiering. A gentle stroll through Gatton Park leads you to the end of the section at Merstham.

Things to look out for

1 Box Hill is one of the best-known beauty spots along the North Downs, thanks in particular to Zig Zag Road, which does exactly that up a series of hairpin bends, and to the many footpaths and bridleways that reach up from all directions. As well as being Britain's first country park, it is a Site of Special Scientific Interest and a Special Area of Conservation because of its wide variety of species. Around 40 per cent of all the naturally occurring box trees in Britain can be found growing on the escarpment here – hence the name. In 1914, the London-based financier Leopold Salomons (1842–1915) acquired the western part of the area to protect it from development, then bequeathed it to the National Trust,

whose centre near the viewing platform has a refreshment kiosk, shop and toilets. A straggling village occupies the eastern part, and it is here that the actual summit lies at 682 feet (208 metres) above sea level; the viewing platform is much lower at 564 feet (172 metres).

Near the viewing platform is a triangulation pillar, commonly known as a trig point. It is one of over 7,000 that were installed around Britain to help create the Ordnance Survey maps by taking accurate measurements using a process called triangulation, which required a direct line of sight between at least three trig points. Now that their function has been replaced by the Global Positioning System (GPS), most trig points are surplus to requirements, but many are maintained by individuals or groups as they still provide a useful aid to navigation in the countryside.

2 **Brockham Lime Works** flourished in this area, with a clanking network of narrow-gauge railways to carry chalk from the quarries to the lime kilns and down to Betchworth. The works closed in 1936 and the area has since been reclaimed by nature. Now managed by the **Surrey Wildlife Trust**, it is a Site of Special Scientific interest, due in particular to the eight species of bat that occupy the old kilns, which you pass along the North Downs Way.

3 **Colley Hill** is managed by the **National Trust** and reaches 738 feet (225 metres) above sea level. The 'Inglis Folly', donated in 1909 to the Borough of Reigate by Lieutenant Colonel Sir Robert William Inglis, VC, was originally a drinking fountain but now houses a topograph, with the night sky depicted on the ceiling. You may find it is, or has been, occupied by cattle – beware droppings!

4 **Reigate Fort**, at 754 feet (230 metres) above sea level near the summit of Reigate Hill, was one of 13 military depots built along the North Downs towards the end of the 19th century as a supply line for defences against a feared invasion by the French – which never came! After a period of occupation by the Scouts, Reigate Fort was refurbished by the **National Trust** and opened to the public in 2007. Several of its buildings can be inspected and have information panels.

5 **Gatton Park** was the home of the Colebrooke family of London bankers. In 1762 they commissioned the great landscape gardener Lancelot 'Capability' Brown to redesign the grounds in his trademark naturalistic style. In 1888 the 600-acre (243-hectare) park was bought by Sir Jeremiah Colman, of mustard fame, and in 1948 it was sold to the Royal Alexandra and Albert School, which can trace its origins back to 1758 and still occupies the eastern part. In 1952 the **National Trust** acquired the western part, which has open access, and in 1996 the **Gatton Trust** was formed to manage the rest of the park, initially to restore the gardens and later to provide educational facilities for local schools and the wider community. The National Trust part has open access; the Gatton Trust area is normally accessible only on public rights of way but has open days on the first Sunday of each month from February to October, when refreshments are available at Gatton Hall. Also within the park is St Andrew's Church, restored in the 1830s from an earlier building.

6 The **Millennium Standing Stones** have found a permanent home in Gatton Park after several years as a travelling exhibition. Clearly a modern representation of Stone Age megaliths, they were created for the Jerusalem Trust by the sculptor Richard Kindersley to commemorate the Millennium by demonstrating the spiritual power of words and artistic lettering. Each of the ten stones represents a 200-year period by featuring the words of St John's Gospel, St Augustine, Anicius Manlius Boethius (a Roman Christian philosopher), John Scotus Erigena (a medieval Irish philosopher), St Anselm, St Thomas Aquinas, St Francis of Sales, Johann von Goethe and T. S. Eliot.

The Inglis Folly houses a topograph – and sometimes a cow or two!

Route description

🚌 *Buses from Dorking stop on the west side of the A24, so you will need to walk on to go through the subway. For those from the Leatherhead direction, the stop is on the east side and is passed soon after the start of the section.*

From Westhumble Street, go through the subway **A** and turn right on the far side (*PC toilets to your left at Burford Bridge car park*), then walk beside the A24 for 440 yards (400 metres). Turn left into the Stepping Stones car park **B**. At its far end you have a choice: the right-hand footpath for the stepping stones, or the left-hand one for the footbridge. After heavy rain, the stepping stones may be slippery or even under water; if, on reaching them, you decide against it, just turn left beside the river to reach the bridge. The alternative routes come together at the foot of the

steep climb up Box Hill **C**. Turn right at the top **D** and continue round to the triangulation column beside the **Box Hill 1** viewing platform.

☕ *PC The National Trust's Box Hill Visitor Centre, with an open-air café, picnic tables and toilets, is 200 yards (220 metres) away – to reach it, climb the steps left of the viewing platform and turn left beside the road.*

Pass the viewing platform, then in 55 yards (50 metres) turn left to climb a footpath into trees, roughly parallel to Zig

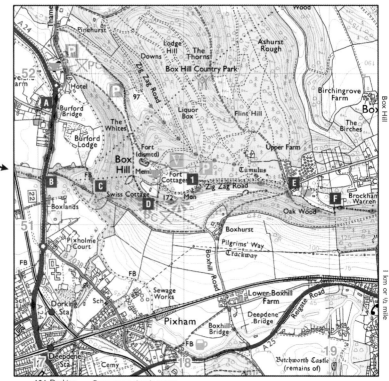

A24 Dorking   Contours are given in metres
The vertical interval is 5m

The viewing platform on Box Hill provides an extensive view across The Weald.

Zag Road. After passing through two gates the route bears right to cross a gully **E** via two short flights of steps to reach a track in a second gully.

🍴 *The South Western bar-grill-diner is just a short distance to your left, up the track in the second gully.*

Cross the second gully then descend through Oak Wood. In 440 yards (400 metres) climb 20 steps to reach a white gate **F**, where the footpath turns right, on the level for a while. Descend 61 steps, then turn left to continue climbing. At the next junction, beside an information panel for **Brockham Lime Works** 2, take the right fork to follow an undulating footpath with garden fences on your left. Just before the next junction, almost hidden in trees on your left, is the gravestone of (presumably) an animal called 'Quick, an English thoroughbred, 26.9.36 – 22.10.44'. Descend steps and turn right, down a gully, to follow an ancient sunken track.

📖 *If you wish to visit the Hand in Hand pub in Box Hill village, turn left after descending the steps, then turn right at the road.*

Keep ahead at the next junction, then, at a fork, use the lower path, as the upper one involves a steep descent. At the next waymark post keep ahead then turn left past another information panel. Contour around the top of a disused, now heavily wooded, quarry, protected by a gated fence. The slope on your left here was for some years a landfill site, now grassed over. Continue downhill between fences to the

next junction G, where you rejoin the Pilgrims Way coming in from the right. Keep ahead to cross the top end of a concrete road H which served the defunct lime works on your right. Go through a metal gate to follow a gravel drive past cottages, then join a lane (The Coombe) to reach the B2032 Station Road I.

🚉 *Betchworth Station is 330 yards (300 metres) to the right down Station Road. Returning from the station, turn left up Station Road, and on reaching The Coombe keep ahead along Pebblehill Road to rejoin the North Downs Way.*

Turn left along Pebblehill Road. When the pavement ends, continue up a footpath in trees, parallel with the road. When this rejoins the road ⚠ you must take great care crossing to the other side, as traffic comes fast around a bend to your right. Turn left along the pavement for 100 yards (90 metres). Just past a house called

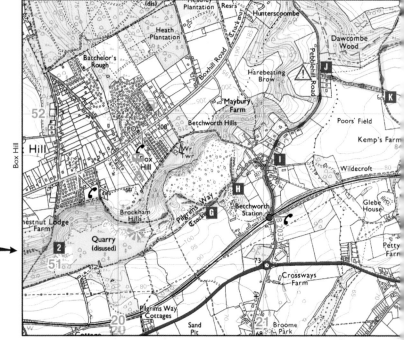

Contours are given in
The vertical interval

Pebbledown **J**, turn right on a footpath into trees. Cross a stile **K** into a field, then turn left along a bridleway, which goes through a gate then continues between fields. Soon after climbing steeply into woodland, turn right on a level footpath at the foot of the scarp, now with a field on your right. At the end, climb steeply to a junction, where you turn right on a deeply rutted byway called Buckland Lane **L**.

When the fence stops, turn left up steps on a footpath, which soon turns right to follow a fairly level, chalky route for 0.5 mile (0.8 km), now at the foot of the Buckland Hills with a field on your right. At the next junction **M** briefly join a bridleway coming down from your left, then immediately fork left and cross another junction to continue along the knobbly, chalky footpath at the foot of the scarp slope for 0.8 mile (1.3 km). Just past a barrier you reach a major junction **N** where the North Downs Way turns left to climb steeply back to the ridge

via a sharp, left-hand bend. This is an old bridleway called Clifton's Lane, where whooping cyclists are known to hurtle down for an adrenalin rush. You reach the top of the hill beside a house called Mole Place **O**.

🔜 *If you wish to visit the Sportsman pub at Mogador, keep ahead here, crossing the M25 motorway on a footbridge.*

Turn right for 35 yards (32 metres), then turn right again between posts along a footpath into trees. Join a bridleway coming in from the left, then go through a gate to enter the wide, open space of the National Trust's **Colley Hill** **3** property. For the next mile or so (1.6 km) you follow a broad, gravel bridleway along the ridge, with Reigate occupying the view to your right and the M25 out of sight (but not out of hearing) to your left. You pass a water tower on your left and the Inglis Folly **P** on your right.

🚆🚌 *The link with **Reigate Station** follows the bridleway down a gully on your right, just before the folly – see page 180.*

M25

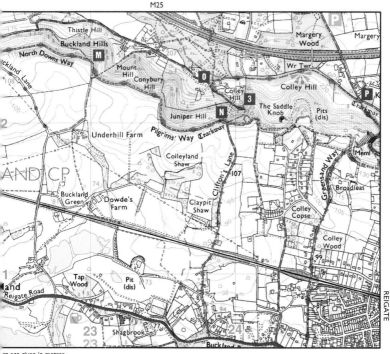

REIGATE

rs are given in metres
ertical interval is 5m

Go through a gate **Q** into trees to reach a huge, white water tank beside a tall mast festooned with aerials. You are now on Reigate Hill, with **Reigate Fort 4** on your right. Continue along the tarmac Fort Lane, then, as it swings sharp left **R**, keep ahead along a bridleway.

🚌 *For buses to Banstead, Sutton or Epsom, turn left along Fort Lane, then right at the roundabout for 220 yards (200 metres).*

The bridleway descends to cross a footbridge **S** over the A217 Reigate Hill to Wray Lane Car Park 🍵 **PC**, which has a refreshment kiosk, toilets, picnic tables and another good view over Reigate and Redhill. At the far end, cross Wray Lane with great care, as you are on the brow of a hill and traffic may come fast and blind from either direction.

Go between bollards into **Gatton Park 5**, looking out for the distinctive black waymark posts. Just past an information panel, take the right fork and follow the winding bridleway as it swings left then right through the estate, following the park's original carriage drive. Near the foot of the hill, the track comes alongside a road called Gatton Bottom, then reaches stone-clad Tower Lodge Cottages **T**. Turn right along a tarmac drive into the part of Gatton

Park that is used as a field study centre for children. Go through a black metal gate, past the **Millennium Standing Stones 6** and stay on the drive as it swings left, with the Hop Garden Pond down to your right.

Pass residences and other buildings on your right (behind which is Gatton Hall) and sports courts on your left, as the drive now swings right to reach a major junction **U** beside the assembly hall, with the entrance to the Royal Alexandra and Albert School on your right, and St Andrew's Church a little further away to your right. Turn left along an avenue of tall Lombardy poplars; you may need to use the grass verge on the left as this busy access road has no pavement. At the thatched North Lodge **V** leave Gatton Park and keep ahead along Rocky Lane 🏃. Keep left as there is a blind right-hand bend and you will shortly turn left anyway.

Take the second left drive, then, at a bend, fork right along a gravel drive between hedges. At its end pass two farm gates, then go slightly left to follow a shady, fenced footpath among trees, soon with a fairway of Reigate Hill Golf Club on your left. Go through a gate and keep ahead across the golf course access drive **W**, with the M25 now close at hand. Continue in the same

Lower Kingswood

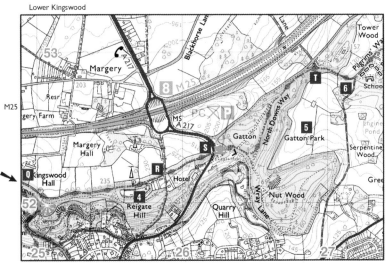

REIGATE

Contours are given in metres
The vertical interval is 5m

direction along a mown path in long grass between fairways, eventually descending between a tee and a green to go through another gate **X**. Follow the fenced footpath beside a cricket pitch, then go through the car park of Merstham Cricket Club and

along its access drive to reach Quality Street **Y** in Merstham, where Section 3 ends.

≋ 🚌 *The link to **Merstham Station** starts by turning right here (see page 180).*

Turn left to continue on to Section 4.

Public transport

Dorking West (1 mile / 1.6 km) ≋
Dorking / Dorking Deepdene (0.8 mile / 1.3 km) ≋
Westhumble Street (on route) 🚌
Boxhill & Westhumble Station (0.3 mile / 0.5 km) ≋
Betchworth (0.2 mile / 0.3 km) ≋
Reigate (1.3 miles / 2 km) ≋ 🚌
Reigate Hill. (0.3 mile / 0.5 km) 🚌
Merstham (0.3 mile / 0.5 km) ≋ 🚌
Taxis/minicabs: Dorking, Brockham, Lower Kingswood, Reigate, Redhill, Merstham

Refreshments and toilets

Box Hill (0.2 mile / 0.3 km) 🍺 National Trust Visitor Centre 🅿 South Western Bar
Box Hill village (0.5 mile / 0.8 km) 🅿 Hand in Hand
Mogador (0.5 mile / 0.8 km) 🅿 Sportsman
Wray Lane car park (on route) 🍺 Kiosk

Merstham (on route) 🅿 Feathers, Railway Arms 🍺 Hunger's End, Quality Café
Food shops: Dorking, Reigate, Merstham
Public toilets: Burford Bridge, Box Hill Visitor Centre, Wray Lane Car Park

Accommodation

Betchworth (1.1 miles / 1.8 km) Hartsfield Manor, Red Lion, Whitelands Country House
Skimmington (2.3 miles / 3.7 km) Dungate Manor
Reigate Hill (0.4 mile / 0.6 km) Bridge House Hotel, Reigate Manor Hotel
Reigate (1.3 miles / 2 km) Cranleigh Hotel, Highview, Maybury Lodge
Harps Wood (1 mile / 1.6 km) Little Orchard
Redhill (1.9 miles / 3 km) Brompton Guest House, Lynwood Guest House, Parklands Guest House
Nutfield (2.8 miles / 4.5 km) Nutfield Priory Hotel

69

Dorking to Merstham

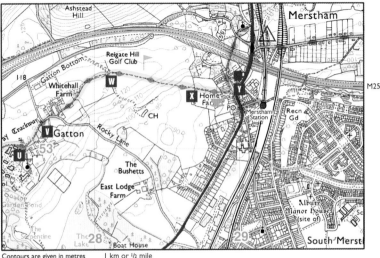

Contours are given in metres
The vertical interval is 5m
1 km or ½ mile
A23 Redhill

4 Merstham to Oxted

via Whitehill Tower and Caterham Viewpoint
8 miles (12.8 km)

Ascent 1,020 feet (311 metres)

Descent 817 feet (249 metres)

Lowest point Merstham 334 feet (102 metres)

Highest point Gangers Hill 780 feet (238 metres)

After passing Merstham's parish church and some desirable properties on the northern edge of the village, a long, steady climb leads back up to the ridge. Then it is easy, level walking at over 650 feet (200 metres) for the next 2.5 miles (4 km), at first in high farmland as far as War Coppice Road, where a very short diversion lets you see the Victorian folly known as the Whitehill Tower. A long stretch in woodland follows, opening up briefly at the popular Caterham Viewpoint. You must descend to cross the A22 as it passes through the Caterham Gap, then the North Downs Way rises and falls twice to reach Chalkpit Lane at Oxted. One of the descents involves a flight of 102 steps, though someone has thoughtfully provided a seat on the way down so that you can rest your knees and enjoy the view.

We forsake the Pilgrims Way on this section, as it has been almost completely subsumed into the M25 motorway. The sprawling 'spaghetti junction' of the M23/M25 intersection is close at hand but fortunately out of sight. Even so, you will have to put up with traffic noise for much of this section as the M25 runs parallel, less than half a mile away.

Things to look out for

1 **Merstham Church** is dedicated to St Katharine of Alexandria, a 4th-century martyr. The present church has parts that date back to the 13th century, but a Saxon one is believed to have pre-existed on the site. Most of it is built of flint, but one of the walls incorporates a stone that has made the return journey from Merstham's sandstone quarries to one of the older incarnations of London Bridge, and back again when that was demolished.

2 **Brambly House Montessori School** is one of many Montessori schools around the world. They are named after Dr Maria Montessori (1870–1952), an Italian educator, who pioneered a method of helping disadvantaged children to achieve their full potential by giving them freedom to develop in their own, natural way.

3 The **Downlands Circular Walks** were set up by the **Downlands Project**, a combined initiative of several local authorities in this area. The routes start and finish on Farthing Downs, near Coulsdon. This section is part of the longest route of 9 miles (14.5 km).

4 **Park Ham** is an area of species-rich chalk grassland that forms part of Quarry Hangers Site of Special Scientific Interest, managed by the **Surrey Wildlife Trust**. It is being maintained and enhanced by cutting back hawthorn scrub, periodic grazing by sheep and hand-pulling of ragwort, which is poisonous to horses and sheep. Look out for the information panel.

5 **Whitehill Tower** (also known as the Sight Tower) is a derelict folly, built by Jeremiah Long, a local farmer, in 1862 as a memorial to his son, who was killed at sea. One of the chain of Victorian forts referred to in Section 3, located on the hilltop a little to the south-west, was known as War Coppice Fort, hence the name of the road.

6 **Caterham Viewpoint** is so named as it is a place where people from the nearby town of Caterham (and surely other places too) come to enjoy a picnic or contemplate the M25.

7 **Pilgrim Fort**, also known as Fosterdown Fort, is another of the Victorian forts referred to earlier. It lies hidden among trees up to the left as you leave Caterham Viewpoint and cannot be seen or visited from the route, but it is very clearly shown on the map. After its abandonment by the military, Pilgrim Fort became a field study centre for schoolchildren and has now been converted to residential use, but remains a Scheduled Monument.

8 **Winders Hill** leads past some old sandstone mines, which are still being explored by the **Wealden Cave and Mine Society**. Two types of the stone were found here: firestone, used as a building stone and in the manufacture of glass, and hearthstone, as the name suggests commonly used as a slab in front of fireplaces. A part of the mines was subsequently used as a mushroom farm, and the Society occasionally offers guided tours of the mines. National Cycle Route 21 (London to Eastbourne) also uses Winders Hill.

9 **Godstone Vineyards** were established in 1985 and occupy 50 acres (20 hectares) of hillside. There is a wine shop, and the Garden Room serves morning coffee, lunch and afternoon tea. You can see the vines from the route, but the shop and Garden Room are about 770 yards (700 metres) away.

10 **Marden Park** is the home of Woldingham School, which lies 0.8 mile (1.3 km) to the north. It is one of the country's leading Roman Catholic schools for girls, established in 1946 by the Society of the Sacred Heart. A predecessor of the present building was the home of a succession of worthies, including Sir Robert Clayton, a Lord Mayor of London in the late 17th century. Part of the estate is farmland. The Woldingham Countryside Walk, another initiative of the Downlands Project, comes up through Marden Park to join the North Downs Way and shares its route to just past the end of this section.

11 **Horse Shaw** is part of the **Woodland Trust**'s Marden Park and Great Church Woods estate. 'Shaw' is a dialect word meaning a rough piece of woodland, with the same root as 'shaggy', and is often found in this part of England.

12 **Oxted Downs**, owned and managed by the **National Trust**, is part of the Woldingham and Oxted Site of Special Scientific Interest. The management policy is to restore grassland through scrub control and the reintroduction of grazing.

13 **Oxted Quarry**, also known as Oxted Chalk Pit, has been worked since the mid-19th century, but operations have increased following planning permission in 1947 granting quarrying rights until 2042. The site is also used for waste landfill. Heavy goods traffic generated by these operations is the cause of much local concern. Prior to a recent extension of the quarry, archaeologists found evidence of late Neolithic and Bronze Age settlement.

14 The **Oxted Railway Tunnel** lies directly below the North Downs Way. It was built in 1878 as part of the branch line from South Croydon to East Grinstead, where it now ends, but originally the line continued to Lewes. A 9-mile (14.5-km) stretch of the line, south of East Grinstead, has been restored as the famous Bluebell Railway.

Merstham to Oxted

Route description

From the cricket club exit **A** continue along Quality Street. At the end, between The Old Forge ('a Tudor Building of Special Interest') and a pillared gateway **B**, bear right along a footpath. Soon you cross a bridge over the M25 to reach a road (Gatton Bottom again). Cross over and climb some steps up to **Merstham Church** **1**. Keep ahead past its door, then turn right at the very busy A23 London Road North **C**, which used to be the main

London–Brighton road until the M23 was built further east. ⚠ Use the pedestrian refuge to cross over, turn right past a bus stop, then shortly left into Rockshaw Road – beware traffic from the right here.

Cross the London–Brighton railway line and then the bypass line, known as the Quarry Line, and climb steadily uphill for 0.5 mile (0.8 km), passing some very attractive houses, including **Brambly House Montessori School** **2**. Just before

A23 Coulsdon
4 km or 2½ miles

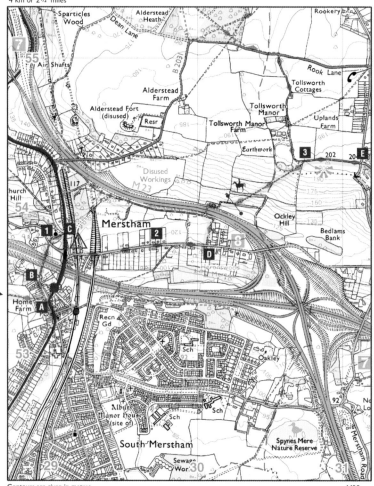

Contours are given in metres
The vertical interval is 5m

M23

The old chalk workings on the Surrey Downs provide secure roosting quarters for the uncommon Bechstein's bat.

The silver-spotted skipper butterfly thrives on the North Downs, having expanded its range in Surrey between Reigate and Guildford as well as at locations in Kent.

Sixty per cent of Britain's orchid species are found on the North Downs. The late-spider orchid is to be seen only in Kent.

The North Downs are the national stronghold for the musk orchid.

the house called Sarum **D**, turn left down a bridleway, which goes under the M23. Bear right with the track as it climbs steadily upwards through scrubland, away from the M23. Go through some bushes, then continue in the same direction up a large arable field.

At the top, look back for a fine view across Redhill, then continue to the right on a bridleway between hedges, from where

the route is shared with one of the **Downlands Circular Walks 3** for the next 1.3 miles (2.1 km). You pass a trig point on your right to reach Hilltop Lane **E** at the edge of Chaldon. Watch out for traffic coming fast around a corner in both directions, then continue along a bridleway (Pilgrims Lane), providing access to the rather swanky Hilltop Farm and other secluded, ridge-top houses.

Continue along the lane for 0.7 mile (1.1 km), ignoring all side turnings. You pass a house called Hilltop, with its wall clock, then an information panel on your right for **Park Ham 4**. The view now is, unusually, to your left, towards Croydon and London. On reaching the small settlement of Willey Park Farm, keep ahead to a junction **F**, where you bear right to follow a metalled drive to Stanstead Road **G**.

The Harrow pub is 130 yards (118 metres) to your left here.

Cross Stanstead Road with care, turn right then immediately left along War Coppice Road, which you follow for 0.6 mile (1 km). *Just 60 yards (55 metres) past the junction, make a short diversion to your left to see **Whitehill Tower 5**.* Pass Pilgrims Cottage and Woodland Way to reach the junction with Hextalls Lane and Weald Way **H**. Go through bollards on your right to follow a footpath, which contours along the scarp slope in woodland for 0.6 mile (1 km), taking the left fork at an X-junction on to a bridleway.

If you wish to visit Godstone, take the right fork here.

Soon after joining a bridleway coming up from the right, although the route officially continues to a road, it is clear that people fork right to reach the extensive grass strip known as **Caterham Viewpoint 6** on Gravelly Hill, which is also the name of the adjacent road.

*The link to **Caterham Station** starts by following the footpath down to the left, opposite the viewpoint (see page 180).*

Keep ahead to the trees, then bear right along a gravel bridleway leading into woodland. At the second bench seat stay on the main track continuing downhill. Just over to your left, out of sight and inaccessible from the North Downs Way, is **Pilgrim Fort 7**. Keep ahead at a path junction, then in 165 yards (150 metres), at a waymark post **I**, fork right to descend steeply on a footpath, via two flights of steps, to reach a road

Caterham St

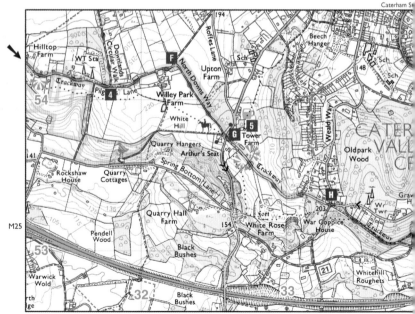

Contours are given in me
The vertical interval is 5

(Tupwood Lane). Turn right along a bridleway to cross a bridge over the dual carriageway A22 Godstone Hill (the London–Eastbourne road). On the far side keep ahead on a short grassy footpath, then turn right on a gravel byway **J**. In 165 yards (150 metres) fork left on a footpath, snaking down to Quarry Road, which provides access to the factory on your left.

☕ *If you wish to visit the wine shop and Garden Room at **Godstone Vineyards**, turn right here.*

Cross the road and keep ahead on a footpath, climbing steeply via two flights of steps to a concrete drive called **Winders Hill 8**. Turn right to ascend past cottages and a yellow barrier, with **Godstone Vineyards 9** on your right, to reach the South Lodge of **Marden Park 10**.

≷ *The link to **Woldingham** Station starts by turning left here (see page 181).*

The route is shared with the Woldingham Countryside Walk (another initiative of the **Downlands Project**) from here to just past the end of this section. Keep ahead on the bridleway, then immediately bear left on an ascending footpath into **Horse Shaw 11** to regain the wooded ridge, passing a viewpoint over Godstone village. Some 220 yards (200 metres) after reaching the top of the hill, you need to turn right, off the main path. Look out for a gnarled, multi-trunked old tree **K**, behind which your onward route continues to a road called Gangers Hill. Cross over beside Hanging Wood Forest Farm (a leisure centre offering a wide range of mainly outdoor activities) and keep ahead on a descending bridleway.

Just before the next road (Tandridge Hill Lane) **L**, turn left through a gate to follow a footpath climbing parallel with the road. In about 350 yards (320 metres) the footpath runs out ⚑, then you must walk along the road

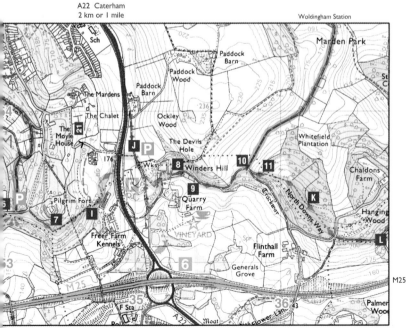

A22 Caterham
2 km or 1 mile

Woldingham Station

M25

:ours are given in metres
: vertical interval is 5m

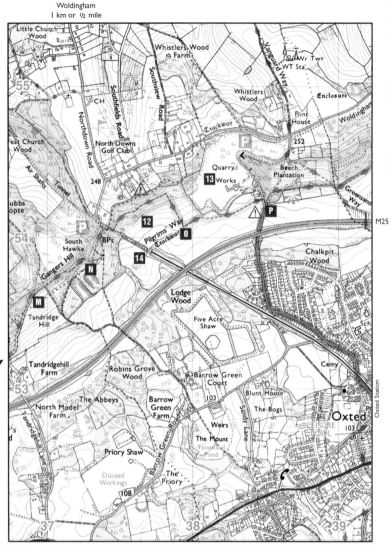

Contours are given in metres
The vertical interval is 5m

to a junction **M** (Gangers Hill again), the highest point of this section at 780 feet (238 metres). Bear right for 80 yards (73 metres), then bear right again along a bridleway (ignoring the footpath that goes sharp right). At the next junction, turn right then soon turn left on a footpath to pass a viewpoint over Oxted with an information panel **N**. Ahead lie **Oxted Downs** **12** and the white scar of **Oxted Quarry** **13**.

🚌 *For bus stops at Woldingham, turn left here, then turn right along the road and left at the next junction.*

Turn right down a long flight of 102 steps. Near the bottom is a fenced resting place with a memorial seat and a good view of trains entering or leaving **Oxted Railway Tunnel** **14** below. Turn left to continue contouring along the slope. ⚠ Take care,

An aerial view of the Surrey landscape looking towards Westerham, Tandridge and Oxted.

as the narrow, chalky footpath is overgrown in places and can be slippery when wet; there is also barbed wire close by and some hidden crevices may trip the unwary.

You now have to divert round the quarry. Turn right at a gate, down a steep slope towards the M25, passing through another gate. At the end of the hedge **O** turn left to follow the left edge of a large field. Just before its end go through a gate on your left and keep ahead to Chalkpit Lane. ⚠

✳ Take care as you emerge on to the road, as its traffic includes heavy lorries travelling at inconsiderate speed to and from the quarry. Turn right down Chalkpit Lane ✳ for 45 yards (40 metres) to a gap in the hedge **P**, where Section 4 of the North Downs Way ends.

⇌ 🚌 🏨 ☕ 🔀 *The link with **Oxted Station** starts by continuing ahead down Chalkpit Lane (see page 181).*

(see page 181).

To continue on to Section 5 of the North Downs Way, turn left through the gap.

Public transport

Merstham (0.3 mile / 0.5 km)
⇌ 🚌
Godstone (1.1 miles / 1.8 km)
🚌 Not Sundays
Caterham (1.6 miles / 2.6 km)
⇌ 🚌
Woldingham Station (2 miles / 3.3 km) ⇌
Woldingham Village (1.1 mile / 1.8 km) 🚌 Not Sundays
Oxted (1.2 miles / 1.9 km) ⇌ 🚌

Taxis/minicabs: Merstham, Godstone, Caterham, Oxted

Refreshments and toilets

Stanstead Road (on route) 🏨 Harrow
Godstone Vineyards (0.4 mile / 0.6 km) ☕ Garden Room
Oxted (1.2 miles /1.9 km) 🏨 Oxted Inn, ☕ several near station
Food shops: Merstham, Oxted
Public toilets: Oxted

Accommodation

Bletchingley (2.1 miles / 3.4 km) Whyte Hart Inn
Godstone (1.1 miles / 1.8 km) Godstone Hotel
Whyteleafe (3.3 miles / 5.3 km) Travelodge Caterham
Oxted (1.2 miles / 1.9 km) Meads, Pinehurst Grange, The Croft

5 Oxted to Otford

over Botley Hill and into Kent
11.8 miles (18.9 km)

Ascent 1,716 feet (524 metres)

Descent 1,922 feet (587 metres)

Lowest point River Darent 193 feet (59 metres)

Highest point Botley Hill 853 feet (260 metres)

The North Downs Way is joined by the Vanguard Way for a while as it contours along the foot of the escarpment, crossing the Greenwich Meridian. Then a steep climb takes you to the highest point of the whole route at Botley Hill. Apart from one more steep ascent near Westerham, the walking is then quite gentle or downhill for the remainder of this section as the Way passes from Surrey into Kent. It also scrapes the Greater London boundary for a while as light aircraft using Biggin Hill Airport pass overhead. But the M25 and M26 motorways have comprehensively carved up the countryside near Sevenoaks, so there is nothing for it but to grit your teeth, cover your ears and dream of better things to come as you trudge beside roads for half an hour and cross the M25. Lavender fields bring relief as you walk into Otford.

The Pilgrims Way runs to the south of and parallel to the North Downs Way for most of this section, though you will often see it from your lofty position atop the scarp. The two routes come together as they enter Otford.

Things to look out for

1 The **Vanguard Way** is a 66-mile (107-km) walking route from Croydon in Greater London to Newhaven in East Sussex. It was opened in 1981 and was devised by members of the Vanguards Rambling Club (including the author of this guide). A free guide is available from the route's website.

2 The **Meridian Plaque** was installed in 2000 to mark both the Millennium and the crossing of the Greenwich Meridian by the North Downs Way and the Vanguard Way.

3 The **Surrey Hills logo sculpture** is one of several that have been erected at locations around the **Surrey Hills Area of Outstanding Natural Beauty**, which covers the North Downs and Greensand Hills in the

county. The logo is based on an original carving by the sculptor Walter Bailey and represents a seed as it starts to germinate.

4 The first **North Downs Way 'milestone'** (see page 32) is passed as you cross the boundary from Surrey into Kent. At this point you are 48 miles (77 km) from Farnham and either 65 miles (105 km) to Canterbury or 77 miles (124 km) to Dover. From this point on, the North Downs Way lies mostly within the **Kent Downs Area of Outstanding Natural Beauty**.

5 **St Botolph's Church** at Chevening is significant for the Pilgrims Way as it lies on that route and St Botolph (a 7th-century Saxon abbot) is the patron saint of travellers.

The church dates from the 12th century and was built on the site of an earlier Saxon one. It contains some fine tombs and monuments and has a full ring of eight bells, including two of the original six cast in 1715.

6 The **Darent Valley Path** is a 19-mile (30-km) walking route that follows as closely as possible the River Darent (or Darenth) from its confluence with the Thames near Dartford to Otford, where the route divides into a western branch to Chipstead (partly shared with the North Downs Way) and an eastern branch to Sevenoaks. The route was devised by the **North West Kent Countryside Project** and the logo is a stylised tree beside a river.

7 The planet **Uranus** is represented by a concrete pillar on the approach into Otford. It is part of Otford Parish Council's Millennium Project to show the relative positions of the planets in our solar system, on a scale of 1:5 billion, relative to the sun at 00.01 hours on 1 January 2000. The panel on the pillar states that this is the world's largest solar system scale model, and tells us that, at this scale, the sun can be found 649 metres away on the recreation ground.

8 **Otford** is a large village (population about 3,500 in 2001) beside the River Darent, with a duck pond as its central feature. St Bartholomew's Church dates from the 11th century, and nearby are the ruins of a 12th-century Archbishop's Palace, which included Thomas Becket among its residents. Henry VIII seized it in 1538, but after his death the palace fell into decline. There is a scale model of the palace in its prime at the **Otford Heritage Centre**. On your way through the village you pass a 40-foot (12-metre)-long mosaic by Oliver Budd, which tells the story of Otford from the dawn of human history to the start of the 2nd Millennium.

The route passes this wooden sculpture at Clarks Lane. It is a representation of a germinating seed – the logo of the Surrey Hills Area of Outstanding Natural Beauty.

Titsey Place lies a few hundred yards down to the right as you leave Botley Hill. Its vast estate, once owned by the Gresham family of London merchants, is now administered by the Titsey Foundation.

Route description

Section 5 of the North Downs Way starts by going up steps through a gap in the hedge in Chalkpit Lane **A**. Bear left uphill, go through a gate into Oxted Downs, then continue steeply upwards. At a bench seat bear right, now with the **Vanguard Way** **1** for the next mile (1.6 km), and parallel with the M25. Go through a gate **B** and between bushes into the next, very large field.

≷ 🚌 *The eastern link with Oxted Station starts by turning right here (see page 181).*

Keep ahead along the top of the field, still parallel with the M25. You pass the **Meridian Plaque** **2** shortly before continuing into a smaller field. Another gate leads on to steps **C** down to a sunken track (Pitchfont Lane). The Vanguard Way turns right here, but the North Downs Way goes left, steeply uphill, to reach the B269 Croydon Road **D** at Botley Hill. You are now at the highest point of the whole North Downs Way – 853 feet (260 metres) above sea level.

🚌 **⌐** *If you wish to visit Botley Hill Farmhouse, turn left along the B269 as it veers right, past The Ridge, for 330 yards (300 metres), passing bus stops –*

northbound towards Croydon on the left, southbound towards Tatsfield on the right.

Turn right, past the mini-roundabout, for 45 yards (40 metres), then carefully cross over and follow a tarmac footpath into trees, with the B269 on your right and Clarks Lane on your left. Take care, as there are many exposed roots. In 700 yards (650 metres) turn left up steps and continue climbing. At a crossing track bear right to continue on the footpath. Take care as you emerge on to White Lane **E**, then go right then immediately left to continue on a footpath through woodland.

Climb steps and cross a stile into a field, where you bear a quarter left to ascend towards a copse. Join a fence, cross a stile and continue along the footpath, now beside the copse. The view to your right includes Pilgrims Farm, so called as the lane that runs past it is the Pilgrims Way. The footpath soon turns right to go beside Clarks Lane, where you cross the line of the Roman road from London to Lewes.

🚌 **⌐** 🌳 *To visit Tatsfield, cross Clarks Lane and take the footpath opposite.*

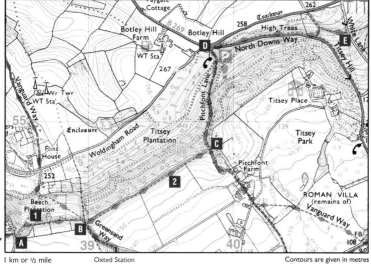

1 km or ½ mile
Oxted

Oxted Station
(Easton Link)

Contours are given in metres
The vertical interval is 5m

As a **Surrey Hills logo sculpture** 🔳3 appears beside the road on your left, keep ahead through a gate into the next field. Just over halfway down turn left through another gate and climb steps to the junction of three roads 🔳F. Taking care as you cross Clarks Lane ahead, turn right over Church Hill, then keep ahead along Chestnut Avenue ✿, beside the sign for Park Wood Golf Club, and with a small car park and a North Downs Way information panel on your right.

Follow this quiet lane for 0.6 mile (1 km), with Hill Park Nature Reserve (owned by **Surrey County Council** and managed by the **Surrey Wildlife Trust**) on your right. You pass the golf club 🍵 (which welcomes visitors for refreshments) and a house called Mole End, on whose wall Mole and Ratty from *The Wind in the Willows* appear in silhouette. At a T-junction 🔳G turn right on a tarmac lane (The Avenue) ✿ and follow it down for 1 mile (1.6 km), passing some sumptuous residences and a **North Downs Way milestone** 🔳4 as you pass from Surrey into Kent. The tarmac turns to gravel halfway down and you eventually reach the very busy A233 Westerham Hill 🔳H.

🚌 *Buses from here go to Westerham (stop opposite) or Bromley (stop 80 yards / 73 metres to your right).*

Cross over ⚠ with extra care (especially in rush hours), as traffic approaches very fast. Descend steps on to a footpath, which bears left to follow a field edge. Cross a stile into trees, swinging right to emerge into a field, with a view of Westerham and the M25. The parallel lane below is the Pilgrims Way again. Just before the end of the field, turn left up 43 steps 🔳I and go through a gate into another field, closely following the poles carrying the power line for a while.

Climb the field, aiming a little to the right of a row of trees. Go through a gate and follow a footpath that swings right, into trees. At a junction with a track, turn right to reach a field, where you follow its top edge, with Pilgrim House down to your right. Go through a gate and turn left, through bushes, then follow the left edge of the next field. Turn right at the field corner 🔳J to stay in the same field. For the next 550 yards (500 metres) you are following the boundary between Kent and Greater London, and the field on your left is in the London Borough of Bromley!

A233 Biggin Hill
2 km or 1 mile

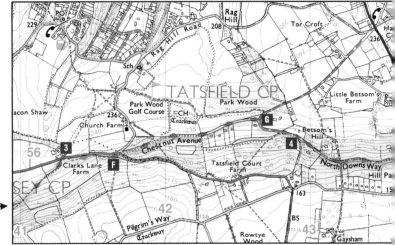

Contours are given in
The vertical interval

Go through two gates (the first commemorating a local rambler), then keep ahead through the next field, now with the power line on your right. Stay close to the field edge as it bears left beside a large tree with low branches to find a gate on your left. Go through it, then turn right along a shady, fenced track (a byway) with a garden on your left. Just after the garden ends, and the byway swings right, go left through a gate and follow a winding footpath through trees, passing some old diggings.

Do not go through the next gate; instead turn right into a field and follow a fence to a hedgerow. Turn left through a gap , then follow the right side of the next field, with a sunken, parallel road (Hogtrough Hill) down to your right. Keep ahead into another field, then cross a minor road (The Nower) via two gates. Follow the left side of a large field, with Brasted Hill Farm

A mile or so to the south of Knockholt Pound is Chevening House, probably designed by Inigo Jones in the 17th century.

away to your right. Cross a stile on to a road (Brasted Hill, close to its junction with Stoneings Lane).

If you wish to visit the Tally Ho! pub, turn left along Stoneings Lane for 750 yards (680 metres).

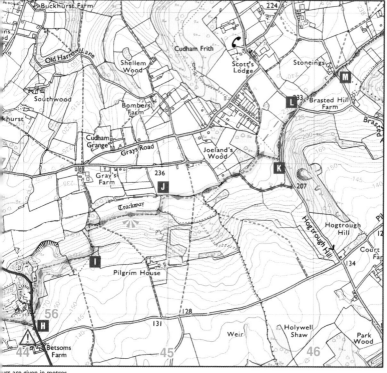

Contours are given in metres
vertical interval is 5m

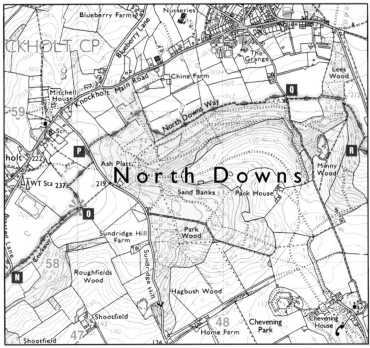

Contours are given in metres
The vertical interval is 5m

Cross the road and go through a gate into another field. Follow its left edge, with Brasted Lane running parallel on your left and an extensive view on your right. Go through a gate into another field. When you reach a field gate **N**, where the lane swings away, go through a kissing-gate to follow the right side of two large fields, with a narrow belt of woodland on your right and two masts away to your left. At the end of the second field, go through a gap **O** and turn left to follow the left side of the next field. Go through another gap and turn right, now following the right side of a field.

At the field corner, do not cross the stile; instead turn left to stay in the same field. In 55 yards (50 metres) descend steps on your right, taking care as you emerge on to a road **P** (Sundridge Hill). Cross over and go through a gate, then keep ahead on a footpath. Shortly turn right through a second gate, then follow the footpath as it veers left, right and left again through a

wood. Go through a third gate, then turn right along the right-hand edge of a field, passing a curvaceous brick gateway, which seems to have lost its reason for existence.

Pass through a gap into the next field, still keeping to the right-hand edge. Go through a gate into another field; a narrow break in the trees to your right gives a 'keyhole' view towards Chevening, the official country residence of the British Foreign Secretary. Keep ahead through a second gate into another field, with cottages ahead, and continue to the end. A third gate beside a bungalow leads on to Chevening Lane **Q**.

If you wish to visit the Three Horseshoes at Knockholt Pound, turn left along the lane for 550 yards (500 metres) to the village centre, or turn right there for 275 yards (250 metres) for the Harrow.

Turn right, then, just before a gate across the lane, turn left through a kissing-gate to the left of a field gate. Follow the left-hand edge of a field – this is a footpath, but horseriders can pay a toll to use it. At the end, go left through a gate, then bear right on a broad footpath between trees, which include some lofty Scots pines on your right. At the next gate, turn right along the field edge for 27 yards (25 metres). Do not go through the gate here; instead turn left to follow the right-hand side of the field. As the field narrows, you come to a fence corner with a fine view ahead. Bear right, beside the fence, into trees, then at the corner go left to a red-topped post and through another gate **R**.

Now start a long descent down Star Hill into the Darent Valley, with the M25 once again intruding on the scene and the sprawling town of Sevenoaks hidden among foliage. The route officially follows a serpentine right of way beside trees, but it is clear that most people follow a more direct permissive path. From a seat near the foot of the slope you can see **St Botolph's Church 5** at Chevening, and the hedge in between marks the line of the Pilgrims Way, though it is not accessible here. At the foot of the hill, cross the Pilgrims Way **S**, then go over a stile. Keep ahead to follow the left-hand

field edge and cross three more stiles as you follow an enclosed footpath to reach the B2211 Sundridge Road **T**.

You must now face one of the most tedious stretches of the North Downs Way, beside the M25 and along busy roads for 0.8 mile (1.3 km). ⚠ ✗ Cross with great care and turn left; for 165 yards (150 metres) there is no pavement, but one is available for the rest of this road-beleaguered stretch. At a roundabout, turn right on the A224 Morants Court Road. Cross the M25 and transfer ⚠ to the opposite pavement to follow the left-hand side of the road, passing the noisily located but charming Shabhall Cottages. Continue to the junction **U** by the Rose & Crown **🅿** on the outskirts of Dunton Green.

🚌 *Buses from here go to Sevenoaks (the stop is on the left, past the pub) and Bromley (the stop is on the right before the pub).*

The western branch of the **Darent Valley Path 6** comes in here, sharing the route all the way into Otford. Cross London Road with care and turn left for 220 yards (200 metres) along its right-hand pavement. Just before the Donnington Manor Hotel **V** 🍴, turn

M25

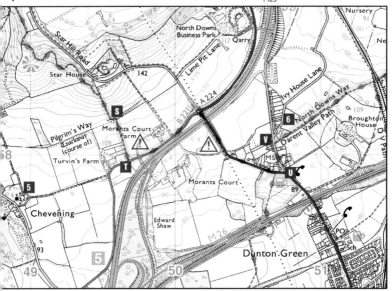

Contours are given in metres
The vertical interval is 5m

Here the North Downs Way joins the Vanguard Way to lead walkers beside the Titsey Plantation on the Oxted Downs.

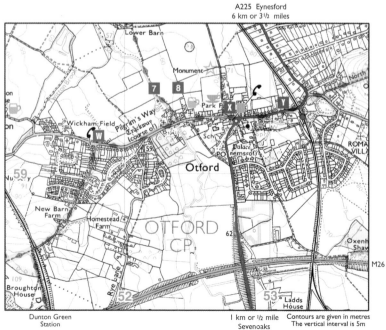

A225 Eynesford
6 km or 3½ miles

Dunton Green
Station

1 km or ½ mile
Sevenoaks

Contours are given in metres
The vertical interval is 5m

right along a footpath, which continues in this direction for 0.5 mile (0.8 km) as a clear path up several fields. Near the top of the rise, the route bears right a little to go through trees, emerging at a junction of tracks. Go ahead through a gap and continue in the same direction on a clear path across a small field. Cross a stile on to a footbridge over the South Eastern main line.

⇌ *The link with **Dunton Green Station** starts by turning right before crossing the stile (see page 182).*

...(see page 182).

Keep ahead down the tarmac Telston Lane, passing a great sea of lavender, and continue in the same direction at a junction to reach Pilgrims Way West **W** at Twitton. Cross over with care and turn right to use a pavement along the left-hand side, where

you pass some impressive small-leaved lime trees, and **'Uranus' 7** beside the Rye Lane bus stop. Cross the River Darent, where the road becomes the High Street, now in **Otford 8**, to the pond **X** at the village centre 🚍☕.

🚌 *Stops for buses to Sevenoaks (left-hand side) and Swanley (right-hand side) are located along Sevenoaks Road to your right.*

Keep ahead for 380 yards (350 metres) to the approach to ⇌ **Otford Station Y** on the Sevenoaks Railway, which opened in 1862 as a branch of the London, Chatham and Dover Railway. Section 5 of the North Downs Way ends here.

To continue on to Section 6, keep ahead over the railway bridge.

Public transport

Oxted (1.1 miles / 1.8 km) ⇌ 🚌
Botley Hill (0.2 mile / 0.3 km) 🚌
Tatsfield (0.6 mile / 1 km) 🚌
Westerham Hill (on route) 🚌
Knockholt (0.2 mile / 0.3 km) 🚌 Not Sundays
Knockholt Pound (0.3 mile / 0.5 km) 🚌 Not Sundays
London Road (on route) 🚌
Dunton Green (0.6 mile /1 km) ⇌
Otford (on route) ⇌ 🚌
Taxis/minicabs: Oxted, Limpsfield, Westerham, Dunton Green, Sevenoaks

Refreshments and toilets

Botley Hill (0.2 mile / 0.3 km) 🍴 Botley Hill Farmhouse
Park Wood (on route) ☕ Park Wood Golf Club
Knockholt (0.4 mile / 0.6 km) 🍴 Tally Ho!
Knockholt Pound (0.3 mile / 0.5 km) 🍴 Harrow, Three Horseshoes
Dunton Green (on route) 🍴 Rose & Crown

Otford (on route) 🍴 Bull, Crown, Horns, Woodman, ☕ Otford Tea Rooms, Willow Rooms
Food shops: Oxted, Knockholt Pound, Dunton Green, Otford
Public toilets: Otford

Accommodation

Clacket Lane Services (1.2 miles / 1.9 km) Premier Inn
Farley Common (1.5 miles / 2.4 km) Worples Field
Westerham (1.4 miles / 2.2 km) Kings Arms Hotel
Cudham (1.8 miles / 2.9 km) Cottage Farm
Brasted (1.7 miles / 2.7 km) Brook Hotel, The Mount House
Brasted Chart (2.7 miles / 4.3 km) Orchard House
Dunton Green (on route) Donnington Manor Hotel
Sevenoaks (2.8 miles / 4.5 km) Moorings Hotel, Royal Oak Hotel
Old Otford Road (1 mile / 1.6 km) Robann

6 Otford to Cuxton

through Wrotham and Trosley Country Park
15 miles (24.1 km)

Ascent 1,716 feet (524 metres)

Descent 1,922 feet (587 metres)

Lowest point Cuxton: 49 feet (15 metres)

Highest point near Otford Manor 711 feet (217 metres)

This long section switchbacks between the high-level track at the top of the Downs and the Pilgrims Way lower down. From Otford, the North Downs Way immediately climbs steeply up Otford Mount to follow the high-level track past Otford Manor. It descends to join the Pilgrims Way through Wrotham, then climbs again to follow an easy-access track through Trosley Country Park. After descending to rejoin the Pilgrims Way briefly, another ascent takes the route through the heavily wooded Rochester Forest. The section ends with some lovely, open walking across two deep valleys and through the delightful hamlet of Upper Bush to finish on the outskirts of Cuxton.

Things to look out for

1 Kemsing Down Nature Reserve straddles the ridge and provides an extensive view, ranging on a clear day from Detling in the east to Leith Hill in the west. The village of Kemsing lies below and Seal church can be seen in the middle distance, but the M26 motorway is out of sight in a cutting. Among the flora are nine species of orchid, fairy flax, burnet saxifrage and squinancywort, while butterflies include brown argus, dingy skipper and grizzled skipper. The reserve is owned by Kemsing Parish Council and managed jointly by **Kent Wildlife Trust** and Sevenoaks District Council.

2 Otford Manor was built in the 1930s for Sir Oliver Lyle, a member of the Lyle family of Tate & Lyle sugar fame. After the Second World War the house passed into the ownership of the Hildenborough Trust, and was bought in 1986 by **Oak Hall**, which arranges Christian conferences there and organises Bible study tours in Israel

and Palestine. The wooden cross on the hillside nearby was erected by the Hildenborough Trust in the 1970s.

3 Wrotham (pronounced Rootam) dates back to the 8th century and was once a market town, but the market has gone and it is now a large village with a population of around 2,000. It is wedged between two motorways (M20 and M26) and a bypass, which means that the price to be paid for a comparatively low level of traffic is the constant roar of those frantic highways. Yet there is still a charm about the village centre, which boasts three old inns within a few minutes' walk of each other. St George's Church dates from the 13th century and is believed to be one of the first in England to be dedicated to the country's patron saint.

4 Wrotham Water Estate is owned by the **National Trust**. Much of its 450 acres (182 hectares) is working farmland, but the estate includes a large area of downland, which is a Site of Special Scientific Interest harbouring endangered orchids as well as being the only known site for the milkwort-feeding micromoth.

5 **Trosley Country Park** was once part of the estate of Trosley Towers, a now-demolished mansion whose site is today occupied by the nearby modern village of Vigo. Trosley is a corruption of Trottiscliffe, the village that lies about half a mile to the south. For about a mile (1.6 km) the North Downs Way follows a level, easy-access trail along the top of the scarp, passing a trim trail and a rustic amphitheatre. The visitor centre

has a café and toilets, as well as an award-winning eco-friendly building. Constructed from the park's own sweet chestnut trees, it has a water-recycling system, natural ventilation and a living green roof.

6 **The Wealdway** is a long-distance walking route of 82 miles (132 km) from Gravesend in Kent to Eastbourne in East Sussex. Launched in 1981, it was originally devised by members of The Ramblers' Kent and Sussex Areas. The route is currently in a state of limbo, as its steering group no longer functions and no publication is in print for the whole route.

Route description

≥ *From Otford station* **A***, turn right up the approach road, then climb the steps and turn right at the top.*

Section 6 of the North Downs Way starts at the top of Otford station's approach road **B**. Continue along Station Road, cross the railway line and keep ahead to a road junction **C**, bearing behind trees with the footway. Turn right up Pennine Way East for 100 yards (92 metres) to the right-hand bend, then cross with care – ⚠ watch for traffic coming fast from the right. Keep ahead up a footpath on the left of a private drive, shortly bearing right to start a long, steady ascent with steps up Otford Mount.

At the top, go through a gate into a field and follow its right-hand side. Another gate leads on to the three-way junction **D** of Row Dow, Row Dow Lane and Birchin Cross Road. With care, cross the central reservation and keep ahead along Birchin Cross Road ✖, signed Oak Hall. In 165 yards (150 metres) turn right through a gap to follow a fenced footpath between a meadow and a wood. Pass three gates, then continue between fields, with farm buildings to your left and Rowdow Wood on your right.

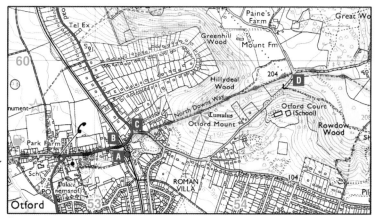

Contours are given in metres
The vertical interval is 5m

Go through a gate on to Shorehill Lane **E** and turn right, passing Silverdale Cottage. Shortly bear left along the drive of Oak Hall, then, just before two brick columns, turn right over a stile and keep ahead along a footpath ahead beside a field, which leads into **Kemsing Down Nature Reserve 1**. Follow the path as it angles several times around field corners, then descend steps to a bench seat with a good view. Go through the gate ahead **F**, then turn left along the top of Whiteleaf Down, contouring along the scarp of Shore Hill. Pass an information panel for the nature reserve, then go through a gate. In 230 yards (210 metres) take the left fork, uphill. Cross a sunken footpath **G** via steps.

🚌 🚊 *If you wish to visit Kemsing, turn right down the sunken footpath.*

Keep ahead, taking care on exposed roots. Turn left across a stile and follow a narrow footpath up steps and past a vast, dead tree, with the brick wall of **Otford Manor 2** on your left. Continue along open downland, with a wooden cross away to your right. Just before the end of the open downland, bear left into trees, passing a farm gate, then cross a stile on the left.

The right of way follows the field edge, but clearly people use a grassy, cross-field footpath.

Cross a stile and keep ahead into trees, then shortly cross two more stiles and a farm track before turning right along a fenced footpath. Cross another stile to join a fenced track ahead between a field and a wood. As the track veers left, keep ahead through a plain gate, then leave the field through a kissing-gate and keep ahead into woodland. Beware of the electric fence on your right and exposed roots along this path. Go through a gate **H** into a field.

🚊 *If you wish to visit the Rising Sun pub at Cotman's Ash, turn left along the footpath here.*

Keep ahead along the right-hand side of the field. Just over halfway along, go through two gates – beware exposed roots – then turn left into woodland. At Cotman's Ash Lane **I** beware traffic coming blind from either direction. Turn left uphill for 120 yards (110 metres) 🏵. Just after a house called Summeryards, turn right through a squeeze-stile to follow a footpath past some barns. At a fork,

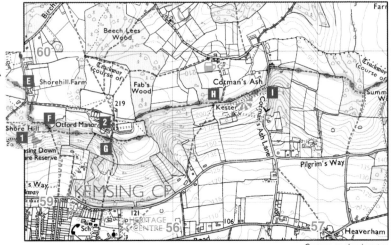

Contours are given in metres
The vertical interval is 5m

keep ahead on a gravel track beside trees. Go through a gate beside another barn, then keep ahead to pass a lone wooden post in the field, with high, rolling fields on your left and a good view on your right. The path closes in on the left-hand side of the field to reach a gate in the corner. Continue along the footpath as it swings right, into Summeryards Wood. Cross a track, where 'White Run' and 'No Entry' signs proliferate, though there is no sign of any recent activity here.

Follow the footpath round to the left and through a gap into a field. Keep ahead along the left-hand side of the field, where you can see the rolling hills of the Kentish Weald through a gap created by the River Bourne. Cross a track junction **J**, then keep ahead in the next field, ignoring grassy tracks leading off to the right. The Pilgrims Way continues on its parallel course below. After passing another North Downs Way milestone (Dover 65 miles / 105 km), and just before the end of this field, bear left to cross a stile, then bear slightly right to pass under the branches of some spreading chestnut trees, with a dry, disused and moss-covered dew pond on your left. Immediately after these, keep

ahead on a rough path between fence and trees to go through a plain gate into a wood. The path bears right and descends gently, finally bending sharp right down to Old Terry's Lodge Road **K**.

Turn right for 35 yards (32 metres), then turn left on a footpath that descends steeply on steps to a gate. Continue down through a field to another gate, with the broad sweep of Exedown to your left and a fine view ahead. The route levels out to follow a clear track across a field to reach a bend in Kemsing Road **L**. The North Downs Way now rejoins the Pilgrims Way for the next 3.1 miles (5 km). Turn left to follow a stony, undulating byway between hedges and along the foot of the escarpment for 1.9 miles (3 km) all the way to Wrotham. Along the way, at Exedown Road **M**, turn right then immediately left to continue in the same direction. Take care when crossing, as traffic comes fast along here. Though its traffic is out of sight, you become ever more aware of the sound of the M20 motorway, which has gouged a great chalk scar down the hillside on your left.

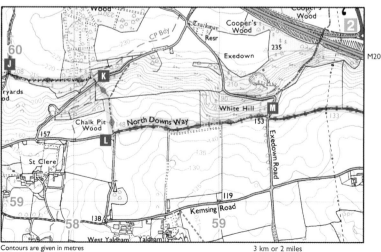

Contours are given in metres
The vertical interval is 5m

3 km or 2 miles
Ightham

The outskirts of Wrotham lie ahead now and you soon join a quiet back road there, unsurprisingly called Pilgrims Way ✳. Keep ahead across Old London Road – a dead end now – and continue along Pilgrims Way, with the M20 hard by your left shoulder. Use the footway along the right-hand side, passing a playing field, to reach a bend in the road beside a recycling centre at **Wrotham** .

🚌 🅿 🍴 **PC** *For Wrotham and the link to Borough Green Station (see page 182), turn right here: the toilets are 165 yards (150 metres) away, the pubs a little further on. Buses go to Borough Green and Meopham stations, Sevenoaks and Gravesend.*

The route continues by turning left along a narrow, tarmac bridleway through bushes, leading to the A20 London Road. Turn left over the M20 towards the roundabout , then cross to the right, via a pedestrian refuge, and keep ahead along a lane – Pilgrims Way again ✳. Follow the lane for 1.1 miles (1.8 km), starting a long, steady climb back up to the ridge. You should use a

parallel footpath that has been provided in three places for North Downs Wayfarers in adjacent fields, as indicated by fingerposts and acorn logos, and taking care as you emerge back on to the lane. There is an extensive view on your right, across fields that are part of the National Trust's **Wrotham Water Estate** . A wide bungalow perched on the hillside above must have one of the best views in southern England.

After passing Nepicar Lane and Hognore Farm, the third parallel path emerges down steps on to a byway, just after the lane makes a sharp right turn. Turn left along the stony byway, then at a farm gate take the left fork (Hognore Lane), leaving the Pilgrims Way to continue ahead. Climb steeply now into Hognore Wood, with widely spaced steps; watch out for cyclists descending apace. At last you reach the top to walk in the shadow of a high, brick wall, which leads you to the A227 Gravesend Road. Continue to the crossroads , and the Vigo Inn , recently reopened after a period of closure.

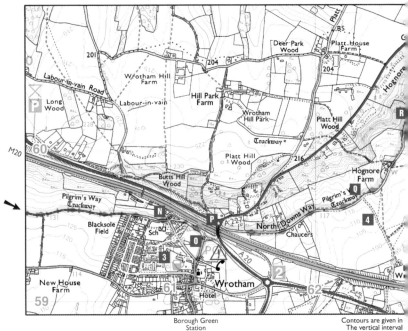

Stanstead
2 km or 1 mile

Borough Green
Station

Contours are given in
The vertical interval

🚌 *Buses from here go to Borough Green and Meopham stations, Sevenoaks and Gravesend.*

Turn right down Vigo Hill ⚒. In 175 yards (160 metres), just before an overhead bridge, bear half left up steps and go through two barriers into **Trosley Country Park 5** 🍽 **PC**, where the park's visitor centre **T** and other facilities lie over to your left. Bear left along a broad, level footpath, which is also an 'easy-access' trail, in company with several waymarked park trails and passing a little amphitheatre with covered picnic tables. There are good views along here, some with bench seats provided. In 0.7 mile (1.1 km) you come to a fork in the track.

🗺 *If you wish to visit the Villager pub at Vigo village, bear left here.*

Keep ahead for another 550 yards (500 metres), the level trail ends and the footpath climbs steeply to the left as a stony track. Go through a gate **U** beside a barrier to leave the country park, then turn sharp right along a byway (Commority Lane), which descends steeply, with steps. At its foot you reach a junction **V** beside a house called Commority, where you turn left along a level bridleway, rejoining the Pilgrims Way. Here you are in brief company with the **Wealdway 6**, which comes in from the right and leaves to the left just 35 yards (32 metres) later. The bridleway follows the foot of the scarp, with

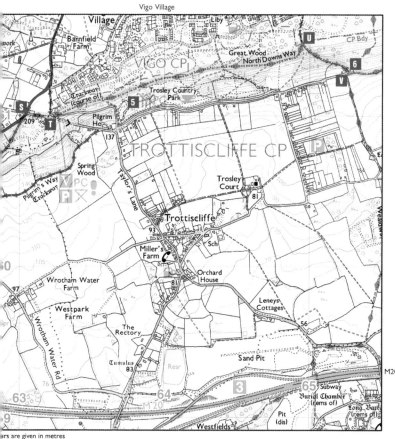

Vigo Village

rs are given in metres
ertical interval is 5m

woods on your left and fields on your right. Keep ahead at a footpath junction , then in 220 yards (200 metres) pass between bollards to join a byway coming down from the left, beside a ruined brick shed. At the next junction , turn left (still a byway). The view on your right now takes in the vast paper mills at Larkfield and New Hythe, beyond which is sprawling Maidstone, the county town of Kent.

In 470 yards (430 metres), at a junction by a gate , turn left to leave the Pilgrims Way on a rather uneven footpath that climbs between fields and hedges. Shortly turn right through a shrubby 'tunnel', then climb very steeply up the scarp. At the top,

go on through a gate to a road  (Birling Hill), cross with care and keep ahead past Holly Hill Lodge along a tarmac lane called Holly Hill ✻. Pass a car park and Holly Hill House, then at a house called West Wing , where the tarmac ends, keep ahead on an earth byway into Greatpark Wood. In 82 yards (75 metres) turn right to follow another byway for 0.6 mile (1 km). On reaching a junction  with an open area on your right, turn right through a black barrier, then immediately left to follow a footpath across a field, passing under a power line. At a second power line , briefly follow a rising track, then halfway round the bend turn left to cross a track via two black metal stiles.

Dean Farm nestles among fields and woods in a dry valley above the River Medway.

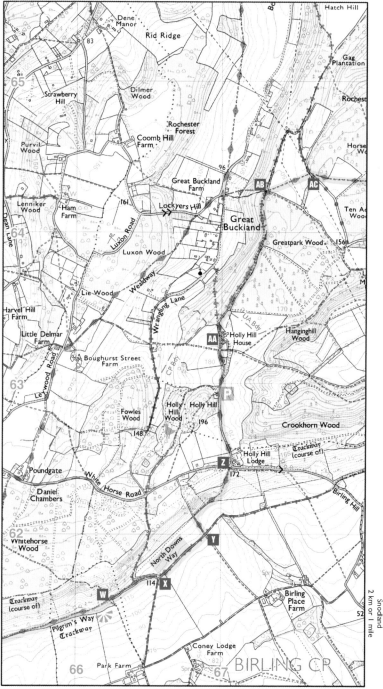

Contours are given in metres
The vertical interval is 5m

Follow a footpath through trees, then across a field. Go through a gate on to a track, where you turn left then immediately right and shortly through another gate into woodland to continue on a narrow footpath in the same direction. You now pass through a number of small woods that are collectively known as Rochester Forest. Keep left at a fork, then cross a field, bearing half right to its far corner **AD**. Keep ahead in woodland again, on a broad footpath which bears left to run beside a field. At a small clearing (a five-way junction) keep ahead past a sunken track **AE**.

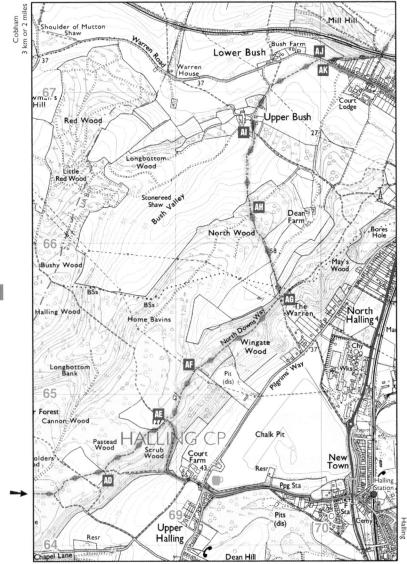

Otford to Cuxton

Contours are given in metres
The vertical interval is 5m

≈ 🚌 *The link with **Halling Station** starts by turning right down the sunken track (see page 182).*

Immediately bear right back into the trees, then in 33 yards (30 metres) turn left along a footpath. The path narrows as it passes under a power line **AF**, then goes between yellow posts to broaden out again through Wingate Wood. First glimpses of the River Medway can be seen on your right. At a junction below another power line **AG**, turn left on a steeply descending footpath with steps, then at a gate go half right down a field. Pass through two gates and cross a farm track to climb between fences, with Dean Farm away to your right. Cross a stile, then follow the path into woods; keep ahead at a junction **AH**. You now descend into Bush Valley across a large field, then bear right beside a clump of trees. Keep ahead into woodland on a rising, sunken track to reach the delightful hamlet of Upper Bush **AI**.

Keep ahead down a tarmac lane (Upper Bush Road), with the houses of Lower Bush ahead. As the lane swings left, bear half right on a footpath across a field to reach Bush Road **AJ**. Cross with care and turn right along the left-hand side for 55 yards (50 metres) to the garage of the first house **AK**, where Section 6 of the North Downs Way ends.

≈ 🚌 *The link to **Cuxton Station** and bus stops starts here by continuing ahead along Bush Road (see page 182).*

To continue on to Section 7, turn left up steps on the left of the garage.

Public transport
Otford (on route) ≈ 🚌
Kemsing village (0.5 mile / 0.8 km) 🚌 Not Sundays
Kemsing railway station (1.5 mile / 2.4 km) ≈
Wrotham (on route) 🚌 Not Sundays
Vigo Inn (on route) 🚌 Not Sundays
Trottiscliffe (0.6 mile / 1 km) 🚌 Not Sundays
Vigo village (0.2 mile / 0.3 km) 🚌
Upper Halling (0.5 mile / 0.8 km) 🚌 Not Sundays
Halling (1.2 miles / 1.9 km) ≈ 🚌
Cuxton (0.9 mile / 1.4 km) ≈ 🚌
Taxis/minicabs: Kemsing, Seal, Wrotham, Borough Green, Vigo, West Malling, Meopham, Cuxton, Strood

Refreshments and toilets
Kemsing (0.5 mile / 0.8 km) 🚍 Bell, Wheatsheaf
Cotman's Ash (0.2 mile / 0.3 km) 🚍 Rising Sun
Heaverham (0.6 mile / 1 km) 🚍 Chequers
Wrotham (0.2 mile / 0.3 km) 🚍 Bull, George & Dragon, Rose & Crown

Little Wrotham (0.6 mile / 1 km) 🚍 The Moat
Trosley Country Park (on route) 🍵 Visitor Centre, 🚍 Vigo Inn
Vigo village (0.2 mile / 0.3 km) 🚍 The Villager
Cuxton (0.6 mile / 1 km) 🚍 White Hart
Food shops: Otford, Wrotham, Cuxton
Public toilets: Otford, Wrotham, Trosley Country Park

Accommodation
Seal (1.6 miles/ 2.6 km) Wendy Wood
Stansted (South) (0.8 mile / 1.3 km) Hilltop Hotel, Thriftwood Camping and Caravan Park
Wrotham (0.2 mile / 0.3 km) Bull Hotel
Wrotham Heath (1.1 mile / 1.8 km) Holiday Inn Maidstone-Sevenoaks, Premier Inn Sevenoaks-Maidstone, Pretty Maid Guest House, Gatehouse Wood Camp Site
Aldon (2.6 miles / 4.2 km) Apple House
Ryarsh (1.3 miles / 2 km) Heavers House
Harvel (1.6 miles / 2.6 km) Amazon & Tiger, Hideaway
Cobham (2.1 miles / 3.4 km) Leather Bottle
Lower Bush (on route) North Downs Barn

7 Cuxton to Detling

across the Medway Bridges and past Kit's Coty House
12.5 miles (20.1 km)

Ascent 1,325 feet (404 metres)

Descent 978 feet (299 metres)

Lowest point Nashenden Farm Lane: 66 feet (20 metres)

Highest point Hermitage Lane: 640 feet (195 metres)

Now the North Downs Way crosses the River Medway – a matter of some importance to the good folk of Kent, because those born west of this noble river call themselves Kentish Men or Maidens, while those born east of it are Men or Maids of Kent. This section starts by climbing over Ranscombe Farm Reserve to cross the Medway Bridges, where you are accompanied by the M2 and Eurostar's high-speed railway line. You can try to ignore them by looking left from your high vantage point above the River Medway towards Rochester's castle and cathedral, while admiring aquatic birds flying gracefully below and feeding on the salt marsh, as well as shimmering yachts at Medway Bridge Marina. The motorway is soon left behind as you steadily ascend Nashenden Down, with some fine views, then it is nearly all level or downhill, apart from one steep ascent after passing prehistoric Kit's Coty House.

The Pilgrims Way follows a different line for nearly all of this section, apart from two short stretches, and you will cross it a couple of times. You must take extra care at an awkward junction at busy Rochester Road, but at least you can take comfort in the knowledge that there is then a long stretch of nearly 20 miles (32 km) with no major road crossings.

Things to look out for

1 Ranscombe Farm Reserve is one of 23 nature reserves in Britain managed by the wild plant conservation charity **Plantlife** – this one jointly with Medway Council. It covers 560 acres (227 hectares) and, as a working farm, includes a substantial amount of arable land as well as extensive areas of ancient woodland. Six species of orchid can be found here, as well as nationally rare plants such as meadow clary and rough marshmallow. Ranscombe Farm, and indeed most of Section 7 of the North Downs Way, falls within the area of the Medway Smile Living Landscape Scheme (so-called as it stretches around the Medway towns like a smile), whose aim is to enlarge and enhance the wildlife reserves that lie within it, under the management of **Kent Wildlife Trust**.

2 Merrals Shaw seems an innocent little wood from our side, but it has given its name to the triple-roundabout junction of the M2 and the A228 on its far side, which is known to many motorists as Merrals Shaw Interchange, opened in 1963.

3 HS1 (High Speed 1) is the name of the 68-mile (109-km) high-speed railway line that whisks Eurostar trains from London St Pancras to the Channel Tunnel, en route to Paris or Brussels, and Southeastern Railway's Javelin trains to East Kent. In the near future they are expected to be joined by Deutsche Bundesbahn trains to such places as Frankfurt and Amsterdam. The line took nine years to construct and the full length was completed in 2007.

4 The **M2** is quite short as motorways go (26 miles / 42 km) – in effect just a bypass for the Medway towns, taking away the traffic that would otherwise pass through them on the A2. It was completed in 1965, but the original plan to extend it to Dover has not materialised.

5 The **Medway Bridges** (sometimes called the Medway Viaducts) are usually referred to in the plural as there are in fact three. The original six-lane bridge opened in 1963 and included a footpath on either side; this was joined in 2003 by a second bridge, resulting in two four-lane carriageways, but at the expense of the footpath on the south side. The bridge for HS1 was completed in 2007. The shared-use track you are walking on, 116 feet (35 metres) above the river, is actually a service road, which can be commandeered for emergency vehicles if necessary – if that were to happen for any length of time you may need to divert via Rochester.

6 The **River Medway** rises in the Ashdown Forest in East Sussex and flows for 75 miles (120 km) to reach the Thames Estuary between the Isles of Grain and Sheppey. It is navigable by craft up to 80 feet (24.4 metres) long as far as Tonbridge and larger, sea-going vessels can pass underneath the Medway Bridges to reach the first lock at Allington. There is a theory that the name, first recorded in AD 764 as Meduwain, was a corruption of ancient British and Celtic words meaning 'golden river'. From 1915 to 1946 this part of the river was used for take-off

and landing by the flying-boats of Shorts Brothers, whose factory was located on the east bank at Borstal. The motorway bridge would preclude such a thing nowadays!

7 Borstal is the name of the village (now part of Rochester) that you are passing through, but it will for ever be associated with the first prison for young offenders, which was established in 1908 (in a former military fort that lies just a short distance ahead) and still functions in a similar capacity, now known as HMP (Her Majesty's Prison) Rochester.

8 Among the buildings at **Nashenden Farm** are a couple of oast houses (from the Old English word *ast* meaning fire). These distinctive buildings with their conical or pyramidal roofs were introduced into England during the 16th century for drying hops, which were spread out on the floor and heated from underneath, while a cowl on top of the roof allowed hot air to escape. You will see many of them as you progress along the North Downs Way – they are no longer in use, but many have been converted into charming and atmospheric homes.

9 Nashenden Down Nature Reserve was established by **Kent Wildlife Trust** in 2009 with the aim of creating a haven for rare and threatened birds, animals and wild flowers. This will be achieved by turning most of its 130 acres (53 hectares) of arable farmland into chalk grassland, extending existing woodland and restoring grubbed-out hedges. The remaining farmland will continue to be managed in a wildlife-friendly way.

10 Shoulder of Mutton Wood, donated to the **Woodland Trust** in 1993, dates from the 17th century and the name is thought to derive from its shape. The north end contains a 'bell barrow' (burial mound) from the Bronze Age, which means it could be 3,100–3,500 years old.

11 Bluebell Hill Picnic Area is a Site of Special Scientific Interest, managed by

The view from the Way where it skirts White Horse Hill between Detling and Thurnham Castle, a country park managed by Kent County Council.

Kent Wildlife Trust, on account of the wealth of specialist species that inhabit this chalk grassland, including flora such as salad burnet, bird's-foot trefoil, horseshoe vetch, fairy flax, pyramidal orchid, bee orchid, false brome grass, hairy violet and bulbous buttercup, and insects such as chalkhill blue, silver-spotted skipper and brown argus butterflies, and the straw belle moth. A memorial here pays tribute to a Kent Air Ambulance crew, who were killed nearby in 1998.

12 Kit's Coty House is one of the best-preserved examples of a rectangular stone chamber, which formed the entrance to one of the many long barrows (burial mounds) that were constructed during the early Neolithic period (4,800–5,500 years ago). 'Kit's Coty' (also the name of the nearby village) is thought to derive from the belief that the site is the burial place of the Celtic leader Catigern (Kit), son of Vortigern, killed in a battle with the Saxons under Horsa in AD 455 – 'coty' being a cot or cottage.

13 The **White Horse Stone** is probably all that remains of a burial chamber, but a legend has grown up that it was part of the tomb of Horsa, one of the 5th-century Saxon warlords brought in by the Celts to help fight off the Picts. He is believed to have become king of Kent, with a white horse as his standard, hence the name of this stone.

14 Jade's Crossing is named after Jade Hobbs, who in 2000, aged eight, was killed while attempting to cross the A249, together with her grandmother Margaret Kuwertz. Following two earlier deaths, there had for some years been a campaign for a protected crossing of this very busy road, and it is tragic that it required the deaths of four people to achieve success.

15 Detling, though now part of Maidstone, is separated from the town by open country and retains a village atmosphere. It was once very noisy, as the A249 passed through the village, but the new road further west has taken away most of the traffic. St Martin of Tours Church dates from Norman times but was extensively restored in the late 19th century. Detling Airfield, to the north-east at the top of the hill, was a famous RAF station during the Second World War, and the memorial in the village centre commemorates the aircrew who were killed. It is now occupied by the Kent County Show Ground (the show takes place in mid July), which is also the location in August of 'People Without Limits', an annual Christian celebration that has come to be known as plain 'Detling'.

Route description

From Bush Road, go up steps on the left of the garage **A** to ascend a footpath into Mill Hill Wood. Pass a memorial seat, then turn left across the railway line from London Victoria to Chatham, Margate and Dover, opened in 1861. Bear right down steps, then cross a large field, passing under a power line. For the next 0.8 mile (1.3 km) the route lies within **Ranscombe Farm Reserve 1**.

Follow the path as it makes a long ascent to the right beside a belt of trees, eventually passing through a gate **B** at the top. Bear left through a gap into another field to continue in the same direction, now with the trees on your right, the houses of Ranscombe away to your left and the M2 motorway in the distance ahead. Follow the track between fields towards the M2, passing a waymark post. On reaching a tarmac farm drive **C**, turn right along it, passing between **Merrals Shaw 2** (on your left) and Longhoes Wood.

As the drive emerges from the woodland, you are greeted by a grand panorama dominated by the River Medway and the Medway Bridges. Follow the drive round to the left, with the Medway Valley Line (opened in 1856) in a deep cutting on your right. Pass a height restriction barrier to reach the A228 Rochester Road **D**. The next 1.3 miles (2 km) of the route follow a 'shared-use' track, where you should bear in mind that cyclists may approach fast from behind.

Turn left along the shared-use track, which heads towards a traffic roundabout, bears left between bollards, then swings right to go through a subway under the A228. Turn left on the far side of the subway, then bear left up a slope to walk beside the A228 across the **HS1 railway line 3** and the **M2 motorway 4**. Keep ahead on the far side for 165 yards (150 metres), with Medway Gate on your left – a major development of new homes occupying a former quarry. Turn right past a barrier **E**, still on a shared-use track, where walkers should keep left. Bear left beside the M2 to reach the **Medway Bridges 5**. (The Pilgrims Way would have followed the river below, on its way to cross Rochester Bridge.)

Cross the **River Medway 6**, keeping left and still bearing in mind that cyclists may approach fast from behind. On the far side, follow the track down past a metal gate on to Wouldham Road **F** in **Borstal 7**. For the next 1.5 miles (2.4 km) your route is shared with the Medway Valley Walk, which closely follows the river for 28 miles (45 km) from Tonbridge to Rochester (details from **Kent County Council**).

🚌 *A bus service goes along Wouldham Road: the stop to the left is for buses to Rochester and Chatham; the stop to the right (past the motorway bridge) is for buses to Maidstone.*

🍺 *To visit the White Hart pub, turn left along Wouldham Road for 300 yards (275 metres).*

🔜 *You can reach Rochester on foot by turning left here to follow the Medway Valley Walk for 2 miles (3.2 km).*

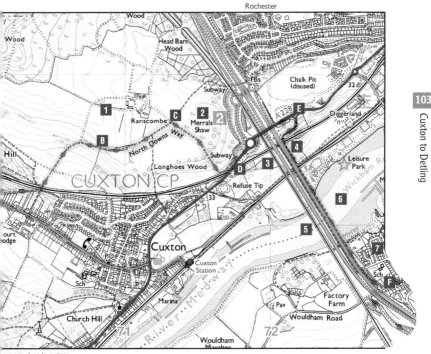

urs are given in metres
vertical interval is 5m

Cross the road with care and turn right under the M2. Turn left to follow Nashenden Farm Lane ✻, which has no pavement but a generous grass verge. In 0.6 mile (1 km), where the road broadens out, turn right on a bridleway to pass through the little community surrounding **Nashenden Farm 8**. Cross the high-speed railway line, then go through a gate into **Nashenden Down Nature Reserve 9**, going uphill between fields.

At a hedgerow, bear right then left to continue in the same direction on a chalky track. You will now be following this ancient ridgeway, keeping ahead and steadily ascending all the time, for the next 2.5 miles (4 km), at first as a bridleway, then as a byway and finally as a tarmac lane. As usual, the views are mostly to your right, but look out for a rare view to your left,

towards the Isle of Sheppey and the Thames Estuary. Ivy Cottage on the Pilgrims Way lies on your right, with **Shoulder of Mutton Wood 10** on your left. You join Hill Road **G**, a gravel byway.

🚌 *The Medway Valley Walk goes off to the right along the byway and you can follow it down to Wouldham for buses to Rochester and Maidstone.*

Pass Wouldham Common viewpoint **H**, with a picnic table, reached past a green bollard on your right. Off to your right is Keeper's Lodge **I**, where the route kinks left and right to resume its original direction. The woodland and grassland on your right now, and for most of the next 1.5 miles (2.5 km), are part of the Burham Down Nature Reserve, managed by the **Kent Wildlife Trust**. At Burham Hill Farm **J**, keep ahead between fields along the tarmac-surfaced

Along the grassy margins of the path the length of the North Downs Way, orchids like the bee orchid are found in sometimes surprising profusion.

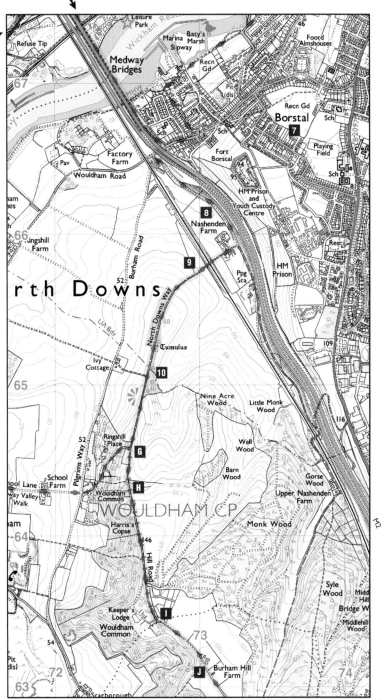

Contours are given in metres
The vertical interval is 5m

The Neolithic remains known as Kit's Coty House are believed to be the burial place of the Celtic leader Catigern.

Common Road ✖, then a swinging pub sign **K** betrays the presence of the Robin Hood pub ⌂ just a short step down a side road on your left.

🚌 *The byway on your right leads down to Burham for buses between Rochester and Maidstone.*

At the top of the long climb, soon after the first houses of the village of Blue Bell Hill, look out for a fingerpost **L** on your right (it may be obscured by shrubbery), which indicates that you should turn off the road to follow a parallel footpath along the top of the escarpment, with an extensive view. Keep ahead past **Bluebell Hill Picnic Area** **11** and car park.

🚌 *For buses from Blue Bell Hill to Rochester and Maidstone, go through the car park then turn right along Common Road.*

Cross a stile, then turn right along a tarmac footpath beside the A229 Maidstone Road. After joining the old A229 **M**, keep ahead on an earth footpath, still beside the A229. ⚠ You must take great care all the way along this next stretch, especially approaching the next junction **N** (Chatham Road), as traffic comes up very fast and close to join the A229. Cross Salisbury Road and keep ahead on a pavement to pass under a footbridge, then a bus stop 🚌 *(buses to Rochester)*. Opposite a road with 'no entry' signs, turn right down some steep steps to follow a footpath that descends past **Kit's Coty House** **12**, which lies in a field on your right and can be reached through a gap in bushes. Continue down the footpath to a road **O**, which is the Pilgrims Way again, but here desecrated as a busy dual carriageway.

⚠ Take very great care as you emerge from the footpath as traffic comes blind from the right. Turn left along a short, narrow pavement (which may be overgrown) to the junction with Rochester Road and cross with equal care to the far side. At busy times, you may find it easier to turn right across Pilgrims Way then left across Rochester Road. This junction is especially bad during rush hours – avoid them if you can.

Rejoin the Pilgrims Way on the far side of Rochester Road and follow it along the foot of the scarp for 0.6 mile (1 km), keeping ahead at a junction **P**.

🛏 🚌 *The footpath up to your left leads to the Lower Bell pub and bus stops serving Maidstone.*

Just before encountering the A229 again, turn left along an access road then turn right, through a subway **Q**. Continue round to the right to Old Chatham Road Service Station (shop, hot drinks, toilets). Pass a National Cycle Network 'Millennium Milestone' signpost and keep ahead on a footpath to the left of a green fence. At its end, turn left to join a byway, crossing the line of a Roman road from Rochester to the south coast, and then the high-speed railway line.

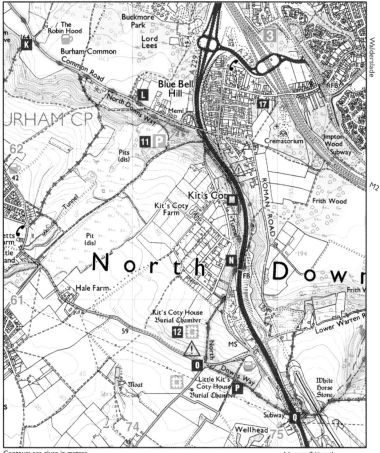

Contours are given in metres
The vertical interval is 5m

4 km or 2 ½ miles
A229 Maidstone

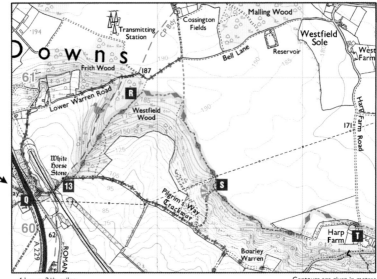

4 km or 2½ miles
A229 Maidstone

Contours are given in metres
The vertical interval is 5m

Keep ahead up a sunken track between trees into Boxley Warren Nature Reserve, passing the **White Horse Stone** 13 (up steps on your left). In 82 yards (75 metres) turn left up a footpath, leaving the Pilgrims Way to continue ahead. This path makes much use of steps as it climbs steeply back up to the ridge, passing another North Downs Way milestone **R** (Dover 54 miles / 87 km) near the top.

Cross a stone stile and turn right along the right-hand side of a huge field. You now follow the line of the ancient ridgeway for most of the next 2.5 miles (4 km). Shortly after a power line **S**, the route dives off to the right, to continue along the ridge but now in trees. Eventually the path turns left then right to pass round some paddocks and reach Harp Farm. Cross Harp Farm Road **T** and keep ahead on a path, past a water tank and along the edge of a field.

Cross Lidsing Road **U** with care and turn right. Opposite the junction with Harp Farm Road, turn left to follow a gravel bridleway for 1.3 miles (2 km). The track rises a little to reach a T-junction **V**, where you turn right down a steep byway (Hermitage Lane). Near

the foot, by the gates of the defunct Detling Lime Works, you join a tarmac access road leading down to the Pilgrims Way **W** – here a tarmac road with no pavement ✳.

Turn left and keep ahead past Harple Lane and the first houses of the village of Detling. Just before reaching the A249 Sittingbourne Road **X**, turn sharp left up a concrete access drive, then turn right up steps to gain access to **Jade's Crossing** 14, a footbridge that takes you across the A249. On the far side, follow the ramp down to rejoin Pilgrims Way. Cross over and turn left to the RAF Memorial (with picnic table). Bear right past the Cock Horse pub 🍺 to the junction **Y** of Pilgrims Way and The Street in **Detling** 15 village centre, where Section 7 of the North Downs Way ends.

🚌 *Bus services go from Detling to Maidstone, Sittingbourne and Faversham. Some go from the village centre, others from the main road – check with* Traveline.

If you are continuing on to Section 8, turn left along Pilgrims Way.

🚆 *The link to Bearsted Station begins soon after the start of Section 8.*

Public transport

Cuxton (0.9 mile / 1.4 km) 🚆 🚌
Borstal (on route) 🚌
Rochester (2 miles / 3.2 km) 🚆 🚌
Wouldham (0.9 mile / 1.4 km) 🚌
Burham (0.5 mile / 0.8 km) 🚌
Blue Bell Hill (0.3 mile / 0.5 km) 🚌
  Not Sundays
Lower Bell (0.2 mile / 0.3 km) 🚌 Not
  Sundays
Detling (on route) 🚌
Bearsted (1.7 miles / 2.7 km) 🚆
Maidstone (2.8 miles / 4.5 km) 🚆
Taxis/minicabs: Cuxton, Strood, Rochester,
  Walderslade, Kit's Coty, Sandling
  (Maidstone), Boxley, Detling, Maidstone

Refreshments and toilets

Borstal (0.2 mile / 0.3 km) 🍺 White Horse
Burham Hill (on route) 🍺 Robin Hood
Burham (0.5 mile / 0.8 km) 🍺 Windmill,
  Golden Eagle
Lower Bell (0.2 mile / 0.3 km) 🍺 Lower
  Bell Inn

Detling (on route) 🍺 Cock Horse
Food shops: Cuxton, Borstal, Rochester,
  Old Chatham Road, Detling, Maidstone
Public toilets: Rochester, Old Chatham
  Road, Maidstone

Accommodation

Borstal (0.8 mile / 1.3 km) Riverview
  Lodge, Sovereign Guest House
Rochester (2 miles / 3.2 km) Wide
  selection – contact **Rochester Visitor
  Information Centre**
Rochester Airport (1.6 miles / 2.6 km)
  Bridgewood Manor Hotel, Holiday Inn
  Rochester-Chatham, Woolmans Wood
  Caravan and Camping Park
Aylesford (1.3 miles / 2 km) Wickham
  Lodge
Sandling (Maidstone) (1.6 miles/2.6 km)
  Premier Inn Maidstone (Sandling)
Detling (0.8 mile / 1.3 km) Detling
  Coach House Hotel
Maidstone (2.8 miles / 4.5 km) wide
  choice – contact **Maidstone Tourist
  Information Centre**

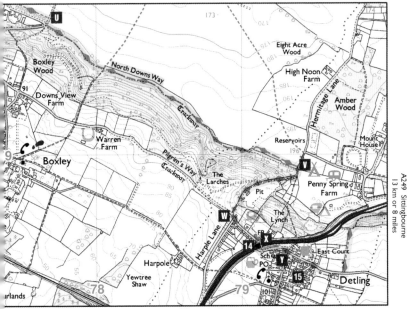

A249 Sittingbourne
13 km or 8 miles

Colours are given in metres
vertical interval is 5m

2 km or 1 mile
A249 Maidstone

8 Detling to Lenham

past Thurnham Castle and the Marley factory
9.3 miles (14.9 km)

Ascent 420 feet (128 metres)
Descent 810 feet (247 metres)
Lowest point Hollingbourne 286 feet (88 metres)
Highest point Allington Hill 617 feet (188 metres)

This section is shared almost equally between the ridge, where you must negotiate several long flights of steps, and the Pilgrims Way, which undulates merrily along lower down. Soon after the start, you can make a short but steep diversion to explore the remains of Thurnham Castle. The transition from high to low level is made halfway at Hollingbourne, whose intriguingly named pub, the Dirty Habit, may be difficult to ignore at lunchtime. Marley is one of the world's best-known tile and roofing manufacturers and you will pass their extensive factory at Harrietsham near the end of the section.

If you have some spare time, you might consider visiting Leeds Castle, which is just 2.5 miles (4 km) from Hollingbourne, with a connecting bus service, and has been described as 'the loveliest castle in the world', situated beside a lake in beautiful grounds..

Things to look out for

1 **White Horse Wood Country Park**, opened in 2007, is managed by **Kent County Council**, who have planted over 20,000 trees and created open grassland from former arable fields. You may see people engaged in hang-gliding and flying model aeroplanes here.

2 **Thurnham Castle** was first mentioned in a document dated 1225, but it may have been built as early as the 11th century, when the Normans were building hundreds of 'motte-and-bailey' castles all over England to subjugate the native population. Some sources suggest that the Norman castle was built on the site of an earlier Saxon fortification known as Godard's Castle, and that this in turn may have occupied the site of a watchtower

guarding the ancient ridgeway along the North Downs. The motte was a tall, steep mound, surmounted by a keep that served as the commander's residence and provided a place to retreat to under attack. The bailey was an enclosed area in front of the motte, containing buildings for soldiers, craftsmen and servants. The whole was surrounded by a high fence or wall and a defensive ditch, guarded by a gatehouse with a drawbridge. Earlier motte-and-bailey castles were built of wood, later ones of stone – flint in the case of Thurnham. The north side of its bailey wall still stands 10 feet (3 metres) high, but the west wall has collapsed. The castle is now owned by **Kent County Council** and has been absorbed into White Horse Wood Country Park.

3 The very large **Hucking Estate** was acquired in 1997 by the **Woodland Trust** with the help of a legacy from John Larking. It consists of 578 acres (234 hectares) of existing woodland, plus arable land that has been planted with over 180,000 native broadleaf trees.

4 The Dirty Habit pub in **Hollingbourne** dates from the 13th century. Its name is a modern invention, though – it was previously called the Pilgrim's Rest, and before that the King's Head. King James II is believed to have stayed there on his way to Dover and France. The 14th-century All Saints Church has a number of impressive memorials to the Culpeper family. The population of the village is about 900.

5 **Harrietsham** is a pleasant village with a population of about 1,500. Its fine church, St John the Baptist, has two towers, one of which is Norman, and an altar floor of medieval tiles.

6 The **Pilgrim's Rest** sculpture near Harrietsham is of a reclining, wooden Brother Percival taking a well-earned rest on his way to Canterbury.

7 The **Marley** factory was established near Harrietsham in 1923 by Owen Aisher, a local builder, who took the name of the nearby farm to create the Marley Joinery Works, at first making doors and windows. The following year he started making tiles, the business expanded and in 1926 the name was changed to the Marley Tile Company. Other factories were established around the country and Marley became internationally famous, now under the management of Owen's son, also Owen, who was knighted in 1981 and died in 1993. After the Second World War, production of the celebrated tiles moved elsewhere and this site turned to manufacturing such products as drainage pipes, guttering and roofing materials. It is now part of the international group Aliaxis, and plastic products are still made here under the Marley name.

8 **Lenham** has managed to retain its village character (despite having been considered a market town in the past) to the extent that it is often selected as a location for period film sets. Many springs in the surrounding meadows contribute to rivers that flow either west (the Len) into the Medway at Maidstone, or east (the Great Stour) through Canterbury to the North Sea near Sandwich. These springs create a wetness that was ideal for the cultivation of watercress.

Detling to Lenham

The picturesque village of Chilham.

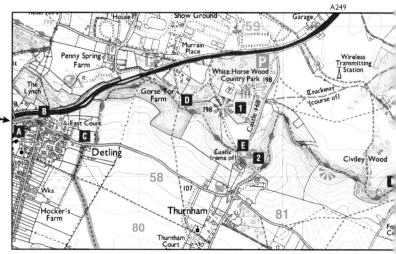

Contours are given in m
The vertical interval is

Route description

🚌 *Buses from Maidstone may stop either in the village centre or on the A249 Detling Hill* **A** *– if the latter, you will need to start at Jade's Crossing, near the end of Section 7. If your bus stops in Detling's village centre, you will need to go to the Cock Horse pub* **B** *at the north end of the village.*

Continue along Pilgrims Way �***** , opposite the Cock Horse, for 440 yards (400 metres) to the entrance of Detling Cricket Club **C**.

⇌ *The link with* **Bearsted Station** *starts by turning right along a gravel track between houses (see page 182).*

Soon after the cricket club entrance, turn left up a footpath beside a field, past a pavilion. At the top, go right then left through a gate and follow the path up the scarp slope. Wayfarer's tree, a kind of viburnum with red and black berries, is in abundance all around here. Behind, on your left, are Gorse Tor Farm and the A249. After an entrance into **White Horse Wood Country Park** **1**, you descend 103 steps and pass through a gate **D** into a field. Keep ahead, using steps up to the left of two lonely holm (evergreen) oak trees. Go through a gate on to a lane **E** (Castle Hill) ✫ and turn right for 220 yards (200 metres). At a sharp right-hand bend, keep ahead through a gate on to a footpath.

🚪🐾 *If you wish to visit the Black Horse at Thurnham, continue down the lane for 275 yards (250 metres).*

In 165 yards (150 metres), at another gate, you can make a strenuous but worthwhile diversion to your left, up 110 steps, to explore the remains of **Thurnham Castle** **2**. Otherwise continue up the left-hand slope of a combe to a third gate. Turn right across the head of the combe, with a fine view over Thurnham Keep Farm, then keep left of a fence that leads down through a gate to follow a fenced footpath. You must now negotiate three long flights of steps: up 63, down 52, up 52, as you contour through woodland around Civiley Hill to a T-junction. Turn right down an old driveway that leads to Coldblow Lane **F**. *If staying at Coldblow Farm, you can continue to the next junction: this involves less road-walking.*

Cross over and ascend a steep footpath, at first through trees, then levelling out across downland. Descend 46 steps via a gate and continue down a field to another gate at Cat's Mount. Turn left up a byway (Coldharbour Lane) around the head of a combe to the top. At a left-hand bend **G**, keep ahead along a footpath.

↩ *For Coldblow Farm, stay on the byway for 100 yards (90 metres), then turn left along a footpath.*

Keep ahead at a path junction **H**, then fork left uphill at the next junction, heading for a hedge corner. Go through a gate then along the lowest faint path among the heather. Pass through a gap, then keep ahead into the next field. Shortly turn left beside a hedge up the left-hand side of a field. Go through a gate, then follow a fenced footpath to your right, along the top of the slope. Keep on past a stile to cross a sunken lane **I** (Broad Street Hill) via steps.

Continue ahead on a fenced footpath along the top of the slope, then descend steps, now in the Woodland Trust's **Hucking Estate 3**. At a T-junction **J** go left up a byway. In 120 yards (110 metres) turn right past a barrier on to a level footpath. Go through a gate and bear left around the hillside to another gate, then follow a fenced farm track along the downs. A third gate leads on to a narrow footpath along the top edge of a field, where Hollingbourne appears down to your right.

The path gradually descends towards the village, but at another gate you bear left to walk on the level again. Approaching the end of the field, turn right at a waymark post and drop down towards the left end of a copse. Go round the back of the copse, through a gate **K** and along the left side of a field, parallel with a road in a cutting below.

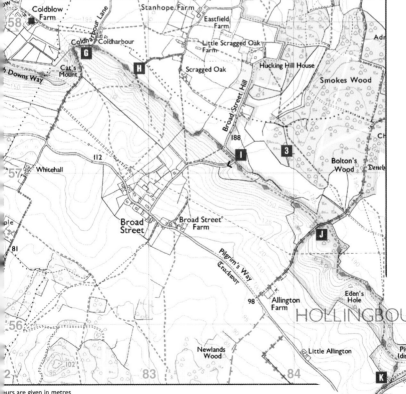

ours are given in metres
vertical interval is 5m

On reaching the road (Hollingbourne Hill) 🏃, turn right to the crossroads **L**, beside the Dirty Habit pub 🍺 in **Hollingbourne** **4**.

≋ 🚉 *The link with **Hollingbourne Station** starts by keeping ahead along Upper Street (see page 183).*

Turn left by the Dirty Habit, rejoining the Pilgrims Way. It undulates between fields for several miles – first as a tarmac lane, then as a gravel byway, passing several path or track junctions. Eventually, in 1.6 miles (2.6 km), The Dutch House comes into view on the hillside ahead – a large, white, timber-framed house with a brown roof. Then, on your right, the huge, black barn of Court Lodge Farm. The byway rises

to meet a metalled drive, beside the entrance to The Dutch House **M**.

≋ *The link with **Harrietsham Station** starts by turning right down a bridleway here (see page 183).*

Follow the drive to a road **N** (Stede Hill) beside Pilgrims Lodge. Cross over and keep ahead, still Pilgrims Way, now on tarmac again for 1.1 miles (1.8 km). **Harrietsham** **5** and the tower of St John the Baptist Church appear on your right, while Stede Court, a luxurious self-catering establishment, dominates the hillside up to your left. The Way chunters along amiably, passing Summoners Farm, and shortly passes Brother Percival, enjoying the view from the **Pilgrim's Rest bench** **6**.

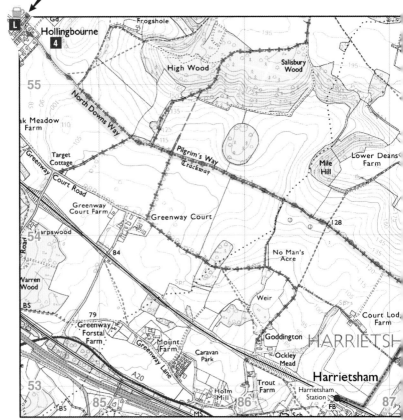

Contours are given in r
The vertical interval i

A house called Serengeti marks the junction with Marley Road **0**, then the vast **Marley 7** works occupy the right-hand side of the Way for the next 440 yards (400 metres), and stretch a similar distance away to the south. If you wish to take a closer look, venture a little way along the public footpath that appears shortly. But look to your left, too, for Marley Court, the house that gave its name to the factory, is a Grade II listed building dating from the 18th century.

After the junction with Flint Lane, a long, brick wall guards a house called The Dorman, then Marlow Farm appears up to your left. When the tarmac lane swings right, keep ahead on a gravel and grass byway between hedges, with the A20 London–Maidstone–Dover trunk road running parallel in the valley below. The large village of **Lenham 8** lies down to your right, but is largely hidden among greenery in summer. You pass a low plaque for the Lenham Millennium Project (in which 2,000 trees were planted to mark the year 2000), then Section 8 of the North Downs Way ends at the junction with Faversham Road **P**.

*The link with **Lenham Station** and buses starts by turning right up steps here (see page 183).*

If you are continuing on to Section 9, cross the road with care and keep ahead along the left-hand side.

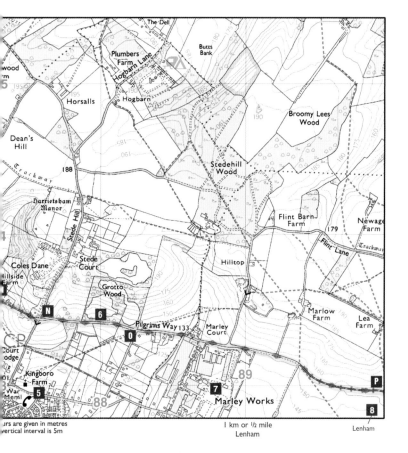

115

Detling to Lenham

Contours are given in metres
The vertical interval is 5m

1 km or ½ mile
Lenham

Public transport

Maidstone (2.8 miles / 4.5 km) 🚄
Detling (on route) 🚌
Bearsted (1.7 miles / 2.7 km) 🚄
Hollingbourne village (on route) 🚌
Hollingbourne (Eyhorne Street, 0.8 mile / 1.3 km) 🚄
Harrietsham (0.6 mile / 1 km) 🚄🚌
Lenham (1.1 miles / 1.8 km) 🚄🚌
Taxis/minicabs: Maidstone, Detling, Harrietsham, Lenham.

Refreshments and toilets

Thurnham (0.2 mile / 0.3 km) Black Horse 🍺
Hollingbourne (on route) Dirty Habit 🍺
Eyhorne Street (0.8 mile / 1.3 km) 🍺 Sugar Loaves, Windmill
Harrietsham (0.6 mile / 1 km) Roebuck 🍺
Lenham (1.1 miles / 1.8 km) Dog & Bear 🍺, Red Lion 🍺, Pippa's Tearoom ☕

Food shops: Maidstone, Detling, Hollingbourne, Harritesham, Lenham
Public toilets: Maidstone, Lenham

Accommodation

Bearsted (2.2 miles / 3.5 km) Marriott Tudor Park, Tollgate
Thurnham (0.2 mile / 0.3 km) Black Horse Inn
Coldblow Farm (0.4 mile / 0.6 km) Camping barn
Maidstone Service Area (1.5 miles / 2.4 km) Day's Inn,
Eyhorne Green (1.4 miles / 2.2 km) Ramada Jarvis Maidstone Hotel
Leeds (2.4 miles / 3.8 km) Kent House
Harrietsham (0.6 mile / 1 km) Roebuck Inn
Lenham (1.1 miles / 1.8 km) Dog & Bear Inn, Lime Tree Hotel
Chilston Park (2.2 miles / 3.5 km) Chilston Park Hotel

'Pilgrim bound with staff and faith, rest thy bones,' says the plaque here, but Brother Percival is oblivious to passing North Downs Wayfarers.

Detling to Lenham

9 Lenham to Wye

through Boughton Lees and Eastwell Park
11.1 miles (17.9 km)

Ascent 420 feet (128 metres)

Descent 810 feet (247 metres)

Lowest point Wye 102 feet (31 metres)

Highest point Charing Quarry 489 feet (149 metres)

If you intend to follow the Canterbury Loop, you will need to branch off soon after Boughton Lees and continue on Section 12 (page 150) to Chilham. The distance from Lenham to Chilham is 14.8 miles (23.8 km).

For a change, a section with comparatively little climbing! The North Downs Way stays with or near the Pilgrims Way all the way to Boughton Lees. You might wish to make a couple of short diversions: into the charming village of Charing, which has many historic buildings, and to inspect the romantic (and supposedly haunted) ruins of St Mary's Church at Eastwell.

It seems that pilgrims arriving at Boughton Lees had the choice of taking alternative routes that went either left or right of the River Great Stour. The Canterbury Loop of the North Downs Way favours the left side, while the Main Line now parts company with the Pilgrims Way altogether and makes a beeline for Dover. It takes a cross-field route past Perry Court Farm, where cream teas, home-made cakes and other temptations are on sale.

Things to look out for

1 Lenham Memorial Cross was constructed in 1922 and paid for by villagers in memory of 42 local people killed during the First World War, whose names were inscribed on a war memorial here. During the Second World War, the 200-feet-(61-metre)-tall cross had to be grassed over to avoid providing a navigational aid for enemy aircraft – and afterwards another 14 names had to be added. An annual memorial service used to be held here, but the long climb proved too much, so it now takes place at St Mary's Church and the war memorial has been moved to the village.

2 Lenham Chalk Cliffs have been designated as a Site of Special Scientific Interest due to the geological structures that were uncovered during its time as a chalk mine, which closed in the early 20th century. If you wish, you can make a short diversion beside the cliffs, following a path that brings you to point **B** a little further along the North Downs Way.

3 The village of **Charing** is a delight, and well worth the short diversion for the wealth and variety of its historic buildings, many of which bear individually designed plaques. They include one for the Venture Works, where the Venture and Invicta

Pilgrims may have stopped at Boughton Aluph's All Saints Church, with a fireplace in the porch, before venturing on their journey through robber-ridden King's Wood

motorcycles were built during the early 20th century, and another for the Cyclists' Touring Club – not actually their headquarters as the plaque misleadingly implies; this only indicated that the establishment was approved by them. Near the 13th-century church of St Peter and St Paul is the crumbling Archbishop's Palace, which in 2004 competed unsuccessfully for funds in the BBC's *Restoration* programme. Dating from the 14th century, it now languishes as part of a farmyard, awaiting a benefactor, while the old hall serves as a barn.

4 'On **Westwell Downs**' is the title of a poem by William Strode (1600–43), a Devonian who married the daughter of the Prebendary of Canterbury and thus became familiar with these parts. In the poem, he extols the peace and beauty of the hilly crests in days when they were speckled with sheep and bushes, and the most intrusive sound was that of a sheep bell, rather than the hum of the M20.

5 **Eastwell Park** consists of a grand mansion and its surrounding land, which today includes a farm, a hotel and the modern mansion that you see when entering the park. The original house (out of

sight behind the hotel) was built in the mid-16th century by Richard de Eastwell, who is believed to have been a son of King Richard III (see St Mary's Church below). This was replaced by a larger house built in 1799 for the Earl of Winchilsea. One of his successors got into financial difficulties, and from 1874 to 1893 the house was rented by the then Duke of Edinburgh, second son of Queen Victoria, and his wife, who had been a Grand Duchess of Russia. Their daughter, Princess Marie, was born here in 1875 and became Queen of Romania by marriage. By all accounts, she seems to have led a colourful life, which involved several extra-marital affairs and pregnancies, and serving as a Red Cross nurse during the First World War. She died in 1938.

6 **St Mary's Church** at Eastwell has lain derelict for six decades. The nearby lake was constructed in the 1840s, and it is thought that the chalk blocks used for building the church were adversely affected by seepage from the lake. During the Second World War, the Eastwell estate was used for tank manœuvres and it seems likely that these weakened the structure still further, to the point where the roof collapsed in 1951 and most of the rest was demolished in 1956. A tomb in the churchyard is thought to be that of Richard, 'last of the Plantagenets', who died in 1550. He was a bastard son of King Richard III and worked as a craftsman in the neighbourhood after the royal lineage of that name was wiped out by the king's death at the Battle of Bosworth Field in 1485. The church is still consecrated, and has been designated a Grade II listed building under the care of the charity **Friends of Friendless Churches**. If you think the church is spooky, be aware that it is said by some to be haunted by the ghost of a monk.

7 The *Grande Randonnée* waymark that appears on a North Downs Way signpost in Eastwell Park is an oddity, as it appears on no other signs along the route; indeed, it may be the only such waymark in Britain. *Grande Randonnée* (generally abbreviated to GR) is the French term for a long-distance walking route, and a formidable network of them extends throughout France. Although the North Downs Way is part of Euroroute E2 at this point, it is not part of a GR.

8 **Boughton Lees** is the public face of the parish of Boughton Aluph (pronounced 'Borton Alluf'), as it jauntily straddles the A251 Ashford–Faversham road around a large village green, where cricket is played in summer, watched by patrons of the Flying Horse pub. Although Boughton Lees has a chapel, the parish church is at Boughton Aluph, a mile or so to the north-east, which you will pass if you have decided to follow the Canterbury Loop of the North Downs Way. Soon after leaving Boughton Lees you pass the point where the branches diverge.

9 The large village of **Wye** (population about 2,500) was once an important market town, occupying a strategic position where a branch of the Pilgrims Way forded the River Great Stour. Then the construction of a turnpike road on the far side of the river during the 18th century resulted in traffic bypassing Wye and the old market fizzled out. However, a farmers' market now takes place every first and third Saturday morning around the green. The arrival of the South Eastern Railway line from Tonbridge to Canterbury and Margate in 1846, and the more recent growth of Ashford as a trading centre, have resulted in Wye becoming a commuter settlement. For over 125 years, from 1849 to 1974, Wye was famous for its racecourse, located a little to the south-west, but it was only a mile in circuit and never achieved much success.

The Archbishop's Palace at Charing is one of three along the North Downs Way. They provided overnight resting places for archbishops and their emissaries travelling between Canterbury and London.

Route description

From where the Pilgrims Way joins Faversham Road 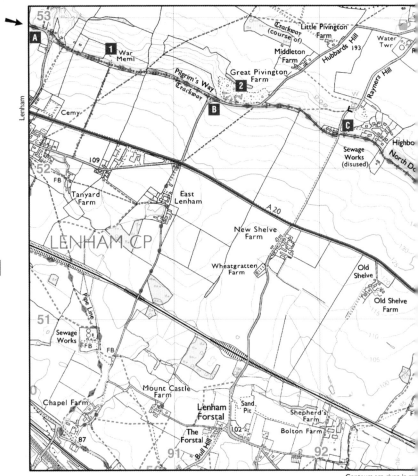, keep ahead along the left-hand side of the road ☀ for 150 yards (140 metres), passing a row of cottages, then bear left up a byway, passing White Lodge. At 'House by the Cross', step over a traffic restriction barrier, which shows that you are about to follow a restricted byway for the next 0.6 mile (1 km). The surface has been levelled and gritted to provide an 'easy-access trail'.

Extensive warehousing appears beside the A20 down to your right, then a fenced seat on your left guards **Lenham Memorial Cross 1**. Another North Downs Way milestone appears shortly: 33 miles (53 km) to Dover, 21 miles (33 km) to Canterbury. The easy-access trail ends and you cross another traffic restrictor to pass an information panel for **Lenham Chalk Cliffs 2**. The Pilgrims Way merges with another road **B** (Hubbards Hill) ☀ for 375 yards (345 metres), where you should keep right as the road ascends. As it swings left, keep ahead (byway again) to reach a metalled

Contours are given in m
The vertical interval is

lane, which passes some cottages in the hamlet of Highbourne. Cross a road **C** (Rayners Hill) and turn left then immediately right, beside the drive of Highbourne Park, a private residential estate that has been developed in the grounds of the former Lenham Hospital.

If you wish to visit the Harrow Inn at Warren Street, turn left up Rayners Hill ✸ for 0.6 miles (1 km).

Soon Cobham Farm comes into view ahead, and you pass the farm to walk along its drive for 100 yards (90 metres) among fields. As the drive swings right, keep ahead on a grassy track, back into trees. At a road (Hart Hill), cross and turn right down the left-hand side, then in 60 yards (55 metres) turn left to regain the byway, with the rambling buildings of Hart Hill Farm on your left. The compact

One of the floral delights of the North Downs Way is viper's-bugloss with its blue, funnel-shaped flowers that appear in June and July.

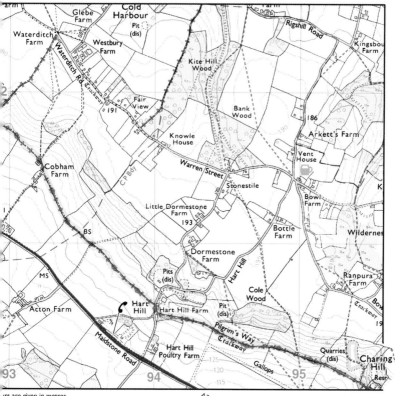

urs are given in metres
ertical interval is 5m

village of **Charing** 3 comes into view ahead, with the tower of St Peter and St Paul Church, while the large building beside the A20 was a hotel (closed at the time of writing). After passing a reservoir on your left, wooden fences lead you to a T-junction D below a large house with a white-painted verandah.

≈ 🚍 🅿️ 🍽️ *The western link with* **Charing Station** *starts by turning right down an unmade road here (see page 183) – this is the shortest route, which takes you through the village. Returning from the station, you may prefer to use the eastern link, which avoids both the village and a double crossing of the busy A252 road.*

Keep ahead on the rough track, passing the charming little Reeves Cottage, to cross (or re-cross) the A252 Charing Hill. ⚠️ Take great care as traffic is coming fast and blind from both directions. Turn left for 44 yards (40 metres), then turn right down Pilgrims Way, which is a tarmac lane here, used by quarry lorries ✱. Looking right, you can see the tower of Charing church poking up among trees. Plod on, passing triangular junctions with Toll Lane E and Wicken Lane F, a hedge-lined bridleway. Soon after white-painted Burnt House Farm, swing left with the lane, now a concrete byway, to pass a wooden bungalow and the entrance to Charing Quarry. The byway continues as a

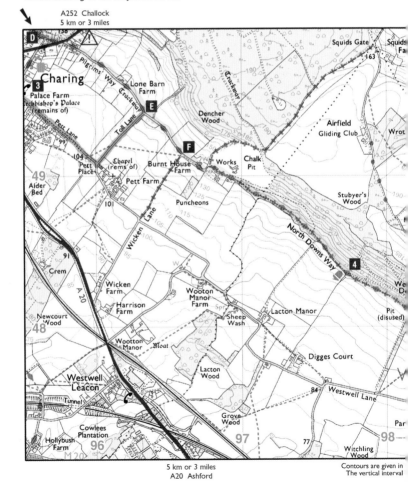

A252 Challock
5 km or 3 miles

5 km or 3 miles
A20 Ashford

Contours are given in
The vertical interval

rough earth track, lined by sycamore and beech trees. The Pilgrims Way is at a comparatively high level here, so you get a view of the 'Garden of England' through the trees. The M2 is there somewhere, but mostly well hidden in cuttings.

After about 0.7 mile (1.1 km), soon after a seat and a little way behind some concrete cylinders, is an information panel for **Westwell Downs** . At a house called Wychling Over, keep ahead, ignoring a lane down to your right. You soon join a road coming in from the right (Pilgrims Way) – note the plaque informing you that this is a roadside nature reserve. Pass a triangular junction with a lane leading left to Blackberry Mead Farm, then in 230 yards (210 metres) a footpath junction .

🥾🍽️🚌 *If you wish to visit Westwell, 630 yards (580 metres) off route, turn right to follow this footpath, which kinks left then right down a field to join a road in Westwell, where you keep ahead to the Wheel Inn and bus stops.*

Keep ahead past Dunn Street Farm, which has a campsite, then at a T-junction the North Downs Way diverges from the line of the Pilgrims Way, whose route is inaccessible for several miles beyond this point. After crossing a stile ahead, the route goes left then shortly right to join a track, at first between fields, then with Skeats Wood on your right. Ignore a gap on your right, then in 275 yards (250 metres), as the track veers left, turn right on a track between trees where you cross the Pilgrims Way.

Shortly turn left to resume the same direction, now with the wood on your left and a field on your right, then as the wood ends continue in the same direction across the field. You are now in **Eastwell Park** . A modern, walled mansion dominates the view, and soon Home Farm appears more coyly on your left. On reaching a private drive , the North Downs Way continues ahead, but take a moment to visit ruined **St Mary's Church** , just 80 yards (73 metres) along the lane to your right.

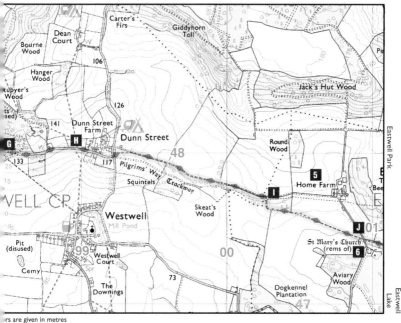

rs are given in metres
ertical interval is 5m

Follow the ascending tarmac avenue ahead, soon with the artificial Eastwell Lake appearing on your right – it was constructed in the 1840s by damming a tributary stream of the River Great Stour. At a T-junction **K** keep ahead through a gate and follow the right-hand side of a field, with the Eastwell Manor Hotel ⛨ over to your left. Note the **_Grande Randonnée_ 7** logo on the North Downs Way fingerpost. In 425 yards (390 metres), follow the waymark arrow pointing half left across the field, to reach the hotel drive a little to the left of a white signboard. Cross the drive diagonally right, then follow a low fence through a gate, with a golf course on your left. Maintain the same direction along a grassy footpath diagonally across a meadow to reach the A251 Faversham Road at **Boughton Lees 8**. Turn left to St Christopher's Church **L** then ⚠ cross the road with great care.

🚌 *Buses between Ashford and Faversham stop on the A251 at the far end of the village green – left-hand side for Faversham, right-hand side for Ashford.*

Turn left along a pavement, following a road along the right side of the village green, with the Flying Horse pub 🍺 off to your left at its far end. At the junction with Wye Road **M**, cross with great care ⚠ by the Give Way sign as traffic comes blind from the right. Turn right then immediately left, rejoining Pilgrims Way ✶ – there is a bit of a verge on the left-hand side. You are now on the pilgrim route that followed the left side of the Stour; the other branch went along Wye Road.

At Malthouse Farm pass a byway on your left, then in 90 yards (80 metres) you reach an insignificant-looking junction **N** with a footpath, but it has great significance for North Downs Wayfarers as this is the point where the Canterbury Loop branches off to the left. One feels that there should be a checkpoint here with marshals pointing you in your chosen direction, but there is just a fingerpost and a rusty old barrier. If you wish to go via Canterbury, turn to page 150.

A251 Challock
3 km or 2 miles

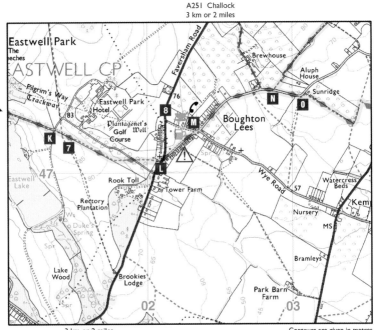

3 km or 2 miles
A251 Ashford

Contours are given in metres
The vertical interval is 5m

Those sticking to the Main Line should continue along the lane. As it starts to swing left, turn right through a gate 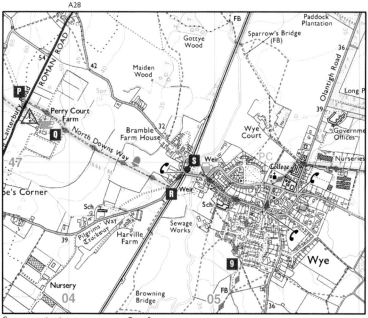, then turn left and soon turn right to follow a narrow field-edge footpath past a shed and beside a hedge. At a corner in the hedge, turn left, still in the same field, then at the next corner turn right at 90 degrees to cross the field. On the far side, turn left beside a hedge to a fingerpost **P** on the A28 Canterbury Road, which follows the line of a Roman road from Canterbury to a settlement that existed near Ashford. ⚠ Cross over with care. On your right now is ☕ Perry Court Farm, which has a tea room and a farm shop where you can buy apple crisps.

Cross a stile and keep ahead along a footpath beside an orchard and past polytunnels – no scrumping! Cross a farm track and keep ahead on a gravel track. As it swings right, keep ahead again, now on grass beside a fence. At a fence corner **Q**,

turn right, so that a line of pine trees is on your right, then shortly turn left on a grassy track between a fence and trees. Away to your left now, on the hillside, is Wye Crown, which you will pass on Section 10. When the fence ends, pass a barrier and disused stile and keep ahead on a worn path across a field. Cross a stile and continue in the same direction to Harville Road **R** at **Wye** **9**. Turn left for 140 yards (130 metres), passing a stop for buses 🚌 to Canterbury (buses to Ashford stop on the other side of the road past the junction ahead). Turn right at the junction (Bridge Street), over the level crossing to **Wye Station** **S** ⇌, where Section 9 of the North Downs Way ends.

If you are continuing on to Section 10, keep ahead along Bridge Street. *If you wish to walk 5 miles (8 km) into Ashford, you can follow the Stour Valley Walk, which starts a little way into Section 10.*

Contours are given in metres
The vertical interval is 5m

Public transport

Lenham (1.1 miles / 1.8 km) 🚆🚌
Charing (0.6 mile / 1 km) 🚆🚌
Westwell (0.4 mile / 0.6 km) 🚌 Not
Sundays
Boughton Lees (on route) 🚌 Not Sundays
Wye (on route) 🚆🚌
Taxis/minicabs: Lenham, Hothfield,
Kennington, Ashford

Refreshments and toilets

Warren Street (0.6 mile / 1 km) 🚽
Harrow Inn
Charing (0.4 mile / 0.6 km) 🚽 Queens
Head, Royal Oak
Westwell (0.4 mile / 0.6 km) 🚽 Wheel
Inn
Boughton Lees (on route) 🚽 Flying
Horse
Perry Court Farm (on route) ☕
Wye (on route) 🚽 King's Head, New

Flying Horse, Tickled Trout, ☕ Latte
& Miele, Wife of Bath
Food shops: Lenham, Charing, Wye
Public toilets: Lenham, Wye

Accommodation

Warren Street (0.6 mile / 1 km) Harrow
Inn
Charing (0.4 mile / 0.6 km) Royal Oak
Inn ('The Oak')
Tutt Hill (1.6 miles / 2.6 km) Holiday Inn
Ashford North
Dunn Street (on route) Dunn Street Farm
Camp Site
Westwell (0.4 mile / 0.6 km) Dean Court
Farm, Tylers, Wheel Inn
Eastwell (on route) Eastwell Manor Hotel
Wye (on route) King's Head, Mistral, New
Flying Horse, Wife of Bath
Ashford (3 miles / 5 km by train or bus
from Wye) Wide selection – contact
Ashford Tourist Information Centre

The Wye Crown – a chalk carving celebrating the coronation of
Edward VII – situated just south of the village of Wye on one of
the most striking sections of the whole North Downs Way.

10 Wye to Etchinghill

past Wye Crown and through Stowting
11.2 miles (18.1 km)

Ascent 1,296 feet (396 metres)

Descent 991 feet (303 metres)

Lowest point 102 feet (31 metres)

Highest point Farthing Common: 600 feet (183 metres)

North Downs Wayfarers had it easy on the last section, but that is about to change! Some of the most outstanding views of the North Downs Way fall in this section, but you will have to work hard to reach them. A long, steep ascent takes you to Wye Crown, where the route was formally launched in 1978. The walking is then fairly level, taking you past the dramatic cleft known as the Devil's Kneading Trough, but there are a couple of dips down to Stowting and Staple Farm. Another long hill leads up to Farthing Common and the combe near Postling, which should be one of the prettiest parts of the route – what a shame that a power line and pylons have been thrust across it! But a stiff climb out is rewarded with a bird's-eye view of the picture-postcard village of Postling.

Things to look out for

1 The **Stour Valley Walk** briefly shares part of its route with the North Downs Way. It follows the River Great Stour (pronounced like 'hour') for 58 miles (93 km) from one of its sources at Lenham through Wye and Canterbury and on to the North Sea at Pegwell Bay, near Ramsgate. Further details about the route can be obtained from **Kent County Council**. (This route should not be confused with the Stour Valley Way in Dorset.)

2 **Wye College** was founded in 1447 by John Kempe (see below) as a training centre for the priesthood. In 1894 it became an agricultural college and four years later was absorbed into the University of London (as an adjunct of Imperial College). Wye College was closed in 2009, and at the time of writing some of its buildings are fenced off, but there is an initiative to re-open it as PhoenixWyeCollege (lack of spacing intentional).

3 The **Kempe Centre** opened in 1996 to serve mainly as the library of Wye College, but at the time of writing, like the college, it lies unused and forlorn with an uncertain future. It is named after John Kempe (or Kemp, 1380–1454), who was born at nearby Olantigh, became Archbishop of York in 1426, a cardinal in 1439, and finally Archbishop of Canterbury in 1452.

4 **Wye Crown** is a special place for the North Downs Way, as this is where the route was officially opened on 30 September 1978 by the then Archbishop of Canterbury, Donald Coggan. And what a spot! There have been grand views aplenty along the route so far, but this one takes some beating, extending on a clear day far across the Weald of Kent and out to sea, with Dungeness Power Station visible at the tip of Romney Marsh, some 20 miles (32 km) away. This is clearly *the* place to install commemorative structures, as there are no fewer than six. In ascending order, they are: Wye Crown itself, cut into the chalk by students of Wye College in 1902 to mark the coronation of Edward VII; Wye Crown Millennium Stone; Floreat Wye ('Let Wye flourish'), a long-distance topograph; a compass rose; a wall commemorating the centenary of Wye Crown and the Golden Jubilee of Elizabeth II; and to top them all, a North Downs Way milestone, which also serves to commemorate Warrick Rance, a local man who loved walking in this area and died in 2000 at the tragically early age of 34.

5 The **Devil's Kneading Trough** is the deepest and most spectacular of the many dry combes in this area (see page 18). The sides are so steep that you can imagine a giant ship coming in to dry-dock.

6 **Postling** (pronounced like 'jostling') is a charming little village of timber-framed houses, with a population of just under 200. The unusually dedicated Church of St Mary and St Radigund dates from Saxon times and has wall paintings thought to date from the 12th century. Pent Farm, on the west side of the village, was the home in turn of the poet Christina Rossetti, the artist Walter Crane and the writer Joseph Conrad.

7 **Tolsford Hill Radio Station** was opened in 1957, originally as the British terminal for Eurovision and to handle telephone calls between Britain and France. It now handles mobile-phone traffic.

8 The **Elham Valley Way** briefly shares its route with the North Downs Way. It leads for 22.5 miles (36.2 km) from Hythe to Canterbury. Elham is actually a village in the valley of the River Nailbourne, known as the Little Stour in its lower reaches. Further details can be obtained from **Kent County Council**.

9 The **Saxon Shore Way** and the North Downs Way share the same route for 13 miles (21 km) from Tolsford Hill all the way to Dover. The Saxon Shore Way is one of the longest recreational walking routes in Britain, extending for 163 miles (262 km) from Gravesend, beside the River Thames in Kent, to Hastings, beside the English Channel in East Sussex. As closely as possible, the route follows the shore as it existed in Roman times, and the name is a reference to the string of forts that were erected along the coast by the Romans to protect Britain from Saxon incursions. Taking something of a liberty, the route's logo is a stylised horned helmet of the type that was supposed to be worn by Vikings. Further details can be obtained from **Kent County Council**.

10 **Etchinghill** is a small village with a population of about 750. A farmers' and craft market takes place in the village hall on the first Saturday in each month.

Route description

After the level crossing at **Wye Station A**, keep ahead along Bridge Street, over the River Great Ouse and, if you can resist its inviting riverside garden, past the 🍺 Tickled Trout pub. At a junction, keep ahead (towards 'Wye Beauty', still Bridge Street), using the left-hand pavement.

At the Co-op pharmacy, the **Stour Valley Walk 1** comes in from the right along

Little Chequers, and the two trails share the same route for the next 0.8 mile (1.3 km). Turn left along Church Street by the Latte & Miele bistro B 🥂, while the Wife of Bath 🍴 ahead advertises itself as a 'restaurant with rooms'. Still keeping to the left-hand pavement, pass the King's Head pub 🍺🍴 to reach Churchfield Way, with the church opposite and a Co-op food shop on your left.

Cross over with care and enter the churchyard, taking the path going half right, so that the church is on your left. The red-brick building on your right is **Wye College** 2. On leaving the churchyard, turn left along a gravel footpath, beside a hedge and past allotments. Turn right at a gate to reach Olantigh Road, cross over with care and keep ahead along Occupation Road, passing the **Kempe Centre** 3. The road then passes several commercial properties, one of which (Furniture Art Co.) has a North Downs Way information panel on its wall.

When the road ends, keep ahead along a stony track, ignoring a sign for the Wibberley Way, which implies that this is a permissive path – it is in fact a public bridleway. Just over halfway along, the Stour Valley Way goes off to the left, and the North Downs Way continues ahead to cross a lane C. Climb the bridleway ahead to regain the ridge.

The gradient is gentle at first, beside a hedge, then you go through a gate beside a rustic bench into a wood (The Junipers) and start to climb in earnest. On either side is Forestry Commission access land (the signs say Forestry Authority, a name no longer in use, whose Wibberley Way signs appear again). At the top D, turn right up a narrow lane for 265 yards (240 metres). As the lane veers left, out of the trees, turn right on a footpath, up steps and through two squeeze-stiles to reach the top of the scarp at Wye Downs. A quite amazing view greets you, extending across the 'Garden of England' to the English Channel and Dungeness Nuclear Power Station.

Turn left along the top of the scarp slope to reach **Wye Crown** 4 – a superb spot for a picnic – where you pass another North Downs Way milestone (Dover 21 miles / 34 km). Keep to the grassy path among old

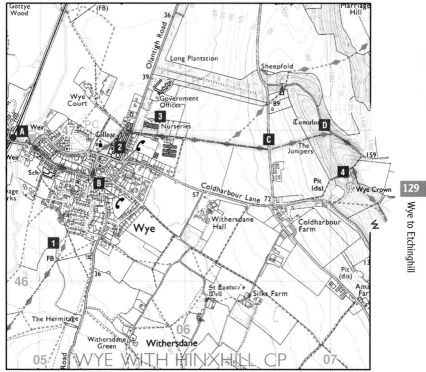

Contours are given in metres
The vertical interval is 5m

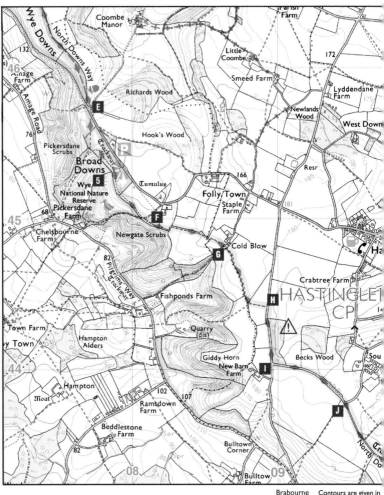

Brabourne   Contours are given in
The vertical interval

chalk pits. At a gate, join a narrow, earth bridleway coming in from your left, which eventually leads to a lane **E**. Turn right to cross Coldharbour Road (beware traffic coming blind from your left), going half left through a gate by an information panel into Wye National Nature Reserve, which harbours an astonishing variety of species, including 2,000 insects, 400 plants (of which 19 are orchids), 90 birds and 28 butterflies.

Turn left across two shallow gullies and keep ahead, following signs to Millstone

Viewpoint on Broad Downs. At the second gate (do not go through it) the route dips a little to go round the head of the **Devil's Kneading Trough 5**. At the bottom of the dip, take the middle of three paths, so that you are ascending slightly with a fence to your right and a seat on the path below. Pass a water tank and keep ahead to a gate **F**.

☕ *If you wish to visit the Devil's Kneading Trough restaurant and tea room, follow the footpath to your left.*

Keep ahead to go through a second gate and continue ahead on an enclosed footpath, with woodland (Newgate Scrubs) on your right and dog kennels on your left. Go through a gate and keep ahead along the left-hand side of a field, then through another gate, now with Cold Blow Farm over to your left. Cross a farm track **G**.

📖 *For the Bowl Inn* ✶ *at Hastingleigh, turn left along the track then right along the road.*

Keep ahead through a meadow and on to follow the right-hand side of a large field. After the next gate, go half left across a field to a road **H**. Turn right ✶ for nearly 425 yards (390 metres) to a junction. Turn left along Tamley Lane **I** (signed for South Hill Farm). In another 635 yards (580 metres), where the lane swings sharp left **J**, keep ahead on an unclassified gravel track and follow this for 0.7 mile (1.1 km) to a lane **K**. Turn right for 450 yards (410 metres) ✶ to the top of the scarp, where non-local motorists screech to a halt and

pull over to admire the view. Follow the lane down the hill, to the point where it swings right **L**.

Turn sharp left through a field gate to follow a gravel byway, gently ascending at first, then contouring around a combe containing Brabourne Chalk Pit and through Long Wood. Emerging from the wood, you reach a junction with a footpath **M**.

📖 *For the Five Bells pub in Brabourne, turn right down the steep field path here.*

The spire of Stowting church appears ahead. The sea is very evident now, and vessels using Folkestone or Dover harbours can be clearly discerned, but Dover is still 18 miles (29 km) away. At Brabourne Lane **N** keep ahead along a stony byway, which descends steadily to another road – Pilgrims Way again – beneath crackling power lines. Turn left past Highfield Farm and Bankside Stables to reach a triangular junction **O**, where you keep ahead.

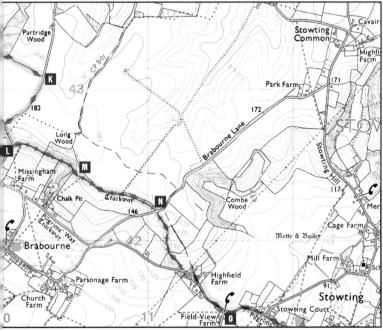

Brabourne   Contours are given in metres
The vertical interval is 5m

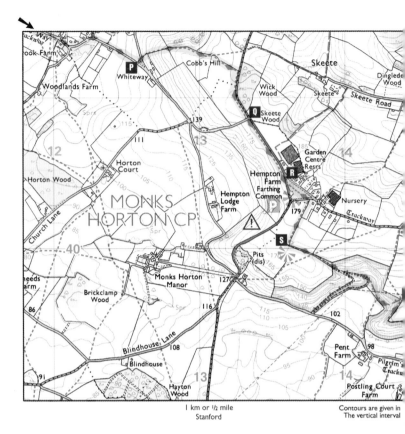

1 km or ½ mile
Stanford

Contours are given in
The vertical interval

The road swings left then right. At this point, North Downs Wayfarers are supposed to cross an overgrown stile on the right and follow a field-edge footpath running parallel with the road and crossing six more rather ancient and awkward stiles, at one point having to leave the field and use the road for a short distance. Or you can continue (at your own risk) for another 460 yards (420 metres) along the normally quiet lane ✳ to reach the 🅿 Tiger Inn at Stowting – note how it proudly proclaims a former association with the now defunct Mackesons Hythe Ales.

Keep ahead on the lane and bear left at a junction, with a stream tinkling among trees on your right. Go past Water Farm and a black gate, then in 275 yards (250 metres) turn left up a steep and narrow footpath ▣. At the top, cross Curteis Lane with care, turn

left then immediately right, up steps to a stile. You now face a very steep climb up Cobbs Hill, following a fence on your right. At the top, cross two stiles – one to the right and one to the left – to resume the same direction, now along the left-hand side of a field. At its end, ignore a yellow arrow on your left and keep ahead across a stile, slightly obscured among trees. On reaching the B2068 Stone Street (which follows the line of the Roman road from Canterbury to Lympne), follow the field-edge path around to the right, so that you are walking inside the field and parallel to the road.

At a side road ▣, keep ahead through a gate to continue through the next field, still parallel to the main road. Note the sign: 'Caution: lawfully permitted bulls may be kept in this field' (see page 34). The view to your right includes Hampton Lodge Farm and Monks Horton Manor. At the next gate , cross Stone Street ⚠ with great care, as traffic approaches blind from both directions.

Enter a small car park at Farthing Common, which is a popular and shady viewpoint with an information panel. Here you encounter the waymarks and dainty information panels of the Discover Postling Downs Circular Walk, with its stylised bird's-foot trefoil logo. Go half right to step over a low fence to a waymark post, then keep ahead along a mown grass footpath into trees. At a fork, go sharp right to a road, then turn left along the grass verge to a fingerpost. Turn right to cross the road with care, then keep ahead on a footpath along the left-hand side of a field. At a field corner 🅂 turn left, still in the same field.

Dominating the view ahead now, and for the next 2 miles (3.2 km), is Tolsford Hill Radio Station, which you will pass later. Go through two gates as you descend into a large, deep and contorted combe in Postling Downs – what should be one of the prettiest locations along the whole North Downs Way, had it not been spoiled by power lines. Follow a slightly sunken, grassy track to the bottom, ignoring another one that veers up to your right. Bear right on a worn footpath to a waymark post, then keep ahead on grass beside a fence. Climb again to pass a gate and turn left up a gully. At the top 🆃, turn sharp right beside a fence, then at a corner turn left, now on a bridleway. You may wish to go ahead a little to a promontory that provides an excellent all-round viewpoint.

The picture-postcard village of Postling, and its church dedicated to St Mary and St Radigund, nestle at the foot of a pretty combe.

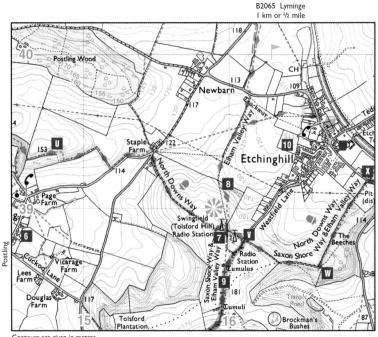

Contours are given in metres
The vertical interval is 5m

Follow the fence, with a grass airstrip down to your right, around the head of the smaller combe and with the little village of **Postling** below, snuggling into the foot of the combe. The hillside ahead contains strip lynchets – evidence of ancient farming. Keep to the higher path, then, soon after veering right, fork left uphill, using rough-hewn steps. *The circular walk continues downhill here into Postling, which is close at hand now.*

Go through a gate and along the right-hand side of a field. After the next gate **U**, the right of way drops down to the right to follow the field edge, but this makes for very uncomfortable walking and clearly people use a worn path down the field ahead. Turn right, across a stile, to follow a field-edge path. At the corner, turn left, still in the same field, now parallel with a lane down to your right. Veer to the right to pass a gate and continue to a lane at Staple Farm. Cross the lane with care, as traffic approaches from the right around a blind

bend. Turn right for 20 yards (18 metres), then bear left through a gate to follow a footpath up the right-hand side of a field. As you ascend, the top of a radio mast pops up ahead and seems to grow ever taller, until its full height is in view, looking like a rocket-launching site: this is **Tolsford Hill Radio Station** **7**.

Do not cross a stile at the field corner, but follow a fence half left, passing two smaller masts, then turn sharp right through a gate, joining the **Elham Valley Way** **8** to swing left past a stile. Go through a gate and keep ahead, past the radio station gates **V**. *If you need to reach Etchinghill quickly, Westfield Lane on your left goes directly there.* Cross a stile, where the **Saxon Shore Way** **9** comes in from a byway ahead and joins the North Downs Way all the way to Dover.

⇒ *The link with **Sandling Station** starts here by going ahead along the byway and following the Saxon Shore Way (see page 184).*

Note the sign warning that you are now in army training land and must keep strictly to the footpath. Go half left to follow a faint footpath, through a long grove of hawthorn trees. As they come to an end, bear left down to a stile and gate **W** and follow a track down through a tunnel of bushes. The deep cleft of Beachborough Combe appears on your right, with the distinctive clump of trees that is Brockman's Bushes, and the conical Summerhouse Hill, on its far side. They will be visible for some time, looking back, as you continue eastwards. Further away to your right are some of the vast marshalling yards of the Channel Tunnel Terminal, but you will get a close-up of these on Section 11.

Turn left through a gate to descend a footpath along the edge of a wood (The Beeches), taking care as there are many exposed roots. Continue through a gate and along the left-hand side of a field, passing under power lines. Go through another gate to follow an enclosed footpath to Canterbury Road **X** on the edge of **Etchinghill 10**, where this section of the North Downs Way ends.

To continue on to Section 11, ⚠ cross the road with great care, as traffic approaches blind from the right, and turn right on the far side.

🚌 *If you wish to finish at or visit Etchinghill, turn left along the road🏃, keeping left as there is a right-hand bend, until you reach a pavement at St Mary's Close, where there are bus stops (left-hand side for Canterbury, right-hand side for Folkestone).*

🍺 *The New Inn is 240 yards (220 metres) further along the main road.*

Public transport

Wye (on route) 🚆 🚌
Brabourne Lees (2.5 miles / 4.0 km) 🚌
Etchinghill (on route) 🚌
Brook, Hastingleigh, Farthing Common and **Postling** are served by a Monday–Friday school bus service; if you think this may be of use, contact Traveline for details.
Taxis/minicabs: Ashford, Kennington, Hythe, Folkestone

Refreshment and toilets

Newgate Scrubs (0.1 mile / 0.2 km) 🍺 Devil's Kneading Trough Restaurant and Tea-room
Hastingleigh (0.8 mile / 1.3 km) 🍺 Bowl Inn
Brabourne (0.4 mile / 0.6 km) 🍺 Five Bells

Stowting (on route) 🍺 Tiger Inn
Etchinghill (0.3 mile / 0.5 km) 🍺 New Inn
Food shops: Wye, Etchinghill
Public toilets: Wye

Accommodation

Hastingleigh (0.8 mile / 1.3 km) Crabtree Farm
Bulltown (0.6 mile / 1 km) Bulltown Farmhouse
Elmsted (1.5 miles / 2.4 km) Elmsted Court Farmhouse, Oak Cottage,
Stowting Hill (0.6 mile / 1 km) Stowting Hill House
Hemsted (0.4 mile / 0.6 km) Roundwood Hall
Saltwood (2.2 miles / 3.5 km) Castle Hotel
Hythe (2.8 miles / 4.5 km) Maccasil Guest House, Malt Guest House, Mercure Hythe Imperial Hotel, Moyle Cottage, Stade Court Hotel

11 Etchinghill to Dover

past Folkestone and over Shakespeare Cliff
12 miles (19.3 km)

Ascent 1,329 feet (406 metres)

Descent 1,657 feet (506 metres)

Lowest point Dover Esplanade: 17 feet (5 metres)

Highest point Shearins Bungalow: 574 feet (175 metres)

This section of the North Downs Way is so utterly spectacular and full of interest that, even if you have chosen to go via Canterbury, you should try to find time to walk at least this part of the southern route.

You start almost immediately with a long, steep climb, but the going is then fairly level for most of the way to Dover – though with a sting or two in the tail. The first half follows the top of the escarpment, with a bird's-eye view over the Channel Tunnel Terminal towards Folkestone and the English Channel, which you reach beside the inspirational and thought-provoking Battle of Britain Memorial. A cliff path takes you to the outskirts of Dover and over the narrow ridge of Shakespeare Cliff, but a final diversion from the coast takes you over the Western Heights for a last grandstand view encompassing the bustling harbour, the mighty castle and the brooding redoubt.

On this section, you will be walking through the territory of the White Cliffs Countryside Partnership, consisting of 14 organisations including Dover and Shepway District Councils and Kent County Council, which was set up in 1989 to conserve and enhance the coastline between Dungeness and Sandwich and the countryside behind it. Much of the work has been supported and financed by Eurotunnel, the company that operates the Channel Tunnel. The North Downs Way runs side by side with the Saxon Shore Way for the whole of this section, and shares its route with the Elham Valley Walk for the first 550 yards (500 metres).

Despite seeming just a stone's throw away, Folkestone is not that easy to reach, due to the sheer drop and the presence of roads and industry that lie in between. Folkestone's West Station is closer than Central, and this section includes a link to it, though it is mostly beside busy roads. If you prefer to go to Central, you can continue on from West, following signs, or you can use our link to Wood Avenue, from where frequent buses go to Central. A more convenient alternative may be to take a bus from any of three points on the town's outskirts: Newington, Canterbury Road or the Valiant Sailor, as indicated in the route description.

⚠ A word of warning: much of this section goes close to the edge of cliffs that are slowly crumbling away. Always keep a safe distance from the cliff edge.

Things to look out for

1 The **Elham Valley Railway**, opened in 1887 for the South Eastern Railway, used to run between Folkestone and Canterbury West. During the Second World War it was closed to passenger traffic and served as a carriageway for an enormous railway-mounted gun, nicknamed 'The Boche Buster'. After the war, traffic declined and the line was closed in 1947. There is a museum of relics from the line at Peene, passed on the link with Newington (see page 184).

2 The vast **Channel Tunnel Terminal** opened for business in 1994, servicing 'Le Shuttle', the Eurotunnel double-deck trains that carry vehicles through the Channel Tunnel. There had been several previous proposals to link England and France beneath the Channel, the first being in 1802, and a start was actually made in 1881 but abandoned the following year. Eurostar trains from London to Paris or Brussels use the tracks along its far side, with the sprawl of Folkestone extending beyond to the English Channel. Note the prominent, white circular structure near the sea – this is one of Folkestone's Martello towers (see below).

3 **Folkestone** started to develop in the 7th century as a fishing village, after a priory and fort had been built on a nearby cliff. It gradually grew into a small port and in 1313 became a corporate (subsidiary) member of the Cinque Ports (see Dover below). For centuries, settlements along the south coast lay open to attacks by the French, and this resulted in the building of fortifications such as the string of 74 'Martello towers' between Folkestone and Seaford during the early 19th century. The port prospered after 1848, when a branch from the South Eastern Railway to the harbour was constructed, and the population rose to its current level of around 54,000. However, the opening of the Channel Tunnel in 1994 has proved a double-edged sword, as the resulting increase in business and employment opportunities has been offset by a wipe-out of ferry services at Folkestone.

4 The top section of the **Folkestone White Horse** is briefly glimpsed as you pass along Cheriton Hill behind the Channel Tunnel Terminal. Despite opposition from environmental organisations, construction

Walking above the Channel Tunnel Terminal you should get a brief glimpse of the 300-foot (90-metre)-tall Folkestone White Horse, completed in 2003 to provide Kent with an exemplar of its county logo.

The North Downs Way follows the top of Folkestone Warren, the scene of many a past landslip, while the railway line from Folkestone to Dover plunges into a tunnel at its foot.

was completed in 2003, with the help of Gurkhas (Nepali soldiers serving in the British Army) based in Folkestone. It is about 300 feet (93 metres) tall and made of chalk slabs, sunk into the grass. The purpose was partly to celebrate the Millennium and partly to provide Kent with a symbolic chalk white horse – the county's traditional logo – which had not previously existed in the county.

5 Corridors to the Countryside Link Routes have been designed and waymarked by the White Cliffs Countryside Partnership, primarily to enable residents of Folkestone to get out into the surrounding countryside, but they can just as easily be used by North Downs Wayfarers to get into Folkestone if necessary.

6 Castle Hill is the location of a Norman castle that was built to subdue the local Saxon population, probably in the 1140s.

Access was via a causeway on the east side, which you will follow as you leave the castle along the North Downs Way. A lower ditch was built in 1940 to serve as a tank trap during the Second World War. Although the site is shown on maps as 'Caesar's Camp', there was no known occupation by the Romans. From the top, you have a bird's-eye view of trains emerging from and entering the Channel Tunnel: Eurostar on the left, Le Shuttle on the right.

7 Dover Hill's trig point marks the spot height 558 feet (170 metres) above sea level. Folkestone Harbour and its pier are now prominent, down to your right. On a clear day you can see the French coast at Cap Gris Nez, 22 miles (35 km) away; and if you have a chance, try to come here at dusk, when the French coast provides a spectacular display of illuminations.

8 From this point on, the **English Channel** (known to the French as La Manche – 'the sleeve') will be your constant companion – more specifically the Strait of Dover, with the French coast in the distance, and ferries plying between Dover and Calais or Dunkerque. They have to thread their way between ships following the two sea lanes: the one nearest England is for westbound vessels – occasionally, one turns out to be a floating palace of a cruise ship heading for Dover. It is fascinating to think that, in past millennia, Britain was joined to Europe and the Channel did not exist. Then a series of ice ages and a catastrophic flood caused water from both the North Sea and the Atlantic Ocean to punch through the unbroken chalk hills. The resulting cliffs have been steadily worn away by erosion, a process that continues until this day, and in places you can clearly see how far back from the shoreline they have receded.

9 The **Battle of Britain Memorial** commemorates the bravery of nearly 3,000 aircrew of Fighter Command who took part in the Battle of Britain between 10 July and 31 October 1940, stopping Hitler's planned invasion. Over 500 died during or soon after the battle, inspiring Winston Churchill's famous words: 'Never in the field of human conflict was so much owed by so many to so few'. The attractively laid out memorial was opened by Her Majesty Queen Elizabeth the Queen Mother in 1993, and was attended by the man who inspired it, Wing Commander Geoffrey Page. The site has a cafeteria, shop and toilets.

10 **Folkestone Warren** has been the location of many landslips, as can easily be seen from your vantage point on top of the cliff. One such slip occurred here on 19 December 1915, when it carried away the undercliff that supported the railway line; fortunately, a watchman stopped a train shortly before it arrived there. There was a railway station here intermittently, but the last one closed for passenger traffic in 1939. The construction of substantial sea defences should stabilise the land

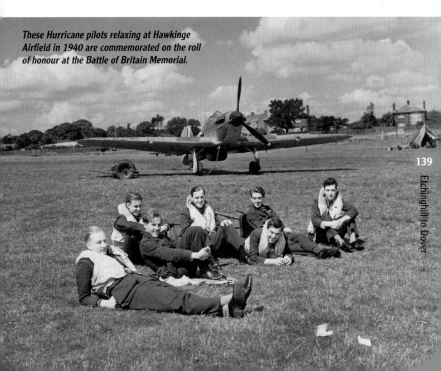

These Hurricane pilots relaxing at Hawkinge Airfield in 1940 are commemorated on the roll of honour at the Battle of Britain Memorial.

supporting the railway for now. Folkestone Warren has been designated a Country Park, a Nature Reserve and a Site of Special Scientific Interest because of its geological interest and the unusual wildlife it supports.

11 Along **Abbot's Cliff** you pass a series of decaying, concrete remnants of the Second World War, especially lookout posts, some of which are set well down the cliff face. One is a 'sound mirror' – a vertical, concrete dish that was designed to listen out for approaching enemy aircraft, though it was soon rendered superfluous by the invention of radar. A tall, grass embankment was there to stop stray bullets from a rifle butts. The circular brick structures are ventilation shafts for the railway tunnel below. Note a large stone in a field on your left marking the boundary of Dover Borough, and look out for some small panels marking the Chalk and Channel Way, a poetic initiative of the **White Cliffs Countryside Project**.

12 As is obvious from its shape, **Samphire Hoe** is an artificial piece of land that was constructed out of spoil from the Channel Tunnel deposited in the sea near Shakespeare Cliff, and has been landscaped to provide a nature reserve, owned by Eurotunnel and managed jointly by them and the **White Cliffs Countryside Project**. The name was chosen in a competition and comes from a reference to samphire (a fleshy edible plant) in the same passage in *King Lear* referred to below. In this instance, a 'hoe' is a piece of land that juts out into the sea. Access is through a 330-yard (300-metre) tunnel.

13 **Shakespeare Cliff** was so named after a passage in Shakespeare's *King Lear*. Some of the action takes place around Dover, which the bard probably visited in 1605 while touring with his company of players. The blinded Earl of Gloucester says to his son, Edgar: 'There is a cliff whose high and bending head looks fearfully in the confined deep' – with the intention of throwing himself off! That cliff has been gradually falling away and is now much narrower than it was in Shakespeare's day.

14 **Western Heights** is the name of both the huge defensive fortifications and the residential district on the west side of Dover. The area has been heavily fortified since Roman times, but the extant structures from Napoleonic days consist mainly of a barracks, known as the Grand Shaft, and two forts – the Drop Redoubt (see below) and the Citadel. Completed in 1815, the Citadel became an institution for young offenders in 1957; it is visible from the North Downs Way but cannot be visited, as it is now the Dover Immigration Removal Centre. The stone foundations that lie beside the route in Citadel Road are thought to be those of a 12th-century church of the Knights Templar, a group of warrior monks who were mandated by the Patriarch of Jerusalem during the 12th century to protect pilgrims to the Holy Land; however, after becoming too rich and powerful for their own good (backed by a widespread belief that they guarded the Holy Grail), the Knights were dissolved by Pope Clement V in 1312.

15 **Dover Priory Station** opened in 1861 and takes its name from the 12th-century priory that stood nearby until it was dissolved by Henry VIII in 1538.

16 The dramatically imposing **Dover Castle** that you see today was started by King Henry II during the 1170s, after his penance for the murder of Archbishop Thomas Becket, and completed in 1185. It replaced an earlier Norman castle, which itself occupied the site of an Iron Age hill fort and a still-standing Roman lighthouse. Since then, the castle has successfully deterred all potential assailants, with two exceptions: in 1216 the forces of King Louis VIII of France only managed to breach its outer walls; and in 1642, during the Civil War, the Parliamentarians took it from the Royalists. During the Second World War the castle served as a command centre for the evacuation from Dunkirk in 1940 and for naval operations in the Dover Strait, and Winston Churchill often based himself here. It is now open to the public and managed by **English Heritage**.

The chalkhill blue butterfly is a regular sight on the downland of the North Downs Way in both Surrey and Kent.

17 The brooding, pentagonal **Drop Redoubt** was completed in 1808. Surrounded by deep, wide ditches, it occupies the sight of another Roman lighthouse. The name comes from a local nickname for the old lighthouse: 'The Devil's Drop of Mortar'. During the Second World War it became a base for commandos, who in the event of invasion would have sabotaged the port. It is in the care of **English Heritage** and open to the public only at certain times.

18 **Dover Harbour** is the busiest ferry port in Europe, and continues to flourish despite the close attentions of the Channel Tunnel. This prime location at the shortest distance across the English Channel has naturally been the place to which people navigated from Europe, and a gap in the cliffs and a wide estuary formed by the River Dour provided the earliest safe landing. Piers and jetties have been constructed since Roman times to create a proper harbour, but silt and shingle combined to make landing difficult, so sometimes Dover became unusable and cross-Channel trade shifted to Sandwich.

The nearest pier that you now see (the Western or Admiralty Pier) was started in 1847. In 1897 work started on the Eastern Pier and the Southern Breakwater (between the two piers), and the Western Pier was extended to create the modern harbour. The Eastern Docks, where roll-on-roll-off car ferries berth, were opened in 1953; until then, vehicles had to be craned on or off at the Western Docks, which are now mainly used by cruise liners.

19 **Dover** owes its existence to the River Dour, which, despite its short length, created a deep valley through the chalk cliffs. Humans are known to have settled here since at least the Bronze Age (3,500 years ago), as a boat from this time has been excavated, but its location must have been a reason for much earlier habitation. The Romans based a fleet here, calling the port Dubris, from the Celtic name Dubra, meaning 'water'. Dover became a major trading centre for the Saxons and, despite its conquest by the Normans in 1066, the port boomed due to the increase in trade between what were now two parts of the Norman kingdom. But in later centuries its highly strategic location also resulted in attacks by the French, the Dutch and, more recently, the Germans. Despite having a greater strategic importance than Folkestone, and being a busier port, Dover is the smaller of the two, with a population of around 33,000. It is also one of the original five **Cinque Ports** (together with Hastings, Romney, Hythe and Sandwich), which date back at least to a royal charter of 1260, set up to maintain and protect English defensive and trading interests in the Channel.

Route description

🚌 *If you are starting from the bus stops at Etchinghill* **A***, walk south-east out of the village centre along the main road (Canterbury Road), using the left-hand pavement. When the pavement runs out at St Mary's Close, keep ahead* ✖ *for 320 yards (295 metres).*

At a 'no through road' sign **1 B**, bear left down a lane. At Coombe Farm, cross a stile on your left and follow a faint grass footpath diagonally down a field. Cross another stile and follow a footpath into a wood. Cross a footbridge over a stream, then shortly turn left over a third stile to a bridge of the former **Elham Valley Railway 1**. The Elham Valley Walk diverges to follow the disused track; the North Downs Way goes under the bridge to ascend a field, keeping right of a pylon. Cross a stile and take the footpath up to your right, passing through a gate.

You now face a long and quite steep ascent up a deep combe. Go all the way up to a waymark post at the top **C**, then turn right to follow a fence. Turn left at a fence corner, cross a stile, then turn left and right, following the field edge. The narrow path continues between a fence and an old chalk pit. Cross a stile and keep ahead in the next, larger field, with Shearins Bungalow to your left. Signs tell you that you are walking through a 'Red Tractor farm' – one that meets high standards of food safety and hygiene, animal welfare and environmental protection. Turn left at a fence corner and go through a kissing-gate to the right of a field gate **D**. Turn right along a bridleway between hedges. Look right for a final view of the distinctive Brockman's Bushes and Summerhouse Hill, passed on Section 10, and on a clear day

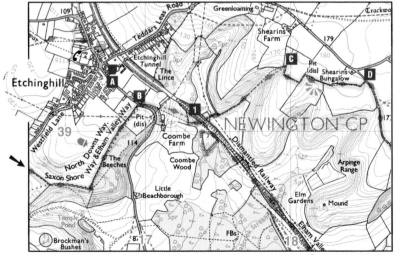

Contours are given in metres
The vertical interval is 5m

you can review the broad sweep of Romney Marsh and Dungeness Power Station.

Continue around the top of another combe to reach a traffic restriction barrier. Cross a lane **E** into a field, then turn right to follow a footpath along the field edge, parallel with the lane. At an embankment, turn right through a gate, then follow the path down to join a track coming in from the right **F**.

🚌 *The link with **Newington**, for buses into Folkestone, starts by turning sharp right here (see page 184).*

A North Downs Way milestone tells you that there are now 9 miles (14.5 km) to Dover, and you may be able to decipher something from a faded information panel for the disused Peene Quarry, which you will shortly pass through, and which has some picnic tables. Pass a gate, bear left through the quarry and climb some steps, preparing to be amazed by the vast **Channel Tunnel Terminal 2**, with **Folkestone 3** stretching beyond to the sea.

You now follow a footpath along the top of the scarp for the next 2.5 miles (4.0 km). The North Downs Way shares this part of its route with walks devised by the **White Cliffs Countryside Partnership**. There are

a few kinks, the first of which goes around the head of a combe, past a concrete pillbox. Soon after this, on Cheriton Hill, you should be able to snatch a brief glimpse of the **Folkestone White Horse 4**, carved on the hillside below. At Danton Lane **G**, turn right then immediately left to regain the scarp-top footpath, which now runs parallel with Crete Road West, passing a small car park. Prominent ahead now is the Arqiva aerial at Creteway Down, with which you will have a close encounter later. You pass through a gate into the Folkestone Downs Nature Reserve beside an information panel. Also here is the first of several circular trig points that you will see along the cliffs.

Pass around another combe with more strip lynchets on the hillside ahead. Keep ahead past a fingerpost beside a stile (do not cross it) and go through a gate to come alongside a wood. Ignore a gate up to the left and go ahead through another gate. Waymarks indicate a **Corridors to the Countryside Link Route 5**. Follow the footpath between Crete Road West and a fence. Take care to avoid a low concrete bollard marked FWC (Folkestone Water Company, now part of the French company, Veolia) – their reservoir lies down to your right. Pass the

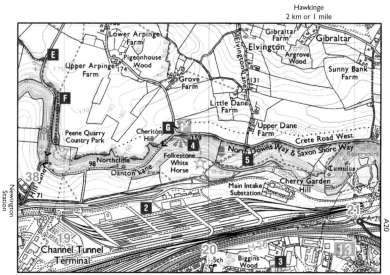

Etchinghill to Dover

Contours are given in metres
The vertical interval is 5m
M20
FOLKESTONE

Dover and Folkestone Kennels to reach a lane (Castle Hill) 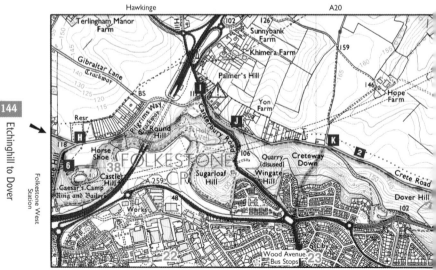 near its junction with Crete Road West.

≋ 🚌 ⟿ *The link with **Folkestone West Station** starts by turning sharp right down Castle Hill (see page 184).*

Pass some black-and-white bollards to a fingerpost, then turn right along a footpath. Go through a gate and keep ahead around the edge of **Castle Hill** 🖟. For a grand panorama over Folkestone, climb to the summit. As you progress around the castle, another tunnel comes into view: this is for the A20 London–Dover road under the aptly named Round Hill. Follow a worn path around to the right, through a gate to ascend Round Hill. Pass a stile (do not cross it) and keep ahead outside a fence. Over to your right is the graceful hump of Sugar Loaf Hill.

Go through a gate and keep ahead to come alongside a road (a detached and incongruously located Pilgrims Way). Do not go through the next gate, but bear a quarter right on a faint grass footpath across a meadow to go through another gate on to ⚠ the A260 Canterbury Road 🖟, which you must cross. Unfortunately, there is as yet no protection for

pedestrians at this busy three-lane carriageway, so carefully choose a spot where you have maximum visibility in both directions.

🚌 *Buses from stops to the left along the A260 serve Folkestone (right-hand side) or Dover (via Alkham and Kearsney) and Canterbury (left-hand side).*

Turn right up Crete Road East ✺, another roadside nature reserve. Approaching the top of the hill, turn right through a gate 🖟, then left to follow a fence, parallel with the road. On the far side of the road comes, first, another concrete pillbox, then the Arqiva mast, which is used for VHF and FM radio as well as mobile phones and emergency services. The white Martello tower is down to your right, but look to your feet, too, as there are several trip hazards along here, including a cracked drainpipe and some badly sawn-off fenceposts. At the entrance to Hope Farm you must cross a side lane 🖟. *NCR2, the National Cycle Route from London to Dover, comes up the side lane, then turns right along Crete Road East.*

≋ 🚌 ⟿ *The link with **Wood Avenue bus stops** (for buses to Folkestone Central Station) starts by turning right down a footpath here (see page 185).*

FOLKESTONE

Contours are given in m
The vertical interval is

Enter the next field, either across a stile or through a gate a little further on. Rejoin the footpath running parallel with the road, now amid gorse and passing a concrete pillbox and the **Dover Hill 7** trig point. At the end of the field, go through a gate and cross Crete Road East. Turn right to cross ⚠ the B2011 New Dover Road **L**, taking great care and watching out especially for traffic coming blind from the right, to the Valiant Sailor 🍺 at Highview Park.

🚌 *The bus stops to the left here are for the frequent service between Dover (left-hand side) and Folkestone (right-hand side).*

Keep ahead on a footpath along the right-hand side of the pub. At a bend, climb an embankment on your left and continue in the same direction to a waymark post. You now turn left and follow the cliff-top path nearly all the way for the next 4.4 miles (7 km) to the outskirts of Dover, taking great care as there is ⚠ a sheer drop on your right.

Dover Harbour is now in sight ahead. Beyond that are the two Dover television transmitters. The view to your right will now always be of the **English Channel 8**. At first, you follow a high, wire fence to reach the **Battle of Britain Memorial 9** 🍺

PC 🚻. The South Eastern Main Line railway between Folkestone and Dover appears below and enters a tunnel, completed in 1844, through Abbot's Cliff ahead. Stay on the footpath past the memorial as it turns away from the cliff to cross a chine, via 47 steps down and 36 up, and reach the drive **M** of a house called Eagles Nest (note: this is not the Eagle's Nest shown on the map further east).

Turn left, then in 33 yards (30 metres) turn right up steps to regain the cliff-edge path. The path is now close to houses on the Old Dover Road at Capel-le-Ferne, with bench seats along the greensward. Ignore a footpath down to the right, which leads to **Folkestone Warren 10**; instead go half left then immediately right to pass the 🍺 Cliff Top Café and a National Cycle Network Millennium Milepost, then the Lighthouse Inn 🍺🛏 and some caravan parks.

Pass through two 'shrubbery tunnels', then turn left just before some cliff-top buildings – you are advised not to use the cliff-top path ahead as it is subject to erosion. Just before the New Dover Road **N**, turn right along a lane, now with National Cycle Network 2, to pass the buildings, and with one of the Dover

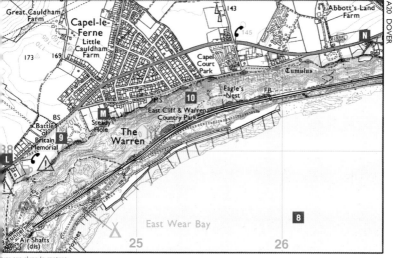

urs are given in metres
vertical interval is 5m

television transmitters away to the left, beyond the A20 London–Dover trunk road. Tarmac eventually gives way to gravel, then the cycle route continues ahead at a gate, but you should turn right then left through another gate along **Abbot's Cliff** **11**, keeping the fence on your right. Pass a brick ventilation shaft and a tall grass embankment, then go through a gate on your right and turn left, back by the cliff.

Dover Harbour makes a grand stage entrance as you come over a brow of the cliff. Its Western Docks seem so close that you think the end of the North Downs Way must be nigh, but there are still 3 miles (5 km) to go. **Samphire Hoe 12** appears down by the sea, then you pass through two more shrubbery tunnels. Follow the path as it dips around to the left of a wartime installation.

Shakespeare Cliff appears ahead like a mountain ridge in miniature, with land falling steeply away on both sides. Cross a dilapidated stile and pass another lookout post, following the right-hand side of a sloping horse paddock. Coming into full view now are Dover's Eastern Docks. Cross over another dilapidated stile to

regain the cliff path, then descend past a tunnel ventilation shaft.

PC *To visit Samphire Hoe, turn left here down a footpath, which leads to the A20, then turn right to the access tunnel.*

Pass another North Downs Way milestone – only 2 miles (3 km) to go, but a fair amount of climbing still to come. A circular triangulation point on your right marks a good viewpoint back along Samphire Hoe towards Folkestone.

With a footbridge over the A20 and the suburb of Aycliff in view on your left, climb **Shakespeare Cliff 13**, to be rewarded at the summit with another grand view of Dover Harbour. Descend to a wooden North Downs Way seat carved in the shape of a stingray, then continue down a concrete footpath beside a railing above Dover's shingle beach and the railway tunnel exit. At the bottom, turn left down steps to go through a subway **0** under the A20, then turn right up steps on the far side to South Military Road in Aycliff.

If needed, there is a bus service into the town centre from here.

Etchinghill to Dover

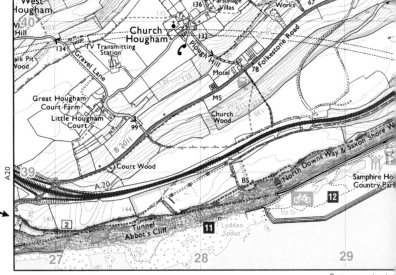

Contours are given in
The vertical interval

Cross the road with care, turn right for 52 yards (50 metres), then turn left up King Lear's Way. Turn right along Kings Ropewalk, then, at the end of this cul-de-sac, turn left up a tarmac footpath behind some houses. Climb 35 steps, then, at the top, by a children's playground, turn right through a gate to follow a worn footpath. You have now reached an area known as **Western Heights 14**. Continue up to join a track coming in from the Citadel on your left. Keep ahead at a lane (Western Close), now with Dover Castle in full view ahead. Join Citadel Road

and keep ahead past the remains of a church of the Knights Templar. At a junction, by BCB Dover, turn left down Centre Road, using a pavement on the left-hand side. Soon after the road swings right, cross over with care to climb 53 steps **P**, passing through a gate at the bottom and the top.

Turn left along a level grass footpath, where cattle may be grazing. Four spectacular sights come into view in quick succession: first an almost aerial view of **Dover Priory Station 15**, followed by the distant bulk of

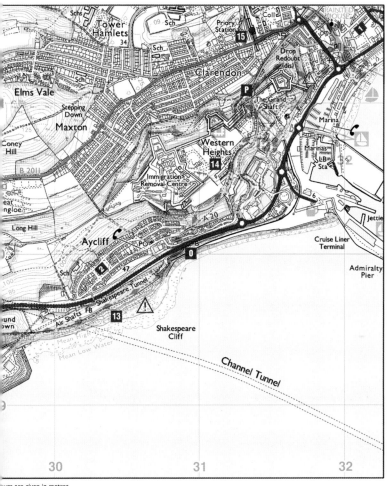

ours are given in metres
vertical interval is 5m

Dover Castle **16**, then the awesome defences of the **Drop Redoubt 17**, and finally a reprise of **Dover Harbour 18**, now seemingly within touching distance.

On reaching an information board for the Drop Redoubt, bear left downhill, past a thoughtfully placed 'pew'. At a gate, turn left to descend a total of 129 steps in two sets, broken by a gate. ⚠ The second set is very steep and can be slippery– a notice advises you to hold the handrail. At the foot, continue ahead, then turn right to reach Adrian Street. Keep ahead to follow it round to the left and down to the main road, York Street **Q**. Turn left, then cross the dual carriageway at the traffic lights. Keep ahead down Queen Street in the centre of **Dover 19**, then turn right to follow pedestrianised streets that lead directly through a subway and across side roads to Marine Parade and Dover's stunning new Esplanade, where you will find the North Downs Way 'End of Trail'

marker **R**, unveiled in November 2010. It is a granite 'start/finish' line, 26 feet (8 metres) long, set in the ground and accompanied by a plaque.

⇌ 🚌 *The links with **Dover Priory Station** and the bus station start by retracing your steps through the subway (see page 185).*

CONGRATULATIONS!

All walkers who complete the North Downs Way from Farnham to Dover are eligible for a certificate, whichever route was followed. Please contact the **North Downs Way National Trail Office**, giving details of your walk and any comments on your experience and a certificate will be sent to you free of charge. If you have now completed at least five National Trails, you are also eligible to be recorded in the National Trails Register maintained by the **Long Distance Walkers Association**.

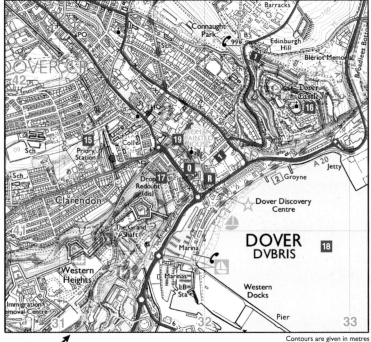

Contours are given in metres
The vertical interval is 5m

Public transport

Etchinghill (on route) 🚌
Newington (1 mile /1.6 km) 🚌
Folkestone West (1.4 miles / 2.2 km) 🚊
Canterbury Road (on route) 🚌
Valiant Sailor (on route) 🚌
Battle of Britain Memorial (on route) 🚌
Capel-le-Ferne (0.1 mile / 0.2 km) 🚌
Aycliff (on route) 🚌
Dover Priory (0.5 mile / 0.8 km) 🚊
Dover Bus Station (0.3 mile / 0.5 km) 🚌

Taxis/minicabs: Saltwood, Hythe, Cheriton, Folkestone, Hawkinge, Capel-le-Ferne, Aycliffe, Dover

Refreshments and toilets

Peene (0.7 mile / 1.1 km) 🍵 Elham Valley Railway Museum
Highview Park (on route) 🚻 Valiant Sailor
Battle of Britain Memorial (on route) 🍵
Folkestone Warren (on route) 🍵 Cliff Top Café
Capel-le-Ferne (on route) 🚻 Lighthouse Inn, Royal Oak, White Cliffs Inn
Samphire Hoe (0.4 mile / 0.6 km) 🍵 Kiosk
Aycliff (0.1 mile / 0.2 km) 🚻 King Lear
Dover (on route) 🚻🍵 Wide selection

Dover Priory Station (0.5 mile / 0.8 km) 🍵
Food shops: Etchinghill, Folkestone, Capel-le-Ferne, Dover
Public toilets: Folkestone, Battle of Britain Memorial, Samphire Hoe, Dover, Dover Priory Station

Accommodation

Cheriton (1.6 miles / 2.6 km) Holiday Inn Express
Arpinge (0.3 mile / 0.5 km) Pigeonwood House
Folkestone (2 miles / 3.2 km) Wide selection – contact **Folkestone Tourist Information Centre**
Crete Down (on route) Crete Down Guest House
Foord (1.1 miles / 1.8 km) Clovelley Guest House, Rob Roy Guest House
Highview Park (on route) Little Switzerland Camping & Caravan Site
Folkestone Warren (on route) Folkestone Camping & Caravan Site
Capel-le-Ferne (on route) Lighthouse Inn
South Alkham (2.5 miles / 4 km) Alkham Court
Alkham (2.8 miles / 4.5 km) The Marquis
Church Hougham (1 mile / 1.6 km) Premier Inn Dover
Dover (on route) Wide selection – contact **Dover Tourist Information Centre**

A fulmar nesting on the cliffs at Folkestone.

12 Boughton Lees to Chilham

through King's Wood and Mountain Street
5.9 miles (9.5 km)

Ascent 512 feet (156 metres)

Descent 561 feet (171 metres)

Lowest point Mountain Street: 85 feet (26 metres)

Highest point Soakham Downs: 528 feet (161 metres)

If you have decided to follow the Canterbury loop from Boughton Lees in Section 9, the total distance from Lenham to Chilham is 14.5 miles (23.3 km).

This section is dominated by King's Wood, where pilgrims banded together as protection against robbers. Approaching its far end, and hoping for clear weather, watch out for a break in the trees to your right, where Canterbury Cathedral, all of 7 miles (4.3 km) away, rises majestically to encourage weary pilgrims onward to their goal. Should you happen to be there in the autumn, as well as enjoying the glorious colours of the foliage you should find the ground covered in sweet chestnuts – and be prepared for one or two to fall at your feet (or on your head) as you pass by.

There is just one ascent of any magnitude, leading up Soakham Downs into King's Wood, where the walking is fairly level. Then a long, gradual descent takes you past ancient, timber-framed houses at Mountain Street into the very pretty hilltop village of Chilham.

Soakham Downs and King's Wood are known to be the haunt of wild boar – if this concerns you, try to walk in company (see page 34).

Things to look out for

1 **Boughton Aluph** is so small you might miss it if engrossed in conversation. Yet it is the location of an impressive 13th-century parish church, All Saints. A wall painting in its north transept dates from about 1440 and depicts the Holy Trinity. The church was extensively damaged by incendiary bombs during the Second World War, and restoration still continues. Boughton Aluph was the last overnight stop for pilgrims on their way to Canterbury, and the church porch is where they gathered to team up for the long walk through the then robber-

infested King's Wood. Note the unusual weathervane atop a barn on your left as you leave the village: though difficult to make out, it is surmounted by a prancing stag (a reindeer?), whose nose, in a moment of whimsy, has been painted red.

2 **King's Wood** is one of the largest woodlands in Kent, covering 1,500 acres (608 hectares), and you will be walking through it for nearly 2 miles (3 km). It is managed by the Forestry Commission and contains sweet chestnut in abundance, as well as beech, Corsican pine and Douglas fir. Fallow deer may be seen, and watch out for adders basking in the early-morning sun. Birds that nest here include nightjars and all three British species of woodpecker.

3 Godmersham Park is the open land on your right as you walk through King's Wood. The brick wall that you pass was a deer leap, a device that allowed the animals to jump into the park, where they could be hunted, but not to return to the wood. The 18th-century house, half a mile away, was owned at one time by Jane Austen's brother, Edward, and she is believed to have written some of *Pride and Prejudice*, *Persuasion* and *Mansfield Park* there.

4 Mountain Street is a quiet hamlet on the old Ashford–Canterbury Road, now a dead-end lane. It contains some delightful old buildings, including the timber-framed Monckton Manor and Heron Manor – the latter dating from 1480 according to a plaque by its front door. The lane used to go past the castle, but in 1728 the new owner, James Colebrooke, diverted it to the east

(you can see where it suddenly veers right) and built the high wall to protect his privacy. One section of the wall was lowered (but provided with railings) to afford a grand view of the castle and the great park that was redesigned by Capability Brown during the 18th century.

5 Chilham is a charming old village. With two sides occupied by historic buildings and the other two by St Mary's Church and the gates of Chilham Castle, the 15th-century square should be an absolute delight, but is spoiled by the cars that hog its centre. They have had to be turfed out, though, when the village has been the location for period films, such as the 1944 classic *A Canterbury Tale*. The Norman keep of the original castle was completed in 1174 for King Henry II and is still occupied, but the mansion now known as Chilham Castle was built in 1616. St Mary's Church dates from the 13th century (but is believed to stand on the site of a 7th-century predecessor), the White Horse pub from the 16th century.

As you emerge from the trees of King's Wood you suddenly behold for the first time, some 7 miles (11 km) ahead, the distant vision of Canterbury Cathedral.

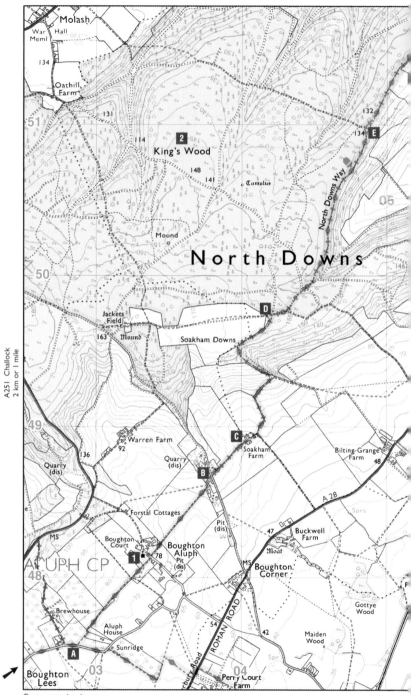

Contours are given in metres
The vertical interval is 5m

Route description

After leaving the lane **A** from Boughton Lees, follow the narrow footpath between fields. Pass All Saints Church at **Boughton Aluph 1**, keeping to the left of a meadow on the right of the church. Cross a tarmac track, then a stile, to continue on a broad, grassy footpath between fences.

Cross a large field and shortly before its end dive between hedges on your right to follow the path as it twists to a road (White Hill) **B**. Keep ahead on a restricted byway for the next 3 miles (5 km). At Soakham Farm **C**, continue on a grassy track and through a gate. You now start to climb up Soakham Downs, twisting left and right. Near the top, turn right, then in 375 yards (340 metres) at a crosstracks **D** turn right again into **King's Wood 2**. Shortly take the left fork and keep ahead as the byway starts to descend. About halfway through the wood, just past a footpath junction **E**, another North Downs Way milestone shows 10 miles (16 km) to Canterbury and 28 miles (45 km) to Dover.

On your right is **Godmersham Park 3**. Just before the end of King's Wood you pass a

wall which is a deer leap. Go through a gate **F**, then turn right, still on a byway and now descending quite steeply. As you turn left at the foot **G**, beware of a partly buried wire fence and some exposed tree roots.

Keep ahead along a tarmac lane, **Mountain Street 4** 🚶, leading through a hamlet of the same name. The ivy-clad brick wall on your left hides Chilham Park, the grounds of Chilham Castle.

You reach the village of **Chilham 5** and immediately ascend School Hill ahead, passing Elephant House and the primary school. None of the streets in this village has a pavement 🚶. If staying at Castle Cottage 🛏️, you will find it on your left at the top. Turn right diagonally across The Square **H** to the White Horse pub 🍺, where this section of the North Downs Way ends.

🚃 🚌 *The link with **Chilham Station** and bus stops starts here by turning right down The Street (see page 185).*

If you are continuing on to Section 13, keep ahead past the church.

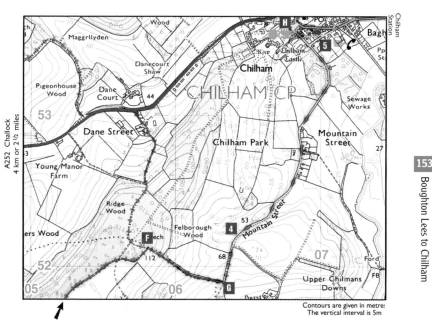

Contours are given in metres
The vertical interval is 5m

Public transport

Boughton Lees (on route) 🚌 Not Sundays

Boughton Corner (0.5 mile / 0.8 km) 🚌 Not Sundays

Bilting (0.9 mile / 1.4 km) 🚌 Not Sundays

Godmersham (0.9 mile / 1.4 km) 🚌 Not Sundays

Chilham Station (0.6 mile / 1 km, at Bagham) 🚈🚌

Taxis/minicabs: Ashford, Kennington, Chartham

Refreshments and toilets

Chilham (on route) 🍺 White Horse, Woolpack ☕ Shelly's

Bagham (0.6 mile / 1 km) ☕ Bagham Barn Tea Room

Food shops: Chilham

Public toilets: Chilham

Accommodation

Chilham (on route) Castle Cottage, Woodchip Guest House, Woolpack Inn

Bagham (0.6 mile / 1 km) Bagham Farmhouse, Folly House, The Old Alma

The rustling of leaves underfoot provides a constant accompaniment as you follow this woodland footpath near Old Wives Lees.

13 Chilham to Canterbury

via Old Wives Lees and No Man's Orchard
7.2 miles (11.6 km)

Ascent 614 feet (187 metres)

Descent 705 feet (215 metres)

Lowest point Canterbury: 39 feet (12 metres)

Highest point Fright Wood: 292 feet (89 metres)

This short section should allow some time for sightseeing in Canterbury. There are several steep but comparatively short ascents; otherwise the walking is quite gentle, much of it through extensive orchards. You pass places with intriguing names – the village of Old Wives Lees and a nature reserve called No Man's Orchard – before enjoying a grand view of the magnificent cathedral on the outskirts of Canterbury and finishing the section at its West Gate.

The North Downs Way passes St Dunstan's Church, where pilgrims nearing their goal paused, like King Henry II, to pray before making the solemn procession to the cathedral. It is difficult to feel solemn these days, as the approach through the city centre is lined by worldly temptations, but at least North Downs Wayfarers will have the satisfaction of knowing that they have completed the journey as it should be done – on foot.

At the time of writing, there is no North Downs Way signage through Canterbury, though it is hoped that this can be provided in the near future.

Things to look out for

1 One source states that **Old Wives Lees** is so called as the widows of workers at Chilham Park were relocated here to leave their estate cottages free for replacements. Another, possibly more likely, explanation is that it is a corruption of Oldwood's Lees, after the 15th-century squire of the manor, John Oldwood – 'lees' may be a variant spelling of 'leas', or meadows. It is now a fairly large agricultural settlement of around 500 people. The neat little village hall was built in 1904 as a mission hall and monthly Christian services still take place there.

2 **Nickle Farm** is the headquarters of F. W. Mansfield & Son, Britain's biggest grower of apples and cherries – you could have guessed this from the extent of their orchards, which you will be traversing for a full 1.5 miles (2.4 km). The company has 16 locations in Kent, covering over 3,000 acres (1,215 hectares), but Nickle Farm is the largest.

3 **No Man's Orchard Nature Reserve** is so called as it straddles the parishes of Chartham and Harbledown, and it was an ancient tradition that such land belonged to no one man. The orchard and surrounding woods were acquired in 1996 by the two parishes, now within the city of Canterbury. It has been designated as a Local Nature Reserve and a Local Wildlife Site, mainly due to the variety of lichens and mosses found here – to say nothing of the apples!

4 Bigbury was an Iron Age hill fort, thought to have been the stronghold to which the ancient Britons retreated after seeing the size of the Roman invading forces under Julius Caesar landing near Deal in 54 BC. Two days later, the Britons were defeated at a battle on the far side of the fort and some of the tribes decided to ally themselves with the Romans. The remainder, under Cassivellaunus, retreated to their home territory north of the Thames, where they were defeated, but problems elsewhere led to Caesar's abandonment of his campaign in Britain and the eventual Roman occupation was delayed by nearly a century. The embankments and ditches that formed part of the fort's walls are clearly visible as you pass through.

5 St Dunstan's Church was founded by Archbishop Lanfranc soon after the Norman Conquest in the late 11th century, though little of that building remains. It was the first church to be dedicated to Dunstan, a 10th-century Archbishop of Canterbury. Here, in 1174, King Henry II, in penance for the murder of Archbishop Thomas Becket, stripped off his usual clothes and, clad only in a rough hair shirt and cloak, walked barefoot to the cathedral. This started the custom for later pilgrims to pause at St Dunstan's and, if they could, complete their journey barefoot.

6 Watling Street has become known as the Roman road from Dover through Canterbury, London and St Albans to Wroxeter in Shropshire, a route now broadly covered by the A2 and A5. The name is a corruption of the Old English *Wæcelinga Stræt*.

7 Canterbury's **West Gate**, built of Kentish ragstone towards the end of the 14th century, is the largest surviving city gate in England, and the last of Canterbury's original seven gates. It suffers the indignity of being penetrated by heavy traffic, including double-decker buses, which rumble gingerly inbound through the central arch, while outbound vehicles creep round the side. For a while the building was used as a prison, but it now houses the West Gate Towers Museum.

8 The post-medieval history of the ancient city of **Canterbury** is inextricably bound up with that of its great cathedral, which holds a very special place in Christianity: the seat of the Archbishopric of Canterbury, one of the most beautiful cathedrals in Europe and, of course, one of the most important objects of pilgrimage following the murder of Archbishop Thomas Becket in 1170. This strategic location by a ford on the River Great Stour was the site of an Iron Age fort, called Durovernon, of the local Celtic tribe known as the Cantiaci, which the Romans called Durovernum Cantiacorum and turned into a walled town. When the Romans left in the early 5th century, the territory of the Cantiaci was invaded by the Jutes, a Germanic tribe, who occupied the Roman town and called it Cantwareburh – the stronghold of the people of Cantia, or Kent. In 597, Augustine was sent by Pope Gregory the Great to convert the Jutes to Christianity, and established his *cathedra* (Latin for 'seat') in Cantwareburh. He was appointed Archbishop of Canterbury, and the city has since developed and prospered amid such prestigious surroundings.

9 Canterbury Cathedral was established soon after the arrival of Bishop Augustine in AD 597 – the site of the original building was under the nave of the present one. It was later rebuilt by the Saxons and again by the Normans in 1070 following a fire. The cathedral has been extensively altered over the centuries, but some parts of that Norman building remain. On 29 December 1170, following a rash outburst by King Henry II, four of his knights took it upon themselves to murder Archbishop Thomas Becket as he prayed before the High Altar. The cathedral was already an object of pilgrimage, but this foul deed led to a surge of pilgrims. Becket's shrine, and possibly his body, were destroyed by King Henry VIII in 1538, though some believe a skeleton found in the crypt in 1888 to be Becket's. Unless you are attending a service, you must pay to enter the cathedral and its precincts.

Chilham to Canterbury

Route description

From the White Horse Inn 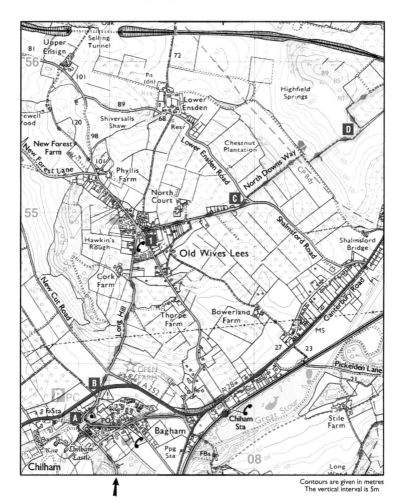, follow the tarmac drive into the churchyard. Keep ahead past the church door across grass then through shrubbery. At the first gravestone bear left to go down a narrow bridleway beside a fence to a lane (Church Hill) ✖. Keep ahead to ⚠ the A252 Chilham Bypass **B** and cross it with great care, especially regarding traffic from the right approaching fast and blind. Keep ahead up a tarmac lane (Long Hill) ✖, shortly crossing New Cut Road, to reach **Old Wives Lees** **1**. At a grassy triangle,

turn right across Cobbs Hill (take care), with the Star Inn 🍺 over to your left, and continue along Lower Lees Road, using the right-hand pavement until it runs out ✖. Just past North Court Oast **C** bear left on a tarmac lane to pass Snowdrop Cottage.

At a junction, turn right then left past a wooden barrier to follow a narrow, fenced footpath. After crossing a field, turn right then shortly left to climb a steep, grassy track beside a belt of trees. Keep to the right-hand side of a field as it turns left **D**

Contours are given in metres
The vertical interval is 5m

around the corner, then in 190 yards (175 metres) turn right to cross or pass a dilapidated stile among bushes. You have arrived at **Nickle Farm** **2**, a vast fruit-growing area, and will be surrounded by apple trees for the next 1.5 miles (2.4 km). Descend a footpath between orchards, with a little right–left kink at one point, to pass a community of mobile homes **E**, where itinerant fruit-pickers are accommodated. Join a track down to the right, then turn left under a railway bridge.

At a five-way junction around an island of grass **F**, bear right up a steep, chalky track beside more fruit trees. At the top, turn left along a concrete track beside Fright Wood, passing 'Roger's Rest' (a rustic seat) and some black-and-white weatherboard cottages. Soon after a large, wooden barn, bear right at a fork, still among fruit trees, still on concrete, which soon deteriorates to gravel and earth. Keep close to a hawthorn hedge, then go left of a fence on to a gravel track. At a large, green barn turn left past a gate into Hatch Farm, now partly residential. Turn right along a gravel drive, passing an ornamental fish pond and oast houses. On reaching a road **G** (Hatch Lane), turn left then immediately right along a tarmac lane (Newtown Street), soon passing a junction with a footpath **H**.

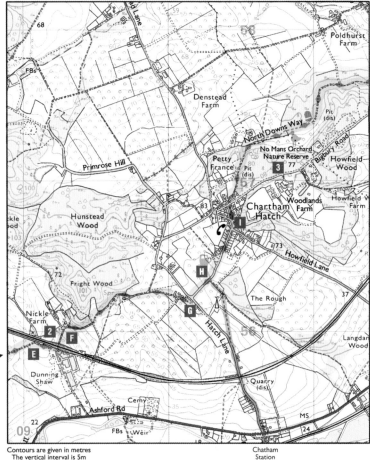

Contours are given in metres
The vertical interval is 5m

Chatham
Station

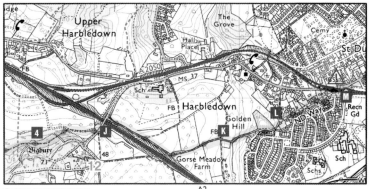

Contours are given in metres
The vertical interval is 5m

A2

⇌ *The link with **Chartham Station** starts here by turning right across a stile (see page 186).*

Still surrounded by fruit trees, you reach the village of Chartham Hatch. The first building is the Chapter Arms pub ⌷. At a T-junction **I** turn left along Howfield Lane, keeping left. Opposite Nightingale Close cross with care, then keep ahead along a fenced tarmac footpath between gardens. Cross the next road (Bigbury Road) and keep ahead along a concrete drive. In 22 yards (20 metres) fork right on tarmac to pass a metal barrier into a playing field. At the corner of a children's playground, follow a footpath beside a fence and past a conifer plantation, part of the **No Man's Orchard Nature Reserve 3**.

At the foot of a hill, keep ahead along the left-hand side of the orchard itself, passing a wooden serpent sculpture and information boards for the Nature Reserve and the North Downs Way. Just before the end of the orchard, turn left through a gate, beside which glares the head of another, larger, wooden serpent. Follow a fenced footpath into Blean Ancient Woodlands nature reserve, part of a vast area of countryside and villages to the west and north of Canterbury known as The Blean. Traffic noise warns you of the approaching A2.

Keeping ahead at a footpath crossing, the steeply rising area on your right was the Iron Age fort of **Bigbury 4**, and you will shortly pass an embankment that was part of its

defensive works. Stay on the main footpath, ignoring side turnings, until it eventually veers right on concrete to join a road **J** (Bigbury Road again). Cross over with care, as traffic approaches blind from both directions, and turn left to cross the A2(T) dual carriageway. On the far side, turn right on a bridleway, parallel with the road, at first on concrete, later on grass, climbing steeply, partly on steps. The route soon turns away from the A2 down a sunken track, with the buildings of Harbledown up ahead, on the western outskirts of Canterbury.

At the foot of the slope, cross a footbridge over a stream **K**, then climb steeply left to join a drive by the gates of a house called Mindora Heights. With the slopes of Golden Hill (a small National Trust property) on your left, follow the drive to a junction by a house called Mill in the Mint **L**, where you bear right along Mill Lane to come alongside the A2050 Rheims Way, named in honour of Canterbury's twin city in France. There is a splendid view of the cathedral from the roadside.

Keep ahead to the traffic roundabout and cross ⚠ Knight Avenue **M** at the pedestrian refuge, but take great care, as vehicles come fast off the roundabout. Dive into the subway on your left, then on the far side keep ahead across a cycle lane to London Road in the St Dunstan's district of Canterbury.

🚌 ↩ *Buses go to the city centre from here. The Victoria Hotel is over to your left.*

Turn right to walk beside London Road to the mini-roundabout by **St Dunstan's Church** ⬛. Note the veteran black North Downs Way fingerpost opposite – it is the last sign for the route that you will see until you reach the city's southern outskirts on the next section.

Turn right along St Dunstan's Street, part of the Roman road known as **Watling Street** ⬛, with the city's West Gate ahead. The building with ancient wooden doors opposite is the Roper Gate, all that remains of Place House, the home of William Roper and his wife, Margaret, daughter of St Thomas More. You may have to wait for a train to pass at the level crossing, or you can use the subway if you are rushing to catch one. Otherwise, use the time to read a graffitied lament on behalf of children, painted on the subway wall. Continue along St Dunstan's Street, passing Station Road West ⬛.

⮞ Canterbury West Station ⬛ is 220 yards (200 metres) to your left along Station Road West. Returning from the station, turn right to the junction with St Dunstan's Street, where you turn left to rejoin the North Downs Way.

One of Canterbury's oldest inns, the 15th-century Falstaff Hotel ⬛, is on your left, just before the West Gate. Cross a branch of the River Great Stour, passing either side of

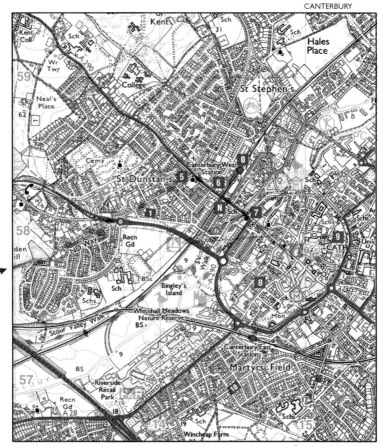

Chilham to Canterbury

A2

Contours are given in metres
The vertical interval is 5m

the **West Gate** **7**. Now within the old city of **Canterbury** **8**, keep ahead along the pedestrianised St Peter's Street. Over to your left at The Friars is the modern Marlowe Theatre. You cross another branch of the Great Stour to continue ahead along the High Street, where you pass more historic buildings: the Canterbury Pilgrims Hospital of St Thomas, the Pilgrims Refectory and Queen Elizabeth's Guest Chamber, whose ground floor is now occupied by Caffè Nero. On your right, a 16th-century inn, formerly well known as the County Hotel 🛏, now trades as ABode.

Turn left along narrow Mercery Lane, beside Pret A Manger, to reach Butter Market and another West Gate, that of **Canterbury Cathedral** **9**. Section 13 of the North Downs Way, and the journey of many a pilgrim, ends here. The Canterbury Visitor Centre is over to your left.

If you wish to continue on to Section 14 of the North Downs Way, turn right along Burgate.

≥🚌 The link to **Canterbury East Station**, which passes the bus station, starts a little way along Section 14.

Oast houses, the drying kilns for the newly picked hops, are a characteristic feature of the Kent countryside.

Public transport

Chilham Station (0.6 mile / 1 km, at Bagham) ≥🚌
Old Wives Lees (on route) 🚌 Infrequent, not Sundays
Chartham (0.7 mile / 1.1 km) ≥
Chartham Hatch (on route) 🚌 Infrequent, not Sundays
Harbledown (on route) 🚌
Canterbury West (0.1 mile / 0.2 km) ≥
Canterbury Bus Station (0.3 mile / 0.5 km) 🚌
Canterbury East (0.7 mile / 1.1 km) ≥
Taxis/minicabs: Chartham, Thanington, Harbledown, Canterbury

Refreshments

Old Wives Lees (on route) 🍺 Star Inn
Chartham Hatch (on route) 🍺 Chapter Arms
Canterbury (on route) 🍺🍴 Wide selection
Food shops: Chilham, Canterbury
Public toilets: Chilham, Canterbury

Accommodation

Shalmsford Bridge (0.9 mile / 1.4 km) Homelea
Chartham (0.9 mile / 1.4 km) Wisteria Lodge
Howfield (0.9 mile / 1.4 km) Howfield Manor Hotel
Thanington (1.2 miles / 1.9 km) Riverside
Harbledown (on route) Highfield Hotel, Victoria Hotel
Canterbury (on route) Wide selection – contact **Canterbury Visitor Centre**

14 Canterbury to Shepherdswell

through Patrixbourne and Higham Park
10.4 miles (16.7 km)

Ascent 814 feet (248 metres)

Descent 519 feet (158 metres)

Lowest point Canterbury: 52 feet (16 metres)

Highest point Shepherdswell: 397 feet (121 metres)

A pilgrimage is best undertaken in the company of like-minded travellers; so, having paid our respects to Canterbury Cathedral, we set off accompanied by those following the Elham Valley Way, which leads to Hythe (see page 128), and the rest of us heading for Dover on either the North Downs Way, Kent Regional Cycle Route 16 or the Via Francigena, as the Pilgrims Way should henceforth be called (see page 24).

This is another predominantly agricultural section, with mostly gentle walking. You will cross some vast fields of up to 105 acres (42 hectares) – large enough to hold 60 football pitches or 1,500 tennis courts. The views are pleasant rather than spectacular, though there is a final view of Canterbury Cathedral, looking back as you leave the city. You pass through the farming communities of Hode, Patrixbourne and Womenswold, and skirt Higham Park, with a fine view of its magnificent Georgian mansion. The section finishes with a steady ascent into Shepherdswell.

Towards the end of the section you cross the defunct East Kent Coalfield, which was discovered in 1890 and developed largely by 'expatriate' Welsh miners. They were renowned for their militancy but were very hard-working, as the coal was extremely difficult to extract from the deep seams. Tilmanstone and Snowdown Collieries even had highly rated male voice choirs. All the collieries had closed by the late 1980s, but their presence has left huge scars.

⚠ For much of this section, the North Downs Way runs parallel with the A2 London–Canterbury–Dover trunk road. To make a diversion to pubs or accommodation that lie on its far side, be aware that some of the rights of way that lead down to the road have no protected pedestrian crossing, so attempting to cross there could be dangerous. You are advised to use crossings that have bridges over or pass under the A2.

Things to look out for

1 **St Augustine's Abbey** was founded in AD 598 as a burial place for the kings of Kent by the man who converted the Jutes to Christianity, and St Augustine himself was buried here just six years later. The abbey was partly dismantled in 1538 during King Henry VIII's dissolution of the monasteries. He turned some of it into a palace for his fourth wife, Anne of Cleves, but it fell out of favour with later monarchs and was sold. A violent storm in 1703 destroyed what was left. The ruins are in the care of **English Heritage** and are open to the public (admission charge).

2 Canterbury Christ Church University was established in 1962 as a teacher-training college, but other fields of study were added and university status was achieved in 1998. The Canterbury campus occupies what were the orchards of St Augustine's Abbey, and the university now has other campuses at Broadstairs, Chatham and Folkestone.

3 St Martin's Church is where Augustine set up his mission soon after arriving from Rome in AD 597, and is thought to be the oldest church still used for worship in the English-speaking world.

4 Bifrons was a 17th-century mansion and the home of the Marchioness of Salisbury. After periods as an old people's home and a hostel for employees of the Ministry of Works, the house was demolished in 1949. *Bifrons* means 'two-faced' in Latin, as the old house had two frontages, but in demonology it is also the name of the two-faced Earl of Hell!

5 Higham Park's 87-room Georgian mansion has a distinguished list of visitors, including Mozart, Jane Austen and Ian Fleming. In the 1920s it was the home of Count Louis Vorrow Zborowski, who constructed racing cars powered by aircraft engines – the inspiration for the film *Chitty Chitty Bang Bang*. The house was requisitioned for use as a hospital during the Second World War and served as the gynæcological department of Canterbury Hospital from 1950 to 1982. It subsequently fell into disrepair, but in 1995 the house and grounds were acquired by cousins Patricia Gibb and Amanda Harris-Deans, who undertook their restoration. In 2005 the estate was sold to Jane Debliek, who has been continuing the work.

6 The **East Kent Railway** was constructed between 1911 and 1917 to link the collieries in the area with the main line at Shepherdswell and the port of Richborough. It never really thrived and most of the line closed in 1948, but the section from Shepherdswell to Tilmanstone Colliery struggled on until 1984. A group of enthusiasts managed to preserve the remaining section of line and re-opened it in 1993 for passenger traffic between Shepherdswell and Eythorne, operating both steam-hauled trains and diesel multiple units.

7 The name of the village of **Shepherdswell** is sometimes seen as Sibertswold, which is probably correct as it derives from the common Saxon name, Sibert. Confusingly, the station name is written as Shepherds Well. The attractive, flint-built St Andrews Church is Victorian, built in 1863.

The Georgian mansion Higham Park has a colourful history. Here were constructed the racing cars that inspired Chitty Chitty Bang Bang, and its doors welcomed Mozart, Jane Austen and Ian Fleming.

Route description

Facing the cathedral's West Gate 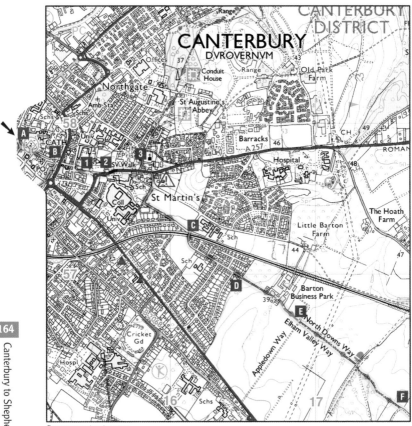, turn right along Burgate, passing Canterbury Cathedral Lodge and the Thomas Ingoldsby pub.

*The link with **Canterbury East Station**, which passes the bus station, starts here by turning right along Burgate Lane (see page 186).*

Cross the A28 Lower Bridge Street (the ring road) and keep ahead along Church Street, passing St Paul's Church and with the Cemetery Gate of **St Augustine's Abbey** ahead. Turn right at Monastery Street, which bends left into Longport.

At the end of a wall you can look left to see the ruins of the abbey, just before the entrance to it. At a mini-roundabout, keep ahead along the A257 (still Longport, signed for Sandwich). Cross over at the traffic lights and continue along the far side. You pass **Canterbury Christ Church University** and Canterbury Prison, built in 1808, which holds foreign nationals – it still bears an old inscription 'County Gaol and House of Correction'. **St Martin's Church** is a short distance along North Holmes Road to your left. Note the black fingerpost opposite the junction, signifying the restart of North Downs Way signage.

Contours are given in metres
The vertical interval is 5m

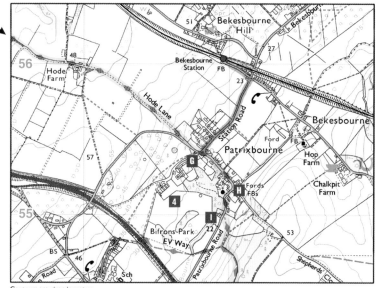

Contours are given in metres
The vertical interval is 5m

When the road veers left, turn right along Spring Lane. Pass the gardens of Hadlow College, then turn right again along a lane – our old friend Pilgrims Way, which you will follow again for the next 2.5 miles (4 km). Pass the university's sports centre then, when the lane swings left, turn sharp left along a tarmac byway beside railings. Keep ahead at the junction with St Augustine's Road, then turn right at the next junction **C** to cross a railway line. The road veers left to skirt the district of Barton, now approaching the south-eastern limits of Canterbury.

When the road ends **D**, keep ahead on a narrow tarmac lane (a bridleway) to pass Barton Business Park, later crossing its access road **E**. You go under three parallel sets of power lines, then fork left past a small orchard. Join Hode Lane **F** **✳** to reach Hode Farm, the thatched outbuildings of which have been converted into desirable residences. The route continues along a sunken lane to a major road (Bifrons Hill) at Patrixbourne. ⚠ **✳** Cross over with great care, as traffic comes

fast from the left round the bend. Turn left to the junction with Station Road **G**, where the Elham Valley Way goes off to the right.

≋ *The link with **Bekesbourne Station** starts here by turning left along Station Road (see page 186).*

Keep ahead along The Street **✳** in the quiet village of Patrixbourne, with **Bifrons Park** **4** on your right. At the junction by Patrixbourne Lodge **H**, the North Downs Way parts company with the Pilgrims Way and the cycle route, both of which continue ahead. Instead, turn right along Patrixbourne Road **✳** to pass St Mary's Church, which dates from the 12th century.

🚌 🚐 🔄 *If you wish to visit Bridge, keep ahead along Patrixbourne Road for 0.6 mile (1 km).*

Immediately after the last house **I** turn left into a field, then follow a footpath diagonally right across it to the corner of a wood. Stay beside the wood to another corner, where you join a bridleway that climbs left, still following the edge of the

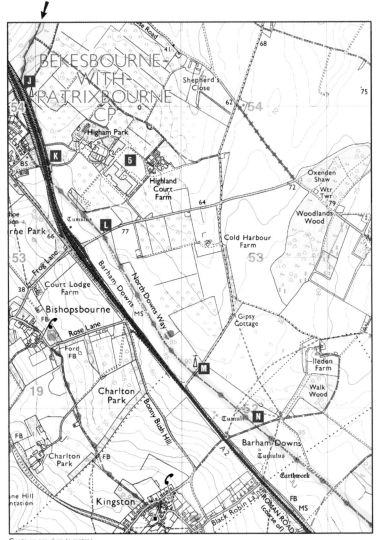

Contours are given in metres
The vertical interval is 5m

wood as it veers right, all the way to the A2, which has been noisily manifesting itself for some time. Down to the right is a pretty little bridge over the infant River Nailbourne, which rises in Bifrons Park. At the top of the hill, a seat provides a welcome opportunity for a rest, and just past it is another North Downs Way milestone: it says 18 miles (29 km) to Dover, but this is wrong – it should say 15 miles (24 km).

Go through a gate **J** to follow the shady bridleway, above and parallel to the A2, passing a mobile-phone mast and a hop field. In 600 metres (660 yards) you reach an estate road **K** in **Higham Park 5**, with the magnificent mansion partially visible away to your left. Keep ahead beside the A2, then shortly go half left through a gap and across a field, with the mansion now fully in view. Join the edge of a wood and continue to a road **L** (Coldharbour Lane), with the A2 running parallel away to your right, where it will remain for the next 2.2 miles (3.5 km).

🚌 🅿️ 🍴 *To visit Bishopsbourne, turn right along Coldharbour Lane ✠ to go under the A2. Turn right (bus stops here), then immediately left along Frog Lane, then turn right at the church.*

Ahead now lies the first of three enormous fields, and you just have to follow the bridleway across it, at first with a belt of black poplar trees away to your left. At its end rises a trio of mobile-phone masts. Cross a lane on to a smaller field, then cross a concrete farm track to find an even larger field – plod on!

🚌 🅿️ 🍴 *To visit Kingston or Barham, turn right at a crossing footpath about 100 yards (90 metres) after the concrete track. Turn left beside the A2 to cross a footbridge to the far side, where turn left for Barham or right for Kingston.*

The bridleway is quite faint here, but you close in on the left-hand side to join a clear track beside a hedge. Eventually you reach Upper Digges Farm, where the bridleway

squeezes along the left of a paddock. At a gravel farm track it would be easy for the unwary to continue in the same direction between fences, but at last the route changes course. Turn left along the track, then immediately keep ahead on grass. Pass a gate and a dilapidated shed, then turn right along another farm track, following a line of telegraph poles between hedges. When the hedges end, go left of a wire fence, leaving the track to follow the bridleway diagonally across a field to the B2046 Adisham Road . Cross with care and continue along the bridleway beside the telegraph poles.

Go between a hedge and a fence, then take the left fork between farm buildings to a road (The Street) in the village of Womenswold (or Wymynswold), with the 13th-century St Margaret's Church on your right. Turn left then immediately right. Pass a brick house, go left through a gap in a hedge, then immediately right on a bridleway along the right of yet another huge field. Cross a road (Woolage Lane)

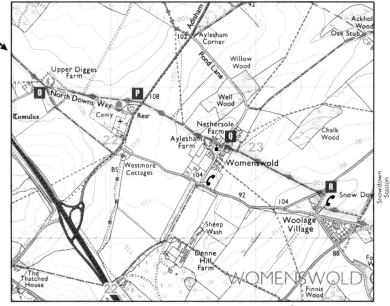

Contours are given in metres
The vertical interval is 5m

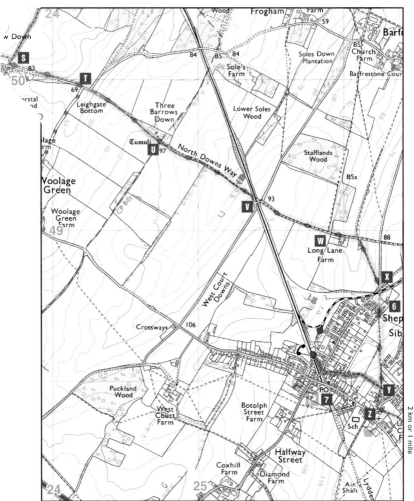

Contours are given in metres
The vertical interval is 5m

to go through a small wood to another branch of the same road, where you turn right ✖ to Woolage Village, built in the early 20th century to provide homes for miners at the now closed Snowdown Colliery and their families. At the name sign on a little white gate, turn left along a footpath beside a field, with a playing field on your right, to a fence corner **S**.

≈ *The link with **Snowdown Station** starts by turning left at the fence corner along a footpath across the field (page 186).*

Follow the fence around the field edge, now with a lane (Nethersole Road) on your right. Pass a gap, then in another 65 yards (60 metres) cross a stile **T** on to the lane ✖. Turn left, then, as the lane bends left, keep ahead along a byway between trees and shrubs – beware exposed roots. At a track junction **U**, keep ahead to a road **V**, then turn left over the Canterbury–Dover railway and turn right on Long Lane ✖. In 770 yards (700 metres), after passing Long Lane Farm **W**, turn right along a grassy footpath.

Go through a gate and continue ahead along the right-hand side of a field, a few yards to the left of a fence.

Emerge on to a road with great care, as traffic comes fast from the right. Cross over and turn right to the junction with another road **[X]** (Eythorne Road), cross that with care, then turn right again to a level crossing over the **East Kent Railway [6]**. Soon after that, turn left through a gate and along a grassy footpath, which climbs through a small playing field with a picnic table. Go through a gate, then keep ahead on a track past houses into trees. Cross a stile beside a gate and keep ahead on a track up a field, between electrified fences. Cross another stile beside a gate and continue in the same direction up the field towards a hedge corner. Go through a third gate to follow a track beside a fence. Follow a narrow footpath on the left of a stableyard to reach a junction with a tarmac footpath **[Y]**.

⇒ *The link with **Shepherds Well Station** starts here by turning right along the tarmac footpath (see page 186).*

Keep ahead along a track between houses, soon reaching Mill Lane **[Z]** at **Shepherdswell [7]**, where Section 14 of the North Downs Way ends.

The Bell Inn is over to your right, beside the village green, with St Andrew's Church nearby. The Bricklayers Arms is at the bottom of Church Hill, near the station.

To continue on to Section 15, facing the village green at Mill Lane, turn left through a gate.

Public transport

Canterbury West (on route) ⇌
Canterbury East (on route) ⇌
Bekesbourne (0.5 mile / 0.8 km) ⇌
Bridge (0.5 mile / 0.8 km) 🚌
Bishopsbourne (0.2 mile / 0.3 km) 🚌
Kingston (0.5 mile / 0.8 km) 🚌
Snowdown (0.8 mile / 1.3 km) ⇌
Woolage Village (on route) 🚌
Infrequent, not Sundays
Shepherdswell (Shepherds Well Station, 0.4 mile / 0.6 km) ⇌
Shepherdswell is served by a Monday–Friday school bus service; if you think this may be of use, contact Traveline for details.
Taxis/minicabs: Canterbury, Barton, Bridge, Aylesham

Refreshments and toilets

Bekesbourne Hill (0.7 mile / 1.1 km) 🍺 Unicorn
Chalkpit Farm (0.7 mile / 1.1 km) ☕ Mama Feelgood's
Bridge (0.5 mile / 0.8 km) 🍺 Plough & Harrow, Red Lion, White Horse
Bishopsbourne (0.6 mile / 1 km) 🍺 Mermaid
Kingston (0.5 mile / 0.8 km) 🍺 Black Robin
Woolage Green (0.6 mile / 1 km) 🍺 Two Sawyers
Shepherdswell (on route) 🍺 Bell, Bricklayers Arms; ☕ East Kent Railway (operational days only)
Food shops: Canterbury, Bridge, Shepherdswell
Public toilets: Canterbury

Accommodation

Barton (0.3 mile / 0.5 km) Best Western Abbots Barton Hotel, Chaucer Lodge, Ebury Hotel, Ersham Lodge, YHA Canterbury
Bridge (0.5 mile / 0.8 km) Bridge Place Hotel, Renville Oast
Bishopsbourne (0.6 mile / 1 km) Beechborough, Court Lodge Farmhouse
Adisham (2.5 miles / 4 km) Lion Hotel, Moor's Head Hotel, Woodlands Farm
Barham (1.3 miles / 2 km) Duke of Cumberland
Shepherdswell (on route) Bishop's Lodge, Oast Cottage

15 Shepherdswell to Dover

through Waldershare Park and along the Roman road
8.5 miles (13.7 km)

Ascent 499 feet (152 metres)

Descent 879 feet (268 metres)

Lowest point Dover Esplanade: 17 feet (5 metres)

Highest point Near Guston: 410 feet (125 metres)

A short final section that should leave you some time to explore Dover and visit its imposing castle. All but the last mile of the route goes through undulating agricultural land, with occasional distant views of the sea. Soon after the start you pass grand Waldershare House and its impressive mews. The second half of the section runs along, or close to, the Roman road that connected the ports of Richborough and Dover. Unsympathetic planners in the 1990s disgracefully failed to provide, for this National Trail, a way through the upgraded A2/A256 junction near Guston, so you must make a half-mile diversion there. However, this takes you fairly close to the Chance Inn at Guston, in an area that has few other opportunities for refreshment. The last mile is downhill all the way into Dover and the end of the North Downs Way.

Things to look out for

1 On entering the **Waldershare Park** estate, the first thing you are likely to notice, over to your right, is the Belvedere Tower, built around 1726 and designed by the architect Lord Burlington as a place of entertainment for guests staying at Waldershare House. The magnificent house was completed in 1712 for Sir Henry Furnesse and later became the seat of the Earls of Guilford. It is thought to be the work of William Talman, a little-known architect of the period, yet he was a pupil of Sir Christopher Wren and designed Chatsworth House. The adjacent mews is almost as impressive as the main house, with its cupola, clock and Latin inscription *disce vivere* ('learn to live'). Both house and mews have been converted into residential apartments, but most of the

estate is still farmland and you pass the Home Farm. You may see gliders from the Channel Gliding Club, which is based over to the right within the park, and an annual steam and country fair is held in the park at the end of July.

2 The **Hornsby Groves** were planted after the 'Great Storm' of 1987 destroyed most of the trees in this part of Waldershare Park. They were funded from the legacy of Mary Hornsby (1910–90).

3 **All Saints Church** dates from Norman times and was substantially rebuilt in the 19th century, with a richly decorated interior. Although no longer in use for regular worship, it remains consecrated and is in the care of the **Churches Conservation Trust**, which protects historic churches at risk.

4 The **Roman road** that will lead you into Dover connected the ports of Rutupiae (Richborough, near Sandwich) and Dubris (Dover). All of Britain's Roman roads were catalogued and numbered by the historian Ivan Margary (1896–1976), and this one is referred to as 'Margary 100'. Like most Roman roads, it is dead straight, and this was achieved not with a compass (the Romans did not have them) but with a *groma*, a contraption consisting of pieces of wood and lead weights.

5 The **White Cliffs Country Trail**, as its name suggests, follows the celebrated white cliffs from Dover to Sandwich, then returns by an inland route (a total distance of 28 miles / 45 km), joining the North Downs Way for its final 5 miles (8 km) into Dover. The route is promoted by the **White Cliffs Countryside Partnership**.

6 **Dover** – see page 141.

7 Dover's **Church of St Mary the Virgin** was extensively rebuilt in 1843 after a period of over 250 years when the earlier church was used as the polling station for Dover's mayors and members of parliament and was often trashed during pitched battles between rival factions. It stands on the site of a Roman building and may have been the location of a Saxon church that was destroyed after the Norman Conquest.

Although Waldershare House and its grand mews have been converted into apartments, they lie in serene parkland that provides a pleasing change from the more dramatic scenery elsewhere.

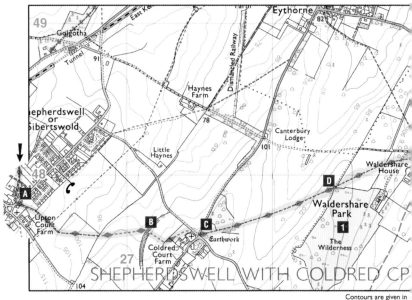

Contours are given in
The vertical interval

Route description

Facing the village green on Mill Lane **A** at Shepherdswell, turn left through a gate to follow a footpath past the churchyard, then go through another gate to continue beside a paddock with an electrified fence. After a third gate turn right, along the right-hand side of a field. Go through shrubbery, then half left on a clear footpath across the next two fields. A gap in a fence **B** takes you into more shrubbery – here you pass between earth banks, the remains of bridge supports on a branch of the East Kent Light Railway that served collieries at Coldred.

Cross a low fence and keep ahead on a faint footpath across a field to a stile. Cross it, then turn left along the left-hand side of a meadow. Cross another stile and go diagonally across a field to its far right corner, with Coldred Court Farm over to your right. Beware exposed roots as you cross a third stile on to a road. Turn right to the junction with Coldred Road **C**.

To visit the Carpenters Arms at Coldred, turn right along Coldred Road for 0.5 mile (0.8 km) and turn left at the village centre.

Cross with care and briefly keep ahead along Singledge Lane, but immediately turn left on to a footpath, which veers right into a wood. Go through a gate and cross a field diagonally right. The building among trees away to your right is the Belvedere Tower in **Waldershare Park 1**. Enter another wood, following a twisting path that emerges on to a large field. Follow a faint footpath across this field, eventually reaching a fence **D** at the corner of a wood called The Wilderness. Look left here for a fine view towards the cooling towers of the now disused Richborough Power Station, nearly 10 miles (16 km) away.

Go through a gate then diagonally left on a faint footpath, passing left of the nearest row of tall trees. Aim about 80 yards (73 metres) to the right of a conspicuous farm gate in the far right corner to go through a black pedestrians' gate, then continue in the same direction to the corner of the next (much smaller) field, crossing an estate road with Waldershare House and its mews down to your right. Go through a gap **E**

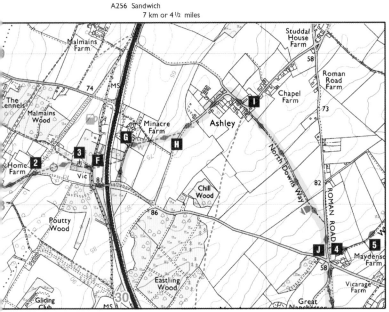

Contours are given in metres
The vertical interval is 5m

beside the grand gates of the house, then turn right along a fenced drive. This swings left and right, passing two footpath junctions and a rather dilapidated white gateway (signed 'private drive'), with Home Farm over to your left. At a fork, keep ahead on grass, passing a commemorative sign for **Hornsby Groves** **2**, then across a field to go through the middle of the circular Piddle Wood.

Continue ahead through two gates, then go to the right of **All Saints Church** **3**, leaving through its lychgate. Turn right, along the drive, to a major road (Sandwich Road) **F**, which was the A256 until the new road was built to the east. It is comparatively little used now, but take care as the traffic that uses it goes very fast.

🍺 *The former High and Dry pub, 350 yards (325 metres) to the left along Sandwich Road � was due to reopen as The Cider Works at the end of 2010.*

Turn right along Sandwich Road ✖ to the junction, by an entrance to Waldershare Park, then turn left to cross a bridge over

the A256, keeping to the left-hand side. On the far side, turn left down a concrete track. Just before Minacre Farm, go through a gate **G** on your right, then cross a field diagonally, continuing in the same direction after another gate to reach a lane **H** (Waldershare Road). Turn left ✖ to follow the road as it swings right, through the village of Ashley.

At the junction **I** with Chapel Lane, turn right into Northdown Close, then immediately fork left along a track (footpath). Maintain this line ahead for the next 0.6 mile (1 km), across and beside fields, to reach the appropriately named **Roman Road** **4**. Shortly before reaching it, note the quirky iron ladder-stile, almost swallowed up in a hedge. It is the only one of its kind along the North Downs Way; fortunately, you can now go through the adjoining gap.

Turn right ✖ to the crossroads **J** beside Maydensole Farm and keep ahead. The North Downs Way now shares its route into Dover with the **White Cliffs Country Trail** **5**. As the tarmac road swings right, keep

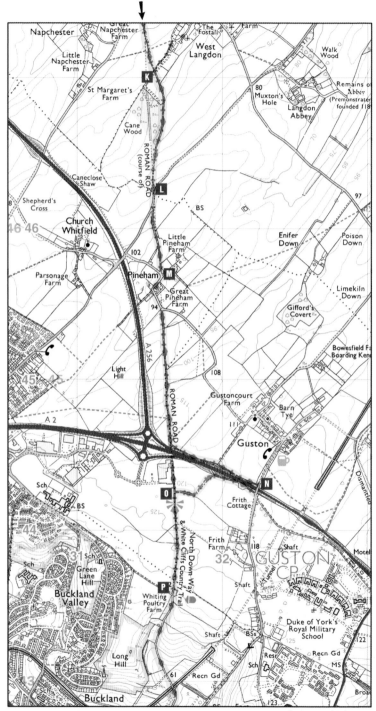

Contours are given in metres
The vertical interval is 5m

ahead up a tree-lined byway, where a fingerpost indicates 4 miles (6.4 km) to Dover. As you start to descend, at a junction with another byway  look back to see the diminutive St Mary's Church in West Langdon. The route diverts a little from the ancient straight line to go left of Cane Wood, but as you reach its far end look right to see the remains of an embankment that may have carried the Roman road.

As you approach the next road , look back for another extensive view, with the port of Ramsgate visible in the distance, and possibly a car ferry on the sea nearby. Just before joining the road, turn right along a track between bushes. Cross the road with care, especially regarding traffic coming fast and blind from the right, then turn right and fork left to resume your journey along the Roman road into the small farming hamlet of Pineham.

Join a tarmac road  to go right then left past Great Pineham Farm. As the road bends left out of the hamlet, keep ahead on the byway – now just 3 miles (4.8 km) to Dover, says the fingerpost. It should be 2.5 miles (4 km), but someone has put the A2

in your way, so on reaching it you must turn left beside the noisy road for 710 yards (650 metres) to reach Dover Road .

🍵 *If you wish to visit the Chance Inn at Guston, turn left here for 330 yards (300 metres).*

There are now 2 miles (3.2 km) to Dover. Turn right, across the A2, then immediately turn right again along a byway, which runs beside the A2 for 330 yards (300 metres) then turns left across a field. On the far side, bear right along a tree-lined track (beware exposed roots) to rejoin your original course along the Roman road .

You soon come to the highest point of this section, altitude 410 feet (125 metres), with a row of cottages over to your left and the clocktower of the Duke of York's Royal Military School in the distance. You can just glimpse the English Channel ahead, while away to your right is the Dover television transmitter. It is downhill all the way into Dover now, and when you reach a tarmac lane  (called, of course, Roman Road) there is just 1 mile (1.6 km) left to go, all on tarmac or pavement. Cross the Dover–Margate railway line to reach the junction

High above the town, Dover Castle stands guard. Its perimeter walls contain both a Roman lighthouse and a Saxon church.

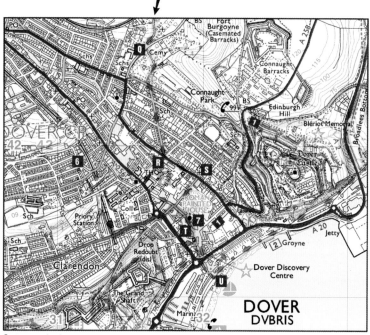

Contours are given in metres
The vertical interval is 5m

with Old Charlton Road **Q** beside the entrance to Charlton Cemetery on the outskirts of **Dover** **6**. Cross the road with care and ascend a footway behind a railing, which goes along a gully between another part of the cemetery and Connaught Park to Connaught Road. Cross it with care, turn left then right down Park Avenue, passing the intriguingly named Blériot's B&B .

You come to traffic lights **R** at A256 Maison Dieu Road. Cross ahead then left at the lights to walk along the right-hand side of Maison Dieu Road. Just before the next traffic lights **S**, turn right along Pencester Road, past the Magistrates Court. Cross the River Dour, then turn left, by the stops of Dover's main bus station, into Pencester Gardens. Cross the park to the right of the bandstand, then go through a car park towards the Roman Quay pub, with public toilets on your left **PC**. Turn right along Church Street, passing the **Church of St Mary the Virgin** **7**, to the fountain in Market Square **T**. Keep ahead along Queen Street and pedestrianised streets that lead directly

through a subway and across side roads to Marine Parade and Dover's stunning new Esplanade, where you will find the North Downs Way 'End of Trail' marker **U**, unveiled in November 2010. It is a granite 'start/finish' line, 26 feet (8 metres) long, set in the ground and accompanied by a plaque.

*The links with **Dover Priory Station** and Dover's bus station start by retracing your steps through the subway (see page 185).*

CONGRATULATIONS!

All walkers who complete the North Downs Way from Farnham to Dover are eligible for a certificate, whichever route was followed. Please contact the **North Downs Way National Trail Office**, giving details of your walk and any comments on your experience and a certificate will be sent to you free of charge. If you have now completed at least five National Trails, you are also eligible to be recorded in the National Trails Register maintained by the **Long Distance Walkers Association**.

Public transport

Shepherdswell (Shepherds Well Station, 0.4 mile / 0.6 km) ≈
Eythorne (0.8 mile / 1.3 km) 🚍 Not Sundays
Whitfield (1.1 miles / 1.8 km) 🚍
Buckland Valley (0.3 mile / 0.5 km) 🚍
Dover (on route) ≈ 🚍
Shepherdswell, **Coldred** and **Guston** are served by a Monday–Friday school bus service; if you think this may be of use, contact **Traveline** for details.
Taxis/minicabs: Kearsney, Dover

Refreshments

Coldred (0.6 mile / 1 km) 🍺 Carpenters Arms
Waldershare (0.2 mile / 0.3 km) 🍺 The Cider Works
Guston (0.2 mile / 0.3 km) 🍺 Chance Inn
Dover (on route) 🍺☕ Wide selection
Food shops: Shepherdswell, Dover
Public toilets: Dover

Accommodation

Coldred (0.6 mile / 1 km) Colret House
Martin Mill (1.9 miles / 3.0 km) Hawthorne Farm Holiday Park (campsite)
Church Whitfield (0.4 mile / 0.7 km) Rolles Court
Connaught Park (on route) Blériot's
Dover (on route) Wide selection contact **Dover Tourist Information Centre**

Journey's end! The North Downs Way 'End of Trail' marker welcomes you to the Esplanade beside Dover Harbour.

Today's orchards, with their serried ranks of small, easy-to-manage trees, are a far cry from Kent's traditional "garden yards"

Link routes

Guildford (1 mile / 1.6 km)

From the foot of Ferry Lane (**AF** in Section 1) turn left along the towpath for a pleasant riverside stroll, which leads past Guildford Lock to a road called Minmead. Stay beside the river to pass High Street pedestrian bridge and continue under Onslow Street and Bridge Street. For trains, turn left up steps, then go through a subway to Guildford Station. For buses, turn right at Bridge Street and go through the Friary Shopping Centre to the bus station.

Returning from the main exit of Guildford Station, turn right through the subway to the Bridge Street exit, go down steps to the riverside walk at Bridge Street then turn right to follow the riverside towpath. From the bus station go through the Friary Shopping Centre, following signs to Bridge Street, where keep ahead to cross the river, then go down steps to follow the riverside towpath. Rejoin the North Downs Way by keeping ahead at the foot of Ferry Lane (**AF** in Section 1).

Shalford (1 mile /1.6 km)

At the gates before Shalford Road (**AG** in Section 1) turn right to follow the cycle track, which at first runs parallel to the road, then veers right, behind houses, to reach Dagley Lane. Keep ahead to the railway bridge, where turn left past the church to cross the A281 The Street with care, then go ahead towards the Queen Victoria pub and right along Station Row to Shalford Station.

Returning from Shalford Station, use the exit from the north side platform (Redhill direction). Go past the Queen Victoria pub, then turn right to cross the A281 The Street with care. Keep ahead on a gravel track past the church, then turn right along a cycle track to reach the gates in Shalford Park (**A** in Section 2), where turn right to re-cross the A281 with care and keep ahead along Pilgrims Way to rejoin the North Downs Way.

Chilworth (1.1 miles / 1.8 km)

From the junction (**D** in Section 2) turn sharp right to follow the Downs Link down to the A248 Dorking Road (bus stops) and cross with care. Turn right to use the pavement along the left-hand side to reach Chilworth Station.

Returning from the ticket office at Chilworth Station, turn right then right again to use the pavement along the right-hand side of the A281 Dorking Road. In 550 yards (500 metres) at bus stops cross the A281 with care and keep ahead up a farm track (Downs Link) past Lockner Farm. At the top, turn left to the sandy junction (**D** in Section 2), where turn right to rejoin the North Downs Way.

Gomshall (2.3 miles / 3.7 km)

At Beggars Lane (**L** in Section 2) turn right to follow the track down to the A25 Dorking Road. Cross with care, then turn right to use the pavement along the left-hand side, which leads through a tunnel under the railway bridge. You will then need to re-cross the A281 carefully to reach Gomshall Station.

Returning from Gomshall Station, go down to the A281 Dorking Road. Cross with care, then turn left to go through the pedestrian tunnel. Follow the pavement for 550 yards (500 metres), then at a small group of houses carefully re-cross the A281 and keep ahead up Beggars Lane to a junction at the top of the hill (**L** in Section 2), where you turn right to rejoin the North Downs Way.

Dorking West (1 mile / 1.6 km)

Keep ahead at the junction (**R** in Section 2) and follow the bridleway down to Ranmore Road. Cross with care and turn left along a footway beside the road. In 385 yards (350 metres) turn right along a footpath and follow this to rejoin the road and turn right to Dorking West Station.

Returning from the north-side platform (Redhill direction) of Dorking West Station, turn right to Ranmore Road, then left for 140 yards (125 metres) and fork left to follow a footpath uphill. On rejoining Ranmore Road, turn left along a parallel verge and footway to a fingerpost, where turn right with care across the road to go up a bridleway. Follow this up to the footpath junction (**R** in Section 2) where you turn right to rejoin the North Downs Way.

Dorking and Dorking Deepdene
(0.8 mile / 1.3 km)

At the A24 London Road (**T** in Section 2) turn right for 0.6 mile (1 km), passing the main entrance to Denbies Wine Centre (Bradley Lane) at a traffic roundabout. Cross the A2003 Ashcombe Road and Croft Avenue, then use the subway. For Dorking Station (main line) keep ahead. For Dorking Deepdene Station turn sharp right to pass the Lincoln Arms pub, cross Lincoln Road, then turn left along the A24 London Road.

Returning from Dorking Station (main line), go ahead and through the subway. From Dorking Deepdene Station turn right along the A24 London Road, right again past the Lincoln Arms pub, then cross over to go through the subway. On the far side, turn left across Croft Avenue and the A2003 Ashcombe Road and keep ahead to pass the main entrance to Denbies Wine Centre at a traffic roundabout. Continue beside the A24 for 465 yards (425 metres), passing another entrance to Bradley Lane, to rejoin the North Downs Way at the next junction (**T** in Section 2).

Boxhill & Westhumble (0.3 mile / 0.4 km)

From the A24 (**U** in Section 2) turn left along Westhumble Street to pass the Stepping Stones pub-restaurant and continue for 400 yards (375 metres) to Boxhill & Westhumble Station. The pavement starts on the left-hand side but continues later on the right-hand side. Watch out for traffic approaching blind as you cross the road.

Returning from Boxhill & Westhumble Station, cross the road and turn right along the footway; you have to cross to the other

side later on. Use the subway (**A** in Section 3) to cross the A24 dual carriageway, then turn right to rejoin the North Downs Way.

Reigate (1.3 miles / 2 km)

Just before the Inglis Folly (**P** in Section 3), take the bridleway in a gully to the right and follow it down, swinging right then left, to the first houses in Reigate. Keep ahead down Underhill Park Road, leading into Beech Road, then turn left at Brokes Road to the A217 Reigate Hill **C**. Turn right to Reigate Station.

Returning from Reigate Station, turn right by the level crossing, up the A217 Reigate Hill. In 550 yards (500 metres) turn left down Brokes Road, then follow it round to the right and fork right up Beech Road. In 330 yards (300 metres) fork left up Underhill Park Road. When this bends left, keep ahead up a bridleway which swings right then left up to Colley Hill. Turn right past the Inglis Folly (**P** in Section 3) to rejoin the North Downs Way.

Merstham (0.3 mile / 0.4 km)

At Quality Street (**X** in Section 3) turn right to the A23 High Street and use the slip road behind a bus stop, from where buses go north to Coulsdon and Croydon. Cross over at the zebra crossing and turn right then immediately left along Station Road to Merstham Station. The bus stop for southbound services to Redhill and Reigate is a little way ahead along High Street when you reach Station Road.

Returning from Merstham Station, turn left along Station Road. At the High Street turn right, go over the zebra crossing, then turn right behind the bus stop. Keep ahead into Quality Street (**A** in Section 4) where you keep ahead to rejoin the North Downs Way.

Caterham (1.6 miles / 2.6 km)

From the central point of Caterham Viewpoint (point **7** in Section 4), cross Gravelly Hill with care and keep ahead along a bridleway that descends through woodland. At a T-junction with an unmade road, turn right (Upper Harestone) and follow this as it swings left then descends Harestone Hill. Follow this all the way down to a church, where you join Harestone Valley Road and keep ahead to the B2030 Church Hill. Caterham Station is almost opposite, but you should cross at the traffic lights to your right.

Returning from Caterham Station, cross Church Hill at the lights to your left, then turn right and shortly turn left along Harestone Valley Road. At a church take the left fork (Harestone Hill) and follow this all the way to the top, keeping ahead where the road becomes unmade. Later, take the right fork into Upper Harestone. At the end of a long, right-hand bend, turn left up a bridleway to a road (Gravelly Hill) and cross with care to Caterham Viewpoint (**7** in Section 4).

Woldingham (1.9 miles /3.3 km)

At South Lodge (**10** in Section 4) turn left to follow the main drive through Marden Park, which swings left then right past the buildings of Woldingham School. Pass the junction for Marden Park Farm then in 520 yards (480 metres) fork right up to Woldingham Station.

Returning from Woldingham Station, use the small school exit on Platform 1. Go down the lane and fork left to follow the main drive through Marden Park, which swings left then right past the buildings of Woldingham School all the way to South Lodge, where you turn left to rejoin the North Downs Way (**10** in Section 4).

Oxted (western link) (1.1. miles / 1.8 km)

From the gap in the hedge (point **P** in Section 4) keep ahead down Chalkpit Lane ⚠ ✳ and under the motorway bridge, after which there is a pavement. Bear left into Gordons Way, then keep ahead along Barrow Green Road. Pass under a railway bridge, turn left along Bluehouse Lane, then immediately turn right along Station Approach, which leads to Oxted Station.

Returning from Oxted Station, follow signs to the ticket office, where you turn right along Station Approach, past a taxi office and parallel with the railway line. At the end turn left then immediately right, along Barrow Green Road, passing under a railway bridge. Bear left with the road, then in 330 yards (300 metres) take the right fork (Gordons Way). In 385 yards (350 metres) turn right up Chalkpit Lane and follow this for 550 yards (500 metres). The pavement runs out as you pass under the M25 ✳, then you should keep right and take care. In 135 yards (125 metres) turn right through a gap in the hedge to rejoin the North Downs Way (**A** in Section 5).

Oxted (eastern link) (1.4 miles / 2.3 km) After the gap in the hedge (**D** in Section 5) turn right down a footpath along the field edge. At a bend, go through a gate and continue to a footbridge over the M25. Follow this twisting footpath through a small wood and beside fields, ignoring side turns through hedges. Beware of a shallow ditch on the left-hand side, which may be hidden. Eventually turn left at a corner to cross a stile and pass the playing fields of Oxted School. Keep ahead along Park Road, then at a junction turn right along Bluehouse Lane. Shortly turn left along Gresham Road, then at its end turn right along Station Road East to Oxted Station.

Returning from Oxted Station, follow signs to Station Approach East. Keep ahead to Station Road East and turn right. In 220 yards (200 metres) turn left along Gresham Road, then at its end turn right along Bluehouse Lane. Shortly turn left along Park Road, and when the road turns right keep ahead past the playing fields of Oxted School. Cross a stile and keep ahead to follow a footpath that twists along field edges and through a small wood towards the M25. Beware of a shallow ditch on the right-hand side, which may be hidden. Cross the M25 then turn left. Go through a gate and keep ahead beside a field to its corner (**D** in Section 5), where you turn right to rejoin the North Downs Way.

Dunton Green (1.4 miles / 2.2 km)

Before crossing the stile (point 7 in Section 5) turn right along a footpath running parallel with the railway line. Pass under the M26 and keep ahead along a footpath beside a fence. At a tunnel under the railway, keep ahead then go diagonally right across fields to reach a tarmac footpath, where turn left back to the railway line and climb steps up to Dunton Green Station.

Returning from Dunton Green Station, from the exit go ahead to a fence, behind which are steps down to a footpath. Follow this to a left-hand bend, where turn right along a faint path across fields to reach a tunnel under the railway line. Do not go through it; turn left to follow the footpath beside the railway line and under the M26 to a stile (7 in Section 5), which you cross to rejoin the North Downs Way.

Borough Green (1.4 miles / 2.2 km)

From the recycling centre (O inSection 6) turn right to the village centre, then right again at the High Street. Turn left along St Mary's Road (opposite the Rose & Crown), then keep ahead to the A227 Borough Green Road. Turn right to use a footway beside the A227 and over the M26 to Borough Green Station.

Returning from the ticket office at Borough Green Station, turn right to the A227 Wrotham Road, then turn left to use a footway over the M26. Turn left at the junction for Wrotham, then turn right into St Mary's Road. Turn right again at the High Street, then follow it round to the left. Fork right at Pilgrims Way to rejoin the North Downs Way by turning right at the recycling centre (O in Section 6).

Halling (1.3 miles / 2 km)

At the junction (AE in Section 6) turn right down the sunken track to pass Court Farm at Upper Halling (some buses serving Halling divert to this point). Keep ahead along Vicarage Road – there is a pavement all the way. As the road swings left to cross the A228, turn right along a footpath and cross the A228 on a stepped footbridge. On the far side, cross with care and turn right along Halling High Street, then turn left along Station Approach to Halling Station. Buses from Halling High Street go to West Malling, Strood, Rochester and Chatham.

Returning from Halling Station, go along Station Approach to Halling High Street, cross and turn right, then turn left past the shop to cross the A228 on a stepped footbridge. Turn left up Vicarage Road to Upper Halling. When the road swings left, keep ahead, passing a grass triangle and Court Farm, then take the right fork. Turn right in 175 yards (160 metres), climb steeply for 380 yards (350 metres) to a track junction (AE in Section 6), where turn right to rejoin the North Downs Way.

Cuxton (1 mile / 1.6 km)

At the first house in Bush Road (AK in Section 6) keep ahead for 0.8 mile (1.3 km). About halfway along, you can use a pavement along the right-hand side. At the A228 Rochester Road B turn right to cross over at the traffic lights, then turn right and left along Station Road to Cuxton station. Buses stop on Rochester Road: northbound (Strood, Rochester, Chatham) on the near side; southbound (West Malling) on the far side, opposite Bush Road. The White Hart is 220 yards (200 metres) further along Rochester Road, past Station Road. There is a Co-op in Bush Road, just before Rochester Road.

Returning from Cuxton Station, go ahead along Station Road, turn right at the A228 Rochester Road (where the bus stops are located), cross at the lights, then turn right and immediately left along Bush Road. When the pavement ends, keep to the right-hand side to reach the last house, then turn right beside its garage (A in Section 7) to rejoin the North Downs Way.

Bearsted (1.7 miles / 2.7 km)

Turn right opposite Detling Cricket Club entrance (C in Section 8) and follow a gravel track between houses. Keep ahead through a gate and along a field edge. At a gate, go half left to follow a footpath diagonally across two fields via stiles into woodland. Turn left and cross two more stiles, now parallel with the high-speed railway line. At Thurnham Lane ✱ turn right for 0.6 miles (1 km), passing under two bridges. Just before a brick railway bridge, turn right up to Bearsted Station.

Returning from Bearsted Station, use the exit on Platform 2 (beside the footbridge) down to Thurnham Lane and turn left along it ✱. In 870 yards (800 metres) pass under two bridges, then 90 yards (82 metres) further on turn left over a stile. Follow a footpath along the field edge, parallel with the railway line, to pass through woodland and cross two stiles before veering right to cross diagonally over two fields and more stiles. On reaching a gate, do not go through it but turn right beside a hedge. Go through the next gate and along a gravel track to rejoin the North Downs Way by turning right opposite Detling Cricket Club entrance (**C** in Section 8).

Hollingbourne (0.8 mile / 1.3 km)

Keep ahead past the Dirty Habit (**L** in Section 8), following Upper Street ✱. After the road swings left, turn right along the approach to All Saints Church, from where buses go to Leeds Castle and Maidstone. Keep ahead along a footpath to the right of the church. Turn right on rejoining the road to go under the railway bridge, then immediately turn right along the approach to Hollingbourne Station (actually in the neighbouring village of Eyhorne Street).

Returning from Hollingbourne Station, turn left to the main road, then left again under the railway bridge. Just before a school, turn left along a footpath leading to All Saints Church and keep ahead to Upper Street. Turn left to the Dirty Habit (**L** in Section 8), where turn right along Pilgrims Way to rejoin the North Downs Way.

Harrietsham (0.7 mile / 1.1 km)

At the Dutch House (**M** in Section 8) turn right down a bridleway and keep ahead at a tarmac lane to meet the railway line, where you turn right to Harrietsham Station

C . 🚌 🚏 🔀 For buses to Maidstone or Ashford and the Roebuck Inn, cross the footbridge, then turn right along Station Road to the junction with West Street, where turn left.

Returning from the ticket office of Harrietsham Station, cross the footbridge and turn sharp right to follow a footpath, which turns left, crosses a tarmac lane then continues up to The Dutch House (**M** in Section 8). Turn right to rejoin the North Downs Way.

Lenham (1.1 miles / 1.8 km)

At the junction with Faversham Road (**P** in Section 8), turn right up steps and cross a stile. Go slightly left to follow a faint footpath down a field to the A20 Ashford Road. Turn left to a junction, then cross to your right with great care ⚠ via a pedestrian refuge. Keep ahead along the left side of Faversham Road ✱ to the village square, where the 🔀 Dog & Bear Inn and Lime Tree Hotel are located, also 🚌 stops for buses to Maidstone and Ashford International Station. Keep ahead along the High Street, bending right then left with it. Just before the railway bridge, turn right along Station Approach to Lenham Station.

Returning from Lenham Station, turn right along the approach road. Turn left to follow the High Street as it bends right then left to the village square, where the bus stops are located. Keep ahead along the right side of Faversham Road ✱ to the A20 Ashford Road, where cross with care ⚠ via a pedestrian refuge then turn left across Faversham Road for 50 yards. At the end of the buildings, turn right into a field and follow a footpath up to its junction with Faversham Road (**A** in Section 9). Turn right to rejoin the North Downs Way.

Charing (western link) (0.7 mile / 1.1 km)

At the house with a white verandah (**D** in Section 9) turn right down a short, unmade lane and carefully cross the very busy A252 Charing Hill ⚠. Keep ahead down a road called The Hill, using a pavement on its right-hand side, to go through Charing village.

Cross the A20 Maidstone Road, using a light-controlled pedestrian crossing, and keep ahead along Station Road to Charing Station.

Returning from Charing Station, go ahead across Hither Field and continue along Station Road to use the pedestrian crossing over the A20 Maidstone Road. Resume the same direction along the High Street and up The Hill. Cross the A252 Charing Hill ⚠ and keep ahead up the unmade lane to the house with a verandah (▣ in Section 9), where you turn right to rejoin the North Downs Way.

Charing (eastern link) (1.1 miles / 1.8 km)

This link is only described returning from Charing Station to the North Downs Way. Go ahead across Hither Field and continue along Station Road. Use the pedestrian crossing over the A20 Maidstone Road, then turn right, past a small private car park. Immediately turn left along a narrow tarmac footpath. Cross a road and go ahead to pass some cottages (Willow House). Turn left to follow the right side of a playing field. At its end, keep ahead beside a wall, then turn right along a tarmac footpath. At another playing field, keep ahead, at first with houses on your left, then between a hedge and a fence. At a small car park, go through a gap, then half left, diagonally across a field to a road. Turn right to a junction, then left along Toll Lane to another junction (▣ in Section 9), where you turn right to rejoin the North Downs Way.

Sandling (2.2 miles / 3.5 km)

From the stile at Tolsford Hill Radio Station (▣ in Section 10) follow the byway (red arrows) and the Saxon Shore Way ahead, down to the A20 Ashford Road. ⚠ Cross with great care, turn left along the verge then shortly right, beside Stone Farm, along a former lane. This has been severed by the M20, which you cross on a footbridge. Keep ahead to a bend, then continue ahead on a bridleway. In 550 yards (500 metres) turn right to follow a former railway line to Sandling Station. Fork right up to the platform, or left through the car park if you need the ticket office.

Returning from Sandling Station, from the main exit turn left through a gate and along a disused platform to follow the disused railway line. In 550 yards (500 metres) turn left on to a bridleway, following the Saxon Shore Way, and join a lane ahead, crossing the M20 on a footbridge. ⚠ Cross the A20 Ashford Road with care and turn left along the verge. Ignore a footpath on the right and keep ahead to turn right along Bluehouse Lane, following Saxon Shore waymarks up to Tolsford Hill Radio Station (▣ in Section 10). Turn right to rejoin the North Downs Way.

Newington (1 mile / 1.6 km)

From the track junction (▣ in Section 11), turn sharp right and cross a stile, then turn sharp left down a lane ✱. Turn sharp right at a junction, continue down to the village of Peene and on to Newington, passing the Elham Valley Railway Museum (see ▣ in Section 11). Stay on the major road through the village to reach the A20 Ashford Road. The stop opposite is for northbound buses to Canterbury; turn right for 100 yards (90 metres) to the stop for southbound buses to Folkestone.

Returning from the bus stops on the A20 Ashford Road, follow the lane (Newington Road) ✱ through Newington and Peene, past the museum. Continue uphill, turning sharp left at a junction. At the top of the hill, as the lane swings left, turn sharp right to cross a stile and go up the track to a junction (▣ in Section 11), where you keep ahead to rejoin the North Downs Way.

Folkestone West (1.3 miles / 2.1 km)

⚠ This link crosses several busy slip roads to and from the M20, where you should take great care.

From Crete Road West (▣ in Section 11) turn sharp right down Castle Hill. At the foot, carefully cross a slip road, to the right of a roundabout, then cross the A20 via the central reservation. Turn left along a pavement, crossing a bridge over the M20. At the next roundabout, turn right to cross two more slip roads (looking left at both parts for traffic), again via a central reservation. Turn left to follow the pavement beside the A20 Cherry Garden Avenue (passing Premier Inn Folkestone) to its junction with the A2034 Cheriton Road. Keep ahead along the B2064 Beachborough Road, then turn right just before a bridge to reach Folkestone West Station.

Returning from Platform 2 of Folkestone West Station, turn right to the B2064 Beachborough Road, turn left to the junction with the A2034 Cheriton Road and keep ahead along the A20 Cherry Garden Avenue to a roundabout. Cross to the right, via the central reservation, then turn left to continue beside the A20 to the next roundabout. Cross to the right, via the central reservation (looking right at both parts for traffic), then cross left over a slip road to the foot of Castle Hill. Follow this road as it swings right, then ascends to meet Crete Road West (**H** in Section 11), where you turn sharp right past black-and-white bollards to rejoin the North Downs Way.

Wood Avenue bus stops (0.5 mile / 0.8 km) (For buses to Folkestone Central)

At the junction of Crete Road East with a side lane (**K** in Section 11), turn sharp right along a footpath leading steeply down to George Gurr Crescent in the Wingate Hill district of Folkestone. Keep ahead down Fleming Way, and as it swings left keep ahead to cross the dual carriageway A260 Hill Road at traffic lights. Turn right and bear left into the A259 Canterbury Road, reaching the Wood Avenue (east side) bus stop in 200 yards (185 metres).

Returning from the Wood Avenue (west side) bus stop, continue ahead along the A259 Canterbury Road. Just before the roundabout, turn right to cross the dual carriageway, via a central reservation, then turn left and bear right into the A260 Hill Road. Cross left over that dual carriageway at the traffic lights, then keep ahead up Fleming Way, keeping to the left-hand side. Cross George Gurr Crescent and keep ahead up a footpath leading steeply up to Crete

Road East (**K** in Section 11), where turn right to rejoin the North Downs Way.

Dover Priory (850 yards / 780 metres)

From the North Downs Way 'End of Trail' marker (**R** in Sections 11 and 15), retrace your steps to King Street and keep ahead to the Market Square. Go slightly left along pedestrianised Cannon Street (by the NatWest Bank). At the next junction turn left along Worthington Street, then cross the dual carriageway York Street at the traffic lights, a little to the left. Turn right to the roundabout, then left up the B2011 Folkestone Road. In 345 yards (315 metres), cross at the traffic lights to Dover Priory station.

Dover Bus Station (385 yards / 350 metres)

From the North Downs Way 'End of Trail' marker (**R** in Sections 11 and 15), retrace your steps to King Street and keep ahead to the fountain in Market Square. Go half right then immediately left along Church Street. By the Roman Quay pub, bear left through a car park into Pencester Gardens and keep ahead past a bandstand to the bus stops.

Chilham (0.6 mile / 1 km)

From the White Horse pub (**H** in Section 12) turn right to go down The Street . At the foot of the hill, beside the Woolpack Inn, turn left along Bagham Road and follow it, eventually turning left at a link road to the A252 Chilham Bypass. Turn right, via a pedestrian refuge, to the junction with the A28 Ashford Road and cross that at another refuge. Keep ahead for 135 yards (125 metres) to find Chilham Station on your right, after passing Bagham Barn tea room, Bagham Farmhouse and The Old Alma.

Returning from Chilham Station, go ahead then turn left beside the A28 Ashford Road. At the junction with the A252 Chilham Bypass, cross via the pedestrian refuge and keep ahead beside the A252. At the next junction, with a link road, cross via the refuge then bear left and right, beside a '¼ mile ahead' sign, to continue in the same

Link Routes

direction along Bagham Road, where the pavement soon runs out ✖. Keep ahead to the Woolpack Inn, then bear right up The Street ✖. At the top of the hill is The Square and the White Horse pub (**A** in Section 13), where you turn right to rejoin the North Downs Way.

Chartham (0.7 mile / 1.1 km)

At Newtown Road (**H** in Section 13) turn right across a stile and follow a farm track through an orchard. Keep ahead through a gap in a hedge, then cross the next two fields diagonally right, with a radio mast on your left, to Hatch Lane ✖. Keep ahead along it and over a level crossing to the A28 Ashford Road. Cross with care and keep ahead for 100 yards (90 metres) to Chartham Station.

Returning from the Chartham Station, turn right at the road, cross the A28 Ashford Road with care, then keep ahead up Hatch Lane ✖. In 275 yards (250 metres) after the level crossing, bear right, up a slope, then go diagonally left over two fields, with the mast on your left. Bear left through a gap in a hedge, then follow the track to Newtown Street (**H** in Section 13), where you turn right to rejoin the North Downs Way.

Canterbury East (0.5 mile / 0.8 km)

At the Thomas Ingoldsby pub (**B** in Section 14) turn right along Burgate Lane, beside the city wall. At the roundabout, cross St George's Street (or use the subway) to rejoin the wall walk, passing the bus station. In Dane John Gardens, turn left across the footbridge to Canterbury East station.

Returning from Canterbury East Station, go ahead to cross the footbridge into Dane John Gardens, then turn right to follow the city-wall walk, passing the bus station. At the roundabout, cross St George's Street (or use the subway), then keep ahead along the wall walk to Burgate, by the Thomas Ingoldsby pub (**B** in Section 14), where you turn right to rejoin the North Downs Way.

Bekesbourne (0.5 mile / 0.8 km)

From the junction at Patrixbourne (**G** in Section 14) turn left along Station Road for 660 yards (600 metres) to the crossroads, then turn left up Station Approach to Bekesbourne Station.

Returning from Bekesbourne Station, turn left down Station Approach to the crossroads, then turn right along Station Road for 660 yards (600 metres) to the junction with Bifrons Hill (**G** in Section 14) at Patrixbourne, where you turn left to rejoin the North Downs Way.

Snowdown (0.8 mile / 1.3 km)

By the fence corner at Woolage Village (**S** in Section 14), turn left to follow a footpath across the field, later with a wood on your right. Keep ahead at a fork to reach a farm track, then go past a broken stile to follow a footpath through the narrow strip of woodland ahead. At a gap, turn right along Woolage Lane to Snowdown Station.

Returning from Snowdown Station, turn left along Woolage Lane, then in 440 yards (400 metres) turn left at a gap. Immediately turn right along a footpath through a narrow strip of woodland. At a farm track, keep ahead on a footpath across a field to a fence corner at Woolage Village (**S** in Section 14), where you rejoin the North Downs Way.

Shepherds Well (0.4 mile / 0.6 km

At the footpath junction in Shepherdswell (**Y** in Section 14), turn right along the tarmac footpath and shortly keep ahead along Approach Road, which leads down to Eythorne Road. Cross over with care, turn left then immediately right down a public footpath, which leads to Shepherds Well Station.

Returning from Shepherds Well Station, follow the ramped footpath up to the right, which leads to Eythorne Road. Cross with care and turn left then immediately right up Approach Road. At the top, keep ahead beside a playing field on a tarmac footpath, then at a footpath junction (**Y** in Section 15) turn right to rejoin the North Downs Way.

Useful Information

Contact details

This list includes details of telephone numbers, websites and email addresses, where available. If no email address is shown, it may be possible to send an email via the website.

North Downs Way National Trail Office
Kent County Council, Invicta House, Maidstone, Kent ME14 1XX
ⓘ www.nationaltrail.co.uk/northdowns
✎ northdownsway@kent.gov.uk
☎ 01622 221525

National Trails Office
Block B, Government Buildings, Whittington Road, Worcester WR5 2LQ
ⓘ www.nationaltrail.co.uk
✎ nationaltrail@naturalengland.org.uk
☎ 01242 603307

County Councils

Hampshire County Council Countryside Department
ⓘ www.hants.gov.uk
✎ countryside@hants.gov.uk
☎ 0845 603 5636

Kent County Council Countryside Access Service
ⓘ www.kent.gov.uk/explorekent
✎ explorekent@kent.gov.uk
☎ 0845 824 7600

Surrey County Council Countryside Department
ⓘ www.surreycc.gov.uk/countryside
☎ 0345 600 9009

Travel Information

National Rail Enquiries
ⓘ www.nationalrail.co.uk
☎ 0845 748 4950 (Traintracker automated service on 0871 200 4950)

Traveline
ⓘ www.traveline.org.uk
☎ 0871 200 2233

East Kent Railway
ⓘ www.eastkentrailway.co.uk
☎ 01304 832042

First Great Western
ⓘ www.firstgreatwestern.co.uk
☎ 0845 700 0125

South Eastern Railway
ⓘ www.southeasternrailway.co.uk
☎ 0845 000 2222

Southern Railway
ⓘ www.southernrailway.com
☎ 0845 127 2920

Tourist Information

Visit Britain
ⓘ www.visitbritain.com

Tourism South East
ⓘ www.visitsoutheastengland.com

Ashford Tourist Information Centre
✎ tourism@ashford.gov.uk
☎ 01233 629165

Canterbury Visitor Centre
ⓘ www.canterbury.co.uk
✎ canterburyinformation@canterbury.gov.uk
☎ 01227 378100

Dover Tourist Information Centre
ⓘ www.whitecliffscountry.org.uk
✎ tic@doveruk.com
☎ 01304 205108

Farnham Tourist Information Centre
ⓘ www.farnham.gov.uk/visit.html
✎ info@farnham.gov.uk
☎ 01252 715109

Folkestone (Discover Folkestone)
ⓘ www.discoverfolkestone.co.uk
☎ 01303 258594

Guildford Tourist Information Centre
ⓘ www.visitguildford.com
✎ tic@guildford.gov.uk
☎ 01483 444333

Maidstone Tourism Information Centre
✎ tourism@maidstone.gov.uk
☎ 01622 602169

Mole Valley Visitor Information Centre
ⓘ www.visitdorking.com
☎ 01306 879327

Rochester Visitor Information Centre
ⓘ www.medway.gov.uk
✎ visitor.centre@medway.gov.uk
☎ 01634 843666

Sevenoaks Tourist Information Centre
ⓘ www.visitheartofkent.com
☎ 01732 450305

Other Contacts

Battle of Britain Memorial
ⓘ www.battleofbritainmemorial.org
✎ battleofbritain@btinternet.com
☎ 01732 870809

Churches Conservation Trust
ⓘ www.visitchurches.org.uk
✎ central@tcct.org.uk
☎ 020 7213 0660

Cinque Ports
ⓘ www.cinqueports.org
✎ enquiries@cinqueports.org
☎ 01424 451751

Denbies Wine Estate
ⓘ www.denbies.co.uk
✎ info@denbiesvineyard.co.uk
☎ 01306 876616

Downlands Project
✎ downlands@surreycc.gov.uk
☎ 01737 737700

English Heritage
ⓘ www.english-heritage.org.uk
✎ customers@english-heritage.org.uk
☎ 0870 333 1181

European Ramblers Association
ⓘ www.era-ewv-ferp.com
✎ secretariat@era-ewv-ferp.com

Farnham Castle
ⓘ www.farnhamcastle.com
✎ info@farnhamcastle.com
☎ 01252 720418

Farnham Maltings
ⓘ www.farnhammaltings.co.uk
✎ info@farnhammaltings.co.uk
☎ 01252 745444

Friends of Friendless Churches
ⓘ www.friendsoffriendlesschurches.org.uk
☎ 020 7236 3934

Gatton Trust
ⓘ www.gattonpark.com
☎ 01737 649068

Godstone Vineyards
ⓘ www.godstonevineyards.com
☎ 01883 744590

Greyfriars Vineyard
ⓘ www.greyfriarsvineyard.com
☎ 01483 813712

Guildford Borough Council
ⓘ www.guildford.gov.uk
✎ enquiries@guildford.gov.uk
☎ 01483 505050

Harvey Maps
ⓘ www.harveymaps.co.uk
✎ sales@harveymaps.co.uk
☎ 01786 841202

Kent Downs Area of Outstanding Natural Beauty
ⓘ www.kentdowns.org.uk
✎ mail@kentdowns.org.uk
☎ 01303 815170

Kent Wildlife Trust
ⓘ www.kentwildlifetrust.org.uk
✎ info@kentwildlife.org.uk
☎ 01622 662012

Long Distance Walkers Association
ⓘ www.ldwa.org.uk
✎ secretary@ldwa.org.uk

Loseley House
ⓘ www.loseley-park.com
✎ enquiries@loseley-park.com
☎ 01483 304440

National Trust
ⓘ www.nationaltrust.org.uk
✎ enquiries@nationaltrust.org.uk
☎ (National Office) 0844 800 1895
(South East Region) 01372 453401

North West Kent Countryside Project
ⓘ www.nwkcp.org
✎ info@nwkcp.org
☎ 01322 294727

Oak Hall
ⓘ www.oakhall.co.uk
☎ 01732 763131

Ordnance Survey
ⓘ www.ordnancesurvey.co.uk
✎ customerservices@ordnancesurvey.co.uk
☎ 0845 605 0505

Otford Heritage Centre
ⓘ http://bit.ly/otfordheritage
☎ 01959 522384

Pillbox Study Group
ⓘ www.pillbox-study-group.org.uk

Ramblers, The
ⓘ www.ramblers.org.uk
✉ ramblers@ramblers.org.uk
☎ 020 7339 8500

Scottish Natural Heritage
ⓘ www.snh.gov.uk
☎ 01463 725000

Surrey Hills Area of Outstanding Natural Beauty
ⓘ www.surreyhills.org
✉ surreyhills@surreycc.gov.uk
☎ 01372 220653

Surrey Wildlife Trust
ⓘ www.surreywildlifetrust.co.uk
☎ 01483 795440

Thomson Local
ⓘ www.thomsonlocal.com

Trosley Country Park
☎ 01732 823570

Vanguard Way
ⓘ www.vanguardway.org.uk
✉ colin@vanguardway.org.uk

Via Francigena
ⓘ www.viafrancigena.com
✉ info@viafrancigena.com

Watts Gallery
ⓘ www.wattsgallery.org.uk
✉ info@wattsgallery.org.uk
☎ 01483 810235

Wealden Cave and Mine Society
ⓘ www.wcms.org.uk

White Cliffs Countryside Partnership
ⓘ www.whitecliffscountryside.org.uk
✉ mail@whitecliffscountryside.org.uk
☎ 01304 241806

Woodland Trust
ⓘ www.woodlandtrust.org.uk
✉ enquiries@woodlandtrust.org.uk
☎ 01476 581135

Yell / Yellow Pages
ⓘ www.yell.com
☎ 118247 (premium rates)

Youth Hostels Association
ⓘ www.yha.org.uk
✉ customerservices@yha.org.uk
☎ 0800 019 1700

Bibliography

Some of these books are no longer in print but may be obtainable from libraries or online booksellers.
Adair, John. *The Pilgims' Way: shrines and saints in Britain and Ireland* (Thames and Hudson, 1978).
Belloc, Hilaire. *The Old Road* (Constable, 1904).
Brandon, Peter. *The North Downs* (Phillimore, 2005).
Charles, Alan. *Exploring the Pilgrims' Way* (Countryside Books, 1992).
Cobbett, William. *Rural Rides* (Penguin, 2005).
Hall, D. J. *English Medieval Pilgrimage* (Routledge, 1967).
Nairn, Ian. *The Buildings of England – Surrey* (Yale University Press, 1971).
Newman, John. *The Buildings of England – Kent: North East & East* (Yale University Press, 1983).
Newman, John. *The Buildings of England – Kent: West & The Weald* (Yale University Press, 1976).

Other publications by Colin Saunders

Navigation and Leadership – a manual for walkers (Ramblers' Association, 1993).
Walking in the High Tatras (with Renáta Nárožná, Cicerone Press, 1994 revised 2006, 2011).
London – the Definitive Walking Guide (Cicerone Press, 2002).
The Capital Ring (Aurum Press, 2003; revised 2006, 2010).
The Vanguard Way (Vanguards Rambling Club, 1997; revised 2009).
The Waymark Story (self-published, 2009).

The Official Guides to all o

Cotswold Way
Anthony Burton

100 miles of quintessentially
English landscape

ISBN 978 1 84513 519 5

Cleveland Way
Ian Sampson

Over 100 miles of magnificent
walking on the North York Moors

ISBN 978 1 84513 520 1

Hadrian's Wall Path
Anthony Burton

Follow the Roman Wall
from coast to coast

ISBN 978 1 84513 567 6

Yorkshire Wolds Way
Roger Ratcliffe

A superbly tranquil walk through the
unspoilt chalk hills of East Yorkshire

ISBN 978 1 84513 643 7

Pembrokeshire Coast Path
Brian John

180 miles of clifftop, beach and cove
around the magnificent Welsh coast

ISBN 978 1 84513 602 4

South Downs Way
Paul Millmore

100 miles of glorious chalk downland
for the walker, cyclist and horse rider

ISBN 978 1 84513 565 2

Pennine Way
NORTH: Bowes to Kirk Yetholm
Tony Hopkins

140 miles of magnificent walking
through remote countryside

ISBN 978 1 84513 562 1

Pennine Way
SOUTH: Edale to Bowes
Tony Hopkins

140 miles of wild country on
Britain's oldest long-distance path

ISBN 978 1 84513 639 0

North Downs Way
Colin Saunders

Follow the chalk ridge across South-East
England all the way to the sea

ISBN 978 1 84513 677 2

Britain's National Trails

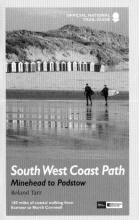

South West Coast Path
Minehead to Padstow
Roland Tarr

160 miles of coastal walking from
Exmoor to North Cornwall

ISBN 978 1 84513 640 6

South West Coast Path
Padstow to Falmouth
John Macadam

From golden beaches to rugged coves
around Britain's southernmost tip

ISBN 978 1 84513 641 3

Thames Path
David Sharp

Follow England's river all the way from its
peaceful source into the heart of the capital

ISBN 978 1 84513 566 9

South West Coast Path
Falmouth to Exmouth
Brian Le Messurier

172 miles of dramatic coves, cliffs and
beaches from Cornwall to Devon

ISBN 978 1 84513 564 5

South West Coast Path
Exmouth to Poole
Roland Tarr

From Jane Austen's Cobb to Lulworth Cove
– over 100 miles of historic coastline

ISBN 978 1 84513 642 0

The Ridgeway
Anthony Burton

87 miles of downland walking
from Wiltshire to the Chilterns

ISBN 978 1 84513 638 3

ISBN 1 85410 957 X

Peddars Way and
Norfolk Coast Path
Bruce Robinson

90 miles from Breckland to
salt marsh and sea cliffs

ISBN 978 1 84513 570 6

Offa's Dyke Path
SOUTH: Chepstow to Knighton
Ernie and Kathy Kay and Mark Richards

Follow the ancient earthwork up the Wye
Valley and alongside the Black Mountains

ISBN 978 1 84513 561 4

NATIONAL TRAIL GUIDES
PENNINE
BRIDLEWAY
Derbyshire to the
South Pennines
Sue Viccars

NATIONAL TRAIL GUIDES
OFFA'S DYKE
PATH NORTH
Knighton to Prestatyn
Ernie and Kathy Kay and Mark Richards

100 miles of walking through the
beautiful Welsh marches

ISBN 978 1 84513 312 2

NATIONAL TRAIL GUIDES
GLYNDŴR'S WAY
Llwybr Glyndŵr
Dave Perrott

ISBN 1 85410 968 5

Definitive guides to Britain's most popular long-distance walks

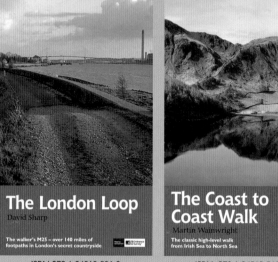

The London Loop
David Sharp

The walker's M25 – over 140 miles of footpaths in London's secret countryside

ISBN 978 1 84513 521 8

The Coast to Coast Walk
Martin Wainwright

The classic high-level walk from Irish Sea to North Sea

ISBN 978 1 84513 560 7

The Capital Ring
Colin Saunders

78 miles of green corridor encircling inner London

ISBN 978 1 84513 568 3

West Highland Way
Anthony Burton

Ninety-three miles of Scottish moor and mountain in Britain's most spectacular long-distance walk

ISBN 978 1 84513 569 0

Published by **Aurum**